Evangelicals and Jews in an Age of Pluralism

Marc H. Tanenbaum,
Marvin R. Wilson,
A. James Rudin,
Editors

Baker Book House
Grand Rapids, Michigan 49506

Copyright 1984 by
Baker Book House Company

ISBN: 0–8010–8871–2

Printed in the United States of America

Contents

Introduction   7

Contributors   9

Part One: **Evangelical and Jewish Relations Today**

1. *Marvin R. Wilson* / Current Evangelical-
    Jewish Relations:
    An Evangelical View   13

2. *A. James Rudin* / Current Evangelical-
    Jewish Relations:
    A Jewish View   29

Part Two: **Moral and Spiritual Challenges
of the Eighties**

3. *Marc H. Tanenbaum* / The Concept of the Human
    Being in Jewish Thought:
    Some Ethical Implications   47

4. *Timothy L. Smith* / Biblical Social Ethics:
    An Agenda for the Eighties   64

Part Three: **The Bible and Biblical Interpretation**

5. *Ellis Rivkin* / A Jewish View
    of the New Testament   85

6. *Bruce K. Waltke* / An Evangelical Christian View
    of the Hebrew Scriptures   105

7. *Asher Finkel* / Jerusalem in Biblical and
    Theological Tradition:
    A Jewish Perspective   140

Part Four: **Atonement and Redemption**

  8. *Donald G. Bloesch* / Sin, Atonement,
                and Redemption   163

  9. *Seymour Siegel* / Sin and Atonement   183

Part Five: **Mission and Proselytism**

  10. *Vernon C. Grounds* / The Problem
              of Proselytization:
              An Evangelical Perspective   199

  11. *Blu Greenberg* / Mission, Witness,
             and Proselytism   226

  12. *Sanford Seltzer* / Mission, Witness,
             and Proselytization:
             A Jewish View   240

Part Six: **The Past and the Future**

  13. *Kenneth S. Kantzer* / Six Hard Questions
              for Evangelicals
              and Jews   257

  14. *David Wolf Silverman* / The Holocaust and
              the Reality of Evil   268

  15. *David A. Rausch* / Prospectus
              for the Future   275

Introduction

The growing relationship between evangelical Christians and the Jewish community is one of the most positive developments on the current American religious scene. In a world where religious pluralism is a scarce reality, evangelicals and Jews are daily developing deepened trust relationships and are cooperating on a broad range of social justice concerns throughout the United States and abroad. The foundation of the evangelical Christian-Jewish encounter is profoundly biblical and theological. Living in an age of pluralism presents both faith communities with many complex challenges as well as many creative possibilities.

This volume is the second collection of essays to be published in recent years. The first, *Evangelicals and Jews in Conversation* (Baker, 1978), contains the perspectives on Scripture, theology, and history shared at the First National Conference in New York City in 1975. This second volume reflects the continuing vitality of that relationship. It contains selected essays presented at the Second National Conference held at Trinity Evangelical Divinity School in Deerfield, Illinois, in December 1980.

The Deerfield Conference was co-sponsored by *Christianity Today* and the Interreligious Affairs Department of the American Jewish Committee. After the initial New York Conference five years earlier, it was heartening to renew friendships and deepen bonds. At the Deerfield Conference there was from the start a much greater openness and candor. Scholars and religious leaders from both communities came prepared to speak from the heart to the gut issues. Mutual stereotypes and hollow caricatures of each other had for the most part vanished. Both the selection of formal addresses found in this volume, and the unpublished discussion which followed each presentation, testified to this fact. Those desiring to be informed about some of the highlights and impressions of this conference may consult news accounts such as those in *Christianity Today* (January 23, 1981, pp. 40, 41) and *The New York Times* (Dec. 14, 1980, p. 32).

While strongly affirming the authentic theological differences that exist between the two communities, this volume also offers many examples of shared interests and concerns. What hopefully emerges from these pages is the clear moral imperative to broaden and deepen the evangelical-Jewish encounter, not only nationally, but on the local and regional level as well.

The editors wish to express their thanks to those who have rendered special assistance in the preparation of this volume: Florence Mordhorst, Rita Reznik, and Daphne Smith for their secretarial skills. The editors also wish to acknowledge the continuing help and support of Baker Book House. Finally, we pay special thanks to Robert I. Lappin without whose generosity this volume could not have been published.

Marc H. Tanenbaum
Marvin R. Wilson
A. James Rudin

Contributors

Donald G. Bloesch, Professor of Theology, Dubuque Theological Seminary, Dubuque, Iowa

Asher Finkel, Professor, Graduate Jewish-Christian Studies, Seton Hall University, South Orange, New Jersey

Blu Greenberg, Chairperson, The Jewish Woman in a Changing Society, Federation of Jewish Philanthropies, New York, New York

Vernon C. Grounds, President Emeritus, Conservative Baptist Seminary, Denver, Colorado

Kenneth S. Kantzer, Immediate Past Editor-in-Chief, *Christianity Today* and Dean Emeritus, Trinity Evangelical Divinity School, Deerfield, Illinois

David A. Rausch, Associate Professor of Church History and Judaic Studies, Ashland Theological Seminary, Ashland, Ohio

Ellis Rivkin, Professor of Jewish History, Hebrew Union College–Jewish Institute of Religion, Cincinnati, Ohio

A. James Rudin, National Director, Interreligious Affairs, The American Jewish Committee, New York, New York

Sanford Seltzer, Director of Research and Planning, Union of American Hebrew Congregations; Director, Task Force on Reform Jewish Outreach, Boston, Massachusetts

Seymour Siegel, Professor of Theology, Jewish Theological Seminary of America, New York, New York

David Wolf Silverman, Professor of Jewish Philosophy and Ethics, Spertus College, Chicago, Illinois

Timothy L. Smith, Professor of History and Director, Program in American Religious History, The Johns Hopkins University, Baltimore, Maryland

9

Marc H. Tanenbaum, Director, International Relations, The American Jewish Committee, New York, New York

Bruce K. Waltke, Professor of Old Testament, Regent College, Vancouver, British Columbia, Canada

Marvin R. Wilson, Harold J. Ockenga Professor of Biblical Studies, Gordon College, Wenham, Massachusetts

Part One

Evangelical and Jewish Relations Today

1

Current Evangelical-Jewish Relations: An Evangelical View

Marvin R. Wilson

"God Almighty does not hear the prayer of a Jew."

This widely quoted remark from the lips of a leading evangelical church spokesman recently ignited a national controversy. Shocked by the off-hand statement, Jews and evangelicals alike immediately jumped into heated debate.

Of particular note was the fact that many evangelical Christians joined with Jews in disassociating themselves from the comment. In the words of one evangelical, "Such remarks come across to the American religious community as insensitive at best and as offensive and arrogant at worst."

Others expressed concern that the statement would undercut respect and love for Jews and Judaism, and that ultimately, if left unchecked, might pave the way for a new wave of anti-Semitism. The reaction of still others—those somewhat wary of the "born-again" politics—was that American pluralism and religious liberty must be underscored, not undermined.[1]

My great concern, and that of many other evangelicals, is that when any member of the Christian community has occasion to speak of Jews and Judaism, it be done in the spirit of true Christian love, with sensitivity and respect. To evade this moral responsibility, especially after the hundreds of years Jews have been slapped and kicked around by professing Christians, will serve only to fortify further the communication barrier which has divided us for nearly two thousand years.

This controversy about prayer has now subsided, and we have learned from it. But we need to remember that clarification of this issue came only after several meetings between evangelical leaders and Jewish leaders, including a visit to Israel. Martin Buber once appropriately observed, "all real living is meeting." Today evangelicals and Jews are talking; they are coming to know and understand each other in more than a superficial way. They are now entering into serious dialogue not only to clarify theological issues like prayer, but for other reasons as well. Indeed, the deepening of evangelical-Jewish relations in this country, and dialogue in regard to Israel, recently was described by church historian Martin Marty as "the most significant religious trend in the United States."[2]

It is fitting, therefore, that we open this Second National Conference of Evangelicals and Jews with an update on the current state of evangelical-Jewish relations. My aim is to present a selective overview by tracing where this dialogue and interaction is going on, why it is happening, and in what direction it may be headed. My focus will primarily be on the interaction taking place within mainstream evangelicalism, which is predominantly Gentile.

The Scope of Recent Interaction

Formal dialogue between evangelicals and Jews is relatively new. The first denominational gathering between both groups took place in 1969 at Southern Baptist Seminary in Louisville. Contact had been infrequent before that time. In the last half of the seventies the first major interfaith discussions began to take place.

On both the national and local levels, in formal and informal settings, evangelicals and Jews are currently interacting with greater frequency than ever before. At these gatherings, the dialogue is for the most part rational, dispassionate, and two-way. The discussions usually avoid superficial themes which would make such gatherings trite or virtually meaningless. Most of the formal conversation deals with issues of mutual interest including the common biblical heritage, Israel, and the current moral crisis. Specific attention is also focused on problems of human rights such as religious liberty, racism, anti-Semitism, and the role of women. Even topics which have historically divided both camps—the Messiah, the crucifixion, and the nature of redemption—are being openly aired.

The First National Conference of Evangelical and Jews was held in 1975. It was co-sponsored by the American Jewish Committee (AJC) and the Institute of Holy Land Studies, an evangelical school of higher education based in Jerusalem.[3] This three-day gathering dealt with issues of Scripture, theology, and history. It was the first extended, interdenominational consultation of evangelicals and Jews held in this country. Consequently, it has served as an archetype and exemplar for other dialogues to follow.

Since 1975 regional dialogues have been springing up in places where both evangelicals and Jews have well-established communities.[4] Many of these dialogues are being spearheaded by the efforts of the AJC and the Anti-Defamation League of B'nai B'rith. In the future we may look for more of these conferences involving religious and lay leadership.

Evangelical higher education is a second realm for increased contact with the Jewish community. Evangelical colleges and seminaries are offering courses in Judaica, modern Jewish culture, rabbinic backgrounds to the New Testament, anti-Semitism, and the literature and history of the Holocaust. Some of these courses involve field trips into the Jewish community for worship services,[5] Hanukkah and Purim celebrations, Passover seders, museum visits, and lectures. Also included have been trips taken to view *mikva'ot* (ritual baths), Jewish day-schools in session, and kosher meat-packing establishments.

Some of these courses are being taught by rabbis under Jewish sponsorship. Since 1976 one evangelical seminary in the West has taken part in an ecumenical program put together by the Center for Judaic Studies at the local university. The evangelical seminarians are able to enroll on a scholarship basis in a number of courses taught by rabbis, including one titled, "Judaism in the Time of Jesus."

A third area of interaction involves evangelical churches. In

New England, one large, suburban, interdenominational church
on a Sunday evening set aside its regular worship service and
held a "Jewish Neighbor Night." Jewish friends and acquaintances were invited for a showing of the Graham-produced
film, *His Land,* a picture one Jewish spokesman calls "the best
loving film about Israel today." The coffee hour that followed
was a climax to a highly successful evening of evangelical-Jewish
interaction and friendship.

Another evangelical church sponsors the Boston Center for
Christian Studies, an adult evening-school of the Bible that
draws several hundred lay people from churches in the Boston
area. Recently a new course was offered called "Evangelicals
and Jews in Dialogue." In this course, evangelical lay people
and their teacher interacted every other week with a different
guest rabbi. The response by the visiting rabbis was most
encouraging as they lectured on topics of vital interest to both
communities. For most of the students, it was their first exposure
to any articulate authority within the Jewish community.

A further area where evangelical-Jewish relations are being
built is in Jewish institutional gatherings at which evangelicals
are invited to speak. Evangelicals who are sensitive and friendly
to the Jewish community are being called on to address
synagogue services, brotherhood breakfasts, Anti-Defamation
League and AJC gatherings, and community center functions.

One such address which received considerable publicity was
given several years ago by Corrie ten Boom at a Conservative
synagogue in the South. Author of *The Hiding Place,* Miss ten
Boom was honored on that occasion by the host Jewish congregation for her and her family's courageous efforts to hide
Jewish people in Holland during World War II.

Perhaps the most publicized and important address by an
evangelical leader at a major gathering occurred in October of
1977 in Atlanta. Billy Graham spoke to two hundred Jewish
leaders on "The Evangelical Christian and the Jew in a Pluralistic Society." On that evening Graham received the AJC's first
National Interreligious Award, being cited for "strengthening
mutual respect and understanding between evangelical and
Jewish communities."[6]

There remains a rather large segment of evangelicals who are either ignorant, suspicious, or unsupportive of dialogue. The growth of dialogue will be closely related to how many of these evangelicals and their organizations—church, parachurch, educational, and other—will be open to provide the impetus, direction, and financial backing for activities with the Jewish community.

Motivation for Meeting

One question to be asked about this new venture in dialogue concerns what is behind it all. What prompts evangelicals and Jews to seek each other out now? Why are evangelicals and Jews engaging in this interaction?

Although history seems to indicate most evangelicals have had but one motive in mind—witness to their faith—when meeting Jews, the new dialogue is making both evangelicals and Jews aware of other things as well.

1. Evangelicals have a genuine interest in deepening their understanding of the Jewish roots of the Christian faith. The Hebrew Scriptures (Old Testament) comprise about 80 percent of the Bible. Orthodox Jewish scholar Michael Wyschogrod has stressed that "the single most important contact between Judaism and Christianity is the centrality of the Bible in the two faiths."[7] The biblical view of reality is profoundly Hebraic. Hence, Karl Barth once stated, "One has either got to be a Jew or stop reading the Bible. The Bible cannot make sense to anyone who is not 'spiritually a Semite.'"[8] Through recent dialogue, evangelicals are becoming alert to the personal benefits which may accrue to them by being able to discuss the Scriptures face-to-face with those people whose ancestors produced this book.

2. The growing impact of relational theology has affected evangelical outreach to Jews. Today evangelicals are seeking more and more to balance the propositional side of truth with its relational and personalizing dimension. Theology is being related to people in the context of their life situation. This has brought about a new freedom and openness in interpersonal

relationships. Evangelicals are being impressed with the importance of relating to others first and foremost as people, not as
repositories into which bags of proof texts may be emptied with
abandon. In the words of evangelical leader Leighton Ford,
"Christians can enter into conversation with Jews, Muslims,
and others on a basis of friendship, of sharing common concerns we have as human beings, of witnessing to our knowledge
of the true God."[9] Evangelicals are now learning that they, like
others, must earn their right to be heard. Indeed, the first step
to lasting friendship and effective communication with one of
another faith is by listening (James 1:19).

   3. Jews are motivated due to the seemingly ubiquitous character of anti-Semitism. Recently there has been a dramatic rise
in anti-Semitic incidents. Jews want anti-Semitism to stop. Dialogue with Christians gives an opportunity to draw attention to
this painful sore which remains unhealed even after such
blood-shrouded atrocities as the Crusades, the Inquisition, and
the Holocaust. Jews point out that some anti-Semitism is theologically motivated. This happens when the majority faith
(Christianity) has suppressed the minority faith (Judaism). An
arrogant attitude of triumphalism has sometimes resulted from
the Christian teaching that views the church as the new and
true Israel. Many Jews fear future persecution because fundamentalist eschatology teaches such persecution before Jesus
returns. Other Jews say Christians today still hold the Jewish
people culpable for the death of Christ. The air needs clearing
on these and other issues.

   4. Jews are curious about the religious commitment of evangelicals who have risen to candidacy for public office and the
parallel impact of the New Christian Right. From the time Jimmy
Carter began his drive to the presidency in 1975 as a "born-
again" Christian, Jews became curious about the nature of this
Southerner's faith. More recently the beliefs of John Anderson
and Ronald Reagan have been viewed with similar interest. In
America most Jews live in the northeast corridor, geographically
isolated from the majority of evangelicals and left in considerable darkness about what evangelicals believe. Hence, Jews
have become curious—even suspicious—of how "born-again"

politicians can lead a pluralistic nation. In addition, with the rise of the New Christian Right, Jews are asking if it is the goal of organizations like the Moral Majority to create a "Christian republic" by "Christianizing" government and politics. Dialogue is providing needed perspective on these concerns.

5. Since the 1960s there has been a general improvement in interfaith relationships brought about by ecumenical endeavors and the easing of racial tensions. The fundamentalist-modernist controversy earlier this century left conservative Christianity largely cultic, culturally closed, doctrinally schismatic, anti-intellectual, and anti-ecumenical. The last two decades, however, have shown great progress in race relations paralleled by major strides in Catholic-Jewish, and mainline Protestant-Jewish relations. Evangelicals, until recently, have been the only major group with which interreligiously minded Jewish organizations have not sought formal dialogue. It was simply a matter of time before evangelicals and Jews would find themselves in conversation. Jews are finding that among evangelicals there is now renewed interest in socio-political concerns, mainline denominationalism, and ecumenical issues that deal with human rights in the context of a pluralistic society.

6. There is recognition of the need to dispel faulty images and popular stereotypes of each other. Lack of personal encounter has resulted in the creation of many prejudices, distortions, and faulty perceptions one of the other. In this vein, Anglican churchman John Stott stresses the importance of evangelicals getting involved: "Dialogue is a token of genuine Christian love, because it indicates our steadfast resolve to rid our minds of the prejudices and caricatures which we may entertain about other people."[10] Many of these unjust portrayals and painfully naive stereotypes of the past are beginning to give way to accurate modern-day images. Accordingly, evangelicals are coming to realize that contemporary Judaism is not simply the blood-sacrifice religion of the Old Testament, but one that developed from it. Jews are coming to see evangelicals as other than "Elmer Gantry" types, as people with a real passion for social justice.

7. Each faith community has an interest to understand the

religious and cultural differences of the other. Christianity and Judaism are—with all their similarities—distinct faiths. Both communities have become increasingly curious about the life, beliefs, and practices of each other. Interfaith dialogue is providing a welcome format to pose a variety of questions—some simple, many probing, but all necessary—to clarify the differences perceived. For instance, evangelicals have often asked Jewish people:

"Why is a glass smashed at a wedding?"

"Why are flowers and music not used at funerals?"

"Jacob was embalmed in Bible times, so why should embalming be forbidden today?"

"Why do Jews eat chicken rather than lamb at Passover?"

"Since there is no more temple where animal sacrifices are offered, how is atonement of sin received?"

"Christians often pray and sing while attending services at a synagogue, but why do Jewish people seldom do the same when visiting churches?"

Some typical questions which have perplexed Jews about evangelicals are these:

"In light of the separation of church and state, why do evangelicals and fundamentalists seem to want prayer and Bible reading in public schools?"

"Why should our rabbi be criticized for questioning the use of city property and funding for a large Christmas nativity display?"

"Why does my child's school-teacher, who is an evangelical, seem to resent my questioning of the class use of numerous traditional Christmas carols, when Hanukkah songs are never included?"

"If evangelical churches try to be so "biblical" in their approach to life, why do they seem to criticize us Jews for celebrating weddings the biblical way with some wine and dancing?"

The search to become enlightened on these and other questions will continue to provide motivation for evangelical-Jewish encounter.

8. We share a common interest in the survival of Israel. Though many within the evangelical world find justification for

their support of Israel in theology (prophetic texts),[11] other reasons are happily being given as well. Political, economic, and sociological factors are also important in arguing for Israel's right to exist as a free and secure state. Indeed, there is growing concern for a just peace among all people in the Middle East, not just between Israel and Egypt or Israel and her Arab neighbors. For a variety of reasons, Jews and evangelicals will continue to find a common bond of interest in Israel's future. Israel *is* the land of the Bible. For evangelicals it is the birthplace of both Jesus and the church; for Jews it is the stage on which thousands of events of Holy Writ have been played out for century upon century. It is a land sacred to both Christian and Jew. And it will always be that way.

An Unfinished Agenda

Being the two different religions that we are, it should never be forgotten that neither of us is seeking to build some symbiotic world-wide religious body. So we must be candid with one another; we must never consciously downplay our differences. To be sure, we have some sensitive areas of tension where theological antitheses of centuries past have resulted in what appears to be a perpetual impasse—an ideological cul-de-sac—which, unless God intervenes, may never be fully resolved until the end of this age. Evangelicals, for instance, are not about to abandon their belief in original sin, nor in the divinity and messiahship of Jesus. Likewise, the Jewish community has never abandoned its commitment to the Oral Law (Talmud), nor proclaimed that man is saved—that is, deemed worthy of the world to come—by faith alone. But these differences should neither stop us from talking nor forbid us to understand the reasons why they exist.

How then do we account for these and other theological disagreements and foundational differences that separate us? Vital to our understanding are two main areas which need extensive clarification. Both these areas must be given high priority on agendas for future dialogue.

First, we must thoroughly explore our differences of approach

in regard to biblical interpretation and theological presupposi
tions. Evangelicals, for instance, hold to the canonicity and
absolute authority of the New Testament writing; Jews do not.
Thus, evangelicals interpret certain Old Testament texts chris-
tologically, through the eyes of—what they believe were—
inspired New Testament authors. It should be readily apparent
then to Christians (but usually it is not) why Jews fail to find
messianic meaning in texts such as the suffering servant passage
of Isaiah 53. Their hermeneutic is different. Evangelical Christians, however, arrive at their interpretation from a different
angle. They find eight of the twelve verses from that prophetic
chapter quoted or referred to in the New Testament. And more
important, each of these texts from Isaiah is tied to the messianic ministry and claims of Jesus. But taken alone, the prophecy
of Isaiah gives no hint of a suffering Messiah, only a suffering
servant. Furthermore, Isaiah gives no indication that the Messiah is Jesus of Nazareth. Contrasted with the evangelical
method of interpretation, the Jewish method does not make
authoritative use of the last twenty-seven books of the Bible.
Rather, biblical interpretation starts with the Hebrew Bible and
then this is understood and interpreted through the Talmud,
the Codes, the Responsa, and the commentaries of scholarly
authorities such as Rashi. In short, Judaism is not bound to one
authority; it embraces many authorities in a long line of living
tradition.

In the nineteenth century, through the rise of Reform Judaism, the issue of biblical authority became more fluid. Reform
Jewry brought in its wake an emphasis on reason and experience. This detracted significantly from the traditionalist's
"Torah-true" or Halakic approach to authority. Furthermore, in
its acceptance of the rationalistic judgments of higher biblical
criticism, the Reform movement departed from the more conservative position common to historic evangelicalism. That is,
evangelicals have usually read the Bible rather literally, producing an express belief in predictive prophecy, and generally
accepting as true the details of historical narrative and the
accounts of miracle-working. Likewise, evangelicals tend to
reject higher critical views such as the Documentary Hypothesis

of the Pentateuch (JEDP), the notion of a "Deutero" and "Trito" Isaiah, and the late (second century B.C.E.) dating of the prophecy of Daniel.

Modern Jewish scholarship, on the other hand, approaches most of these same issues from a radically different perspective. Thus, questions such as what is Scripture, the accuracy and trustworthiness of the Bible, biblical hermeneutics, the appropriate use of higher criticism, and the nature of religious authority represent major points of difference between the two faiths. It is indeed a strange and ironic phenomenon that the one written authoritative source that in so many ways unites evangelicals and Jews, at the same time so radically divides them. Fully aware of these differences, at some time in the future a thorough study of the history of canon and the early schools of biblical interpretation could be undertaken jointly with considerable profit.

A second area of conflict and difference that calls for exploration and clarification is that of mission and outreach. Of special concern is the way in which evangelical witness is being communicated to Jewish people. Happily, a number of evangelical leaders are now taking a clear stand against "singling out Jews as Jews" in evangelistic efforts. Accordingly, evangelist Leighton Ford has stated that "good news we have no right to withhold from anyone. But we do reject the neurotic approach which would select out Jews alone as some uniquely needy objects for proselytism."[12]

Many evangelicals now publicly disassociate themselves from contacting Jews by any evangelistic method considered to be deceptive or devious or coercive or manipulative. In a word, they strongly shun "hard-line conversionary tactics." Let it be clearly affirmed that high-pressure witness—wherever directed—has never yielded results worthy of the name Christian. No souls can be brought into the kingdom against their will; this is a myth to be quickly dismissed. The evangelical community, however, must continue to struggle with what it means for an evangelical to be genuinely "evangelical." How can an evangelical be faithful to tradition and the Christian call to spread the gospel to all men (Matt. 28:18–20; Acts 1:8), and yet do so in an

honest, open, humble, and nonmanipulative way? Is the evangel, in the very nature of the case, to be always reckoned a
"stumbling block" (see I Cor. 1:23)? Is it possible for evangelicals
and Jews to agree on the ethics of bearing witness to that
evangel?[13] Granting the long history of abuses in this area,
evangelical and Jewish leaders must become more sensitive to
the deep feelings of each other and seek to establish some
agreed-upon guidelines pertaining to the ethics of legitimate
witness.

The last two thousand years painfully reveal that neither of
us can impose or force faith on the other. The heavy-handed,
overly zealous witness, unfortunately seen in certain Christians,
has been largely due to a deep conviction regarding the finality
of Jesus as the Christ. Regretfully, this has often been tied to a
depreciation and lack of respect for Jewish beliefs and practices.
But this should never be the case with evangelicals. They, as
recipients of the grace of God, have no ground for boasting,
arrogance, or triumphalism. There is nothing inherent in
Christianity that makes one individually, or Christians corporately, better than Jews. It is indeed a blight on the name *Christian* that a proud and elitist spirit has sometimes been openly
displayed. Such hubris seems to have little respect for religious
pluralism, a concept on which this nation was founded. Furthermore, attitudes of Christian superiority have often resulted in
the denegration of Judaism, preparing the ground for the
sowing of the seeds of anti-Semitism.

Christians who truly care about the feelings of others will
hold to their own deepest commitments of faith with a spirit of
genuine humility without compromising the conviction of truth.
A Christian's friendship, respect, and love for Jewish people—as
with all people—should be unconditional, genuine, and irrevocable, never preconditioned or governed by the acceptance of
any given Christian belief or dogma. The evangelical community must recognize, as one of its spokesmen Clark Pinnock has
stated, that "There is nothing to boast of in ourselves. We are
just human beings speaking to other human beings, testifying
to what we have found. We do not assume we are completely
right and infallible or have nothing left to learn."[14] Growth

comes through mutual sharing and a willingness to risk self-exposure. On this level, the deepest sensitivities and convictions of each other are laid bare. Yet, it is this two-way street that gets to the very heart of dialogue.

Is There a Future?

Where is the current dialogue going? What prospects for the future can be offered? From an evangelical perspective there is a broad range of speculation at this point.

One large segment of evangelicals stands in great fear of dialogue and others are, at best, passive. Many of these come from fundamentalistic church backgrounds. For the most part they feel that the evangelical movement has everything to lose by interreligious activity with any group outside its own self-contained evangelical world. By involvement in interfaith dialogue, evangelicalism is headed nowhere, they say, but to its own destruction. This will come because of a fatal loss of its evangelical distinctives. So, it is argued, dialogue is to be avoided lest evangelicals become lukewarm and succumb to compromising ecumenical pressures. Those who will mount these pressures, these evangelicals insist, though appearing friendly at first, will eventually convince evangelicals not to be an offense religiously to others. There will be strong insistence that evangelicals display great tolerance and broad-mindedness, for this is an age of "live and let live." Where does this "garden path" eventually lead, they ask; it ends when evangelicals suddenly and tragically find themselves part of some doctrineless ecumenical religious body. Then New Testament Christianity will have lost its uniqueness, and biblical warnings about compromise will be vindicated.

In contrast to that, there is another segment of evangelicals—and I number among them—who are enthusiastic about the future prospect of dialogue. They refuse to believe God has rejected his people (Rom. 11:1), and that there is no place for Israel in God's redemptive and messianic program. Such evangelicals affirm that there is much yet to be learned from those

who from biblical times have been his people. Still included in
the mystery of God's election love, the Jews remain a "holy"
people (Rom. 11:16). While affirming the centrality of a Christian
witness which sees the gospel message open to all peoples
everywhere, these evangelicals believe that Romans 9–11 teaches
that in God's plan Judaism and Christianity will co-exist until
the end of this age. At that time, according to the metaphor
employed by Paul, God will regraft into the olive tree (Rom.
11:23) those natural branches (Jews) beside the place where the
wild olive branches (Gentiles) presently grow, so finally, "all
Israel will be saved" (Rom. 11:26).

It would appear from the context that the apostle Paul's
understanding of this future salvation of Israel is tied clearly to
Jesus, the one he called the Messiah. But most evangelicals are
conscious that the when and how of God's sovereign outworking of his plan for "Israel after the flesh" remains shrouded in
a great mystery which no man can fathom (Rom. 11:33–34). For
the Jewish community, the question of Messiah has never
focused so much on who that person would be, but upon the
empirical evidence of world-wide redemptive activity.

How will the Spirit of God and the will of man allow this new
dialogue to be shaped in the future? That remains to be seen.
Both evangelical and Jew recognize that God is the Lord of
history; He is the ultimate judge of men and movements. He
controls for his own purposes the affairs of his people. He
omnisciently sees as no mere mortal can presently see.

What is important now is that barriers of communication are
being broken down between evangelicals and Jews. This new
dialogue is enabling evangelicals—many for the first time—to
learn from, and make lasting friendships with, a people who
brought riches to the Gentile world (see Rom. 11:12).

For hundreds of years the evangelical has had something to
offer the Jew; but for thousands of years the Jew has had
something to teach the rest of the world. Witness to the tradition
of one's faith cuts both ways. So, dialogue need not be written
off out of peril, but pursued for its potential. For both evangelicals and Jews, more riches have yet to be discovered.

Notes

1. In viewing prayer theologically, from one side, we may ask whether God—apart from his grace—has ever listened to the prayers of any of his children when broken commandments and other sins have placed a barrier between themselves and him (Ps. 66:18; I John 3:22). From another side, we know that God is loving, merciful, and just; he knows and understands the inmost desires of every heart. God is also sovereign. When he hears prayer, it is not because he has to, but because he is a compassionate Father and is moved when man reaches out toward him in faith. Accordingly, it is evident why many evangelicals felt drawn to the reflective response made by the Rev. Jerry Falwell to this matter of whose prayer God hears. Said Falwell, "God hears the cry of any sincere person who calls on him."

2. Martin Marty, *Context* (Jan. 1, 1978), p. 1.

3. The Institute of Holy Land Studies attracts most of its students and its greatest support from the American evangelical community. The founder and first president of the Institute, G. Douglas Young (deceased, May, 1980), served as cochairman with Rabbi Marc H. Tanenbaum at the First National Conference.

4. Two regional conferences held in 1977 will be cited by way of example. In Philadelphia, a dialogue was held at the evangelical Tenth Presbyterian Church. Religious leaders gathered under the sponsorship of the AJC and *Eternity* magazine (The Evangelical Foundation, Inc.). Major addresses, a kosher luncheon, and a vigorous panel discussion on evangelical-Jewish relations highlighted the day. In Dallas, Texas, a dialogue cosponsored by the AJC and the Southern Baptist Convention was held at Southern Methodist University. The theme of this three-day conference was, "Agenda for Tomorrow: Baptists and Jews Face the Future." Several hundred lay people, pastors, and rabbis interacted in special interest sessions focusing on such issues as human rights, world hunger, and religious liberty. A key address was delivered by Senator Mark Hatfield, an evangelical Baptist from Oregon. At the end of the conference a joint statement was informally adopted indicating areas where continued cooperation would be pursued between the two groups.

5. For the past decade, groups of my students have been involved in an interesting kind of interaction with the Jewish community. Annually, they have been invited to local synagogues to put on an hour-long program following the Friday evening worship service. As a practical outworking of their college course in modern Jewish culture, these Christian students have made use of the Hebrew Scriptures, music, art, film, literature, drama, and dance to present themes related to the Jewish rootedness of the common biblical heritage.

6. See *Newsweek* (Nov. 28, 1977), p. 126. A condensed version of Graham's address, retitled, "Be Strong," is found in *Decision* (June, 1978, p. 6). In six

areas Graham called for evangelical-Jewish cooperation: 1) working and praying together for the peace of Jerusalem; 2) working together for improved race relations between black and white; 3) joint honoring, supporting, and undergirding of our nation; 4) hammering out together a common agreement so that moral law may be taught to the young people in our public schools; 5) working together for world peace, freedom, and justice; 6) working jointly for a national, spiritual, and moral awakening.

7. Michael Wyschogrod, "Judaism and Evangelical Christianity," *Evangelicals and Jews in Conversation,* ed. Marc H. Tanenbaum, Marvin R. Wilson, and A. James Rudin (Grand Rapids: Baker, 1978), p. 35.

8. Quoted in Thomas Merton, ed., *Conjectures of a Guilty Bystander* (Garden City, New York: Doubleday, 1968), p. 14.

9. "A Conversation with Leighton Ford," *The Reformed Journal* (November, 1976), p. 14.

10. John Stott, *Christian Mission in the Modern World* (Downers Grove, Illinois: InterVarsity, 1975), p. 81.

11. For elaboration of this point, see my study, "Zionism as Theology: An Evangelical Approach," *Journal of the Evangelical Theological Society* (March, 1979), pp. 27–44.

12. Leighton Ford, "A Letter to Richard," *Evangelicals and Jews in Conversation,* p. 307.

13. I have discussed this question and others related to it in "Christians and Jews: Competing for Converts?" *Christianity Today* (March 21, 1980), pp. 28–30.

14. Clark Pinnock, "Why Is Jesus the Only Way?" *Eternity* (December, 1976), p. 14.

2

Current Evangelical-Jewish Relations: A Jewish View

A. James Rudin

It has been said, half in jest and half in truth, that geography as much as theology has helped keep evangelicals and Jews separate from one another. Historically, the largest concentration of Jews has been in the urban centers of the northeast and the upper midwest, while the major evangelical population has generally been located in the southeast and the southwest.

Thus, for more than two centuries evangelicals and Jews have moved past each other like the proverbial "ships in the night," never really encountering one another as vibrant and unique spiritual communities. In such a situation it is little wonder that mutual ignorance, negative stereotypes, and caricatures have emerged. Martin Buber taught that "real living is meeting," but for too long a fruitful and "real" encounter between Jews and evangelicals simply did not take place partly because of history, demography, and, yes, evangelicals' geography.

Thus, the formative American experience for both faith communities was decisively shaped in distinctly separate areas of the nation; and only in recent decades have Jews and evangelicals, like millions of other Americans, moved into all parts of the United States. Our incredibly mobile society has brought all groups closer together, and evangelicals and Jews have been no exception to this phenomenon. This condition of limited

contact between the two religious groups is ending, but unfortunately we still encounter some of the negative images and
false generalizations that have plagued evangelical-Jewish relations. Can anyone honestly believe that terms such as "red-
neck," "cracker," "Elmer Gantry," or "bigot" fairly describe the
contemporary evangelical? And can anyone honestly believe
that the epithets of "Christ killer," "scribes and Pharisees," and
"Shylock" have any basis in fact as accurate descriptions of
Jewish history, religion, and culture? Yet, these pernicious
images have poisoned and bedeviled relations between evangelicals and Jews for many years.

It was not until the late 1960s and early 1970s that a systematic
national program was undertaken to overcome the centuries of
mutual suspicion and ignorance. The first evangelical-Jewish
national conference took place in December, 1975, in New York
City, cosponsored by the Institute of Holy Land Studies and the
American Jewish Committee.

The conference was historic not only for the participants,
but also because New York City energized our two communities
in a profound and lasting way. All of the important and difficult
issues and themes of Scripture, theology, and history were
addressed in New York City. The meanings of Israel, Messiah,
Bible, salvation, conversion, and faith were fully explored; and
the modern moral questions of war, racism, anti-Semitism,
church-state relations, and social justice were discussed and
debated. The 1975 meeting has served as the model for many
other successful evangelical-Jewish conferences throughout
America.

New York City was extraordinary for several reasons. First, it
revealed a real hunger for true dialogue between responsible,
knowledgeable, and thoughtful representatives from each community. Academicians, local pastors and rabbis, seminarians,
national officials, and lay people were all present at New York
City; and they interacted with one another in a remarkable way.
Second, it was as if decades of pent-up energy among Jews and
evangelicals were released at the conference. Two great faith
communities discovered many shared concepts and concerns;
and when they differed, as they did, the atmosphere was not

one of triumphalism or confrontation, but rather the differences were clearly articulated in an irenic spirit. Finally, and not the least important, the "human chemistry" between evangelicals and Jews was extremely positive. Follow-up conferences have been held. The last five years has seen a remarkable proliferation of such meetings, and the 1980s promise to be no different. The 1975 New York City Conference proceedings became the basis for the book, *Evangelicals and Jews in Conversation* (Baker Book House, Grand Rapids, 1978). This pioneering work is acknowledged as an important source book for all current evangelical-Jewish relationships and programs.

These conferences have developed a generation of evangelical and Jewish leaders who possess the inner security and knowledge to engage in deep and meaningful dialogues with each other. No longer can a seminary professor or an editor of religious teaching material commit egregious errors based on ignorance when describing Jews or evangelicals. A significant body of literature has emerged along with a growing sense of mutual trust and respect. Much serious work on a variety of issues remains to be done, but the New York City meeting broke important new ground and was an interreligious milestone of the first order.

American Jews discovered a serious and deeply theological evangelical commitment to American social justice concerns. At the New York City meeting Paul E. Toms, a past president of the National Association of Evangelicals, declared: "Evangelicals are actively engaged in varying ministries. These ministries include adoption agencies, programs for unmarried parents, foster care, family counseling, family life education, tutoring, and assistance in meeting other demands of our society. We are concerned with the place of Christians in government, the obtaining of justice by minority groups, the feeding of the hungry and starving, and the meeting of physical needs. . . . Evangelicals operate hospitals, clinics, health centers, schools, feeding stations, and clothing depots. These projects often afford opportunities for witness to our faith, but we feel a responsibility to engage in them for their own sake as well." Today Jews and evangelicals are both working on a host of

contemporary social and moral issues that impact on the
general American society: the integrity of the family, quality
public education, equal employment opportunities, open hous-
ing, morality in government, and a fair energy program.

Another important area of evangelical-Jewish cooperation
has been the continuing campaign for human rights and religious liberty, especially in the Soviet Union. There are currently
an almost equal number of evangelicals and Jews in the USSR;
and both communities of believers currently face persecution,
discrimination, and repression. The National Interreligious
Task Force on Soviet Jewry, a unique instrumentality that brings
Christians and Jews together on this issue, recently sent a
seven-person delegation, including evangelicals, to the 1980
Madrid Conference on European Security and Cooperation.
They pressed for full compliance of the human rights provisions of the Helsinki Final Act that was signed in 1975 by
thirty-five governments. In Madrid the Interreligious Task Force
outlined five specific rights that evangelicals and Jews demand
of the USSR: the right of Soviet Jews and Christians to leave the
Soviet Union to resettle elsewhere and to be reunited with their
families; an end to the official virulent Soviet campaign of
anti-Semitism; the right of Soviet Jews and Christians to fully
exercise the right to employment; the right to provide religious
education for children under the age of eighteen; and the right
to maintain houses of worship in the Soviet Union, houses that
are well-maintained and not in disrepair.

In April, 1979, the free world rejoiced when five Prisoners of
Conscience were released by the USSR. Among the five were
two Soviet Jews, Eduard Kuznetzov and Mark Dimshitz, and
evangelical pastor, Georgi Vins. However, there are still many
Jews and Christians imprisoned in the Soviet Union. It is clear
that the twin issues of human rights and religious liberty have
brought evangelicals and Jews together in a significant way.

These specific events, programs, and projects are important
to recount in any description of current evangelical-Jewish relations. Too often such relationships are clouded over in a fog of
rhetoric or in a haze of ambiguity. Yet, it must be remembered
that the evangelical-Jewish encounter, a late-blooming flower,

is really the story of individual people in contact with one another. Reports from around the country confirm a central fact: evangelicals and Jews are entering into more cooperative projects and programs than ever before. Many churches and synagogues have begun serious interreligious dialogues that involve not only pastors and rabbis but lay people as well.

Whenever Jews and evangelicals meet in dialogue, they soon discover five areas of mutual interest and agreement:

1. A similar congregational polity and structure.

2. A deep respect and reverence for the integrity and authenticity of the Hebrew Bible, the foundation of both Jewish and evangelical spiritual values.

3. An abiding commitment to the security and survival of both the people and the state of Israel.

4. A shared commitment to the principle of separation of church and state in the United States.

5. A mutual involvement in the struggle to achieve human rights and religious liberty for their co-religionists in the Soviet Union.

Volumes have been written on each of these areas, but a brief description is necessary, particularly since the points represent the basis for the increasing number of evangelical-Jewish dialogues. Evangelical church life and Jewish congregational life are strikingly similar. Both are free of any hierarchical structures, and each congregation is uniquely (sometimes defiantly) independent. It selects its own pastor or rabbi, conducts the kind of religious service it desires, and operates as a free entity within the community. Synagogues and evangelical churches are usually members of a convention, federation, or union of like-minded congregations. Such unions often provide educational and liturgical material, allow individual congregations to work together on national or global issues of concern, and provide a host of support services for the church or synagogue. It is the power source of the evangelical and Jewish religious experience, and bitter history has taught both communities to treasure that sense of congregational independence.

The evangelical and Jewish respect and reverence for the Hebrew Bible is a self-evident truth that nonetheless needs to

be restated again and again. In a time when theological fads
come and go with dizzying speed, it is important to reaffirm the
obvious: Jews and evangelicals stake their spiritual lives on the
Bible's message and teachings. The men and women of Scripture are theologically alive for our two communities, and the
God of Scripture is eternal. That is why the Jewish and evangelical communities seemed less buffeted by the "God is dead"
message of a decade ago; nor are we often fazed by today's "in"
theologies. We are both peoples of the living God rooted to
Scripture and its moral message. The biblical view of humanity
is especially precious to us as we look to the Bible for values
and meanings for our own day. The sanctity of men and women
in a brutal and dehumanizing world, the preciousness of each
life that God created, the belief that there is meaning in human
history, and the need for an unchanging ethical view of the
universe all stem from our commitment to Scripture. This does
not mean, however, that evangelicals and Jews do not differ on
biblical interpretation. Indeed they do! In fact, there are profound differences within each community as well, but we both
share the belief that the Hebrew Bible has transcendent meaning for the entire human family. One of the most fruitful results
of the evangelical-Jewish dialogues has been an increased
awareness of the spiritual richness the Bible can offer modern
men and women. As Jews and evangelicals plumb Scripture's
depths in dialogue, they often discover profound truths that
illuminate and enhance their individual and congregational
lives. Marvin Wilson warns his fellow Christians that "the heresy
of Neo-Marcionism thrives today in those churches where
Christians fail to form in themselves a truly Biblical way of
viewing man and the world."

One of the results of this scriptural anchoring has been the
abiding commitment to the security and survival of the State of
Israel and its people by both evangelicals and Jews. Jews have
yearned and prayed for thousands of years: "Next year in Jerusalem!" Zionism, the liberation movement of the Jewish people,
is no "johnny come lately" nineteenth or twentieth-century
brand of nationalism. On the contrary, Zionism had its origin
in Scripture with the haunting verses from Psalm 137: "If I

forget thee, O Jerusalem, let my right hand forget her cunning."
"Zion" and "Jerusalem" appear hundreds of times in the
Hebrew Bible. The Jewish link to the land of Israel is etched in
Scripture and is an indestructible historical reality. The land,
the language, the people, and the religion of the Bible have all
been reinvigorated in modern Israel. That passionate commitment by Jews throughout the world to Zion, to Israel, is one
of the two powerful historic realities that fuel and sustain contemporary Jewish life. Israel reborn has set off an earthquake
of Jewish emotions, passions, and intellectual fervor that has
radically transformed the entire Jewish people. To be at home
on one's ancestral soil is a powerful sentiment that is daily
being fulfilled in modern Israel. Evangelicals, by and large,
understand and even share in the redemptive meaning of the
State of Israel. With Jews, they know that Israel, like any other
nation, is not free of imperfections and defects. Yet evangelicals
are profoundly stirred by the rebirth of a democratic Jewish
State in the Middle East and by the remarkable spectacle of
Jews from 120 countries "coming home" to Zion at last. Evangelical leaders, as well as the often-forgotten person in the
church pew, maintain a bedrock commitment to Israel's survival
that cannot be shaken by the international machinations of
"realpolitik," nor by American extremists who would weaken
the State of Israel or undermine its security. Jews and evangelicals are not unaware of the claims of the Palestinian people in
the Middle East, and both communities seek the maximum
amount of justice for all the peoples of that region with the
minimum amount of injustice. We have witnessed the single
most important move toward Middle East peace in our lifetime:
the Camp David Accords and the Egyptian-Israeli peace treaty.
The process of direct negotiations between nations provides
the single best hope for a true and just peace in the area. It is
encouraging to see many evangelicals support this positive and
fruitful move toward rapprochement and peace.

The other powerful force in modern Jewish life is the
memory of the Holocaust. Those awful years from 1933–1945
in which six million—one third of all the Jewish people in the

world—were murdered by German Nazis and their sympa-
thizers stagger the imagination and assault the religious spirit.
Only now, a generation later, has the full and overwhelming
impact of the Holocaust begun to register on the world. Plays,
books, poems, TV programs, academic courses, liturgical services, community commemorations, sermons, interreligious visits
to the Nazi death camps in Europe, the President's Commission
on the Holocaust, and many other activities represent the
human mind's attempt to deal with the infinite evil and brutality
of the Holocaust. The poignant and yet energizing "Eleventh
Commandment" of Professor Emil Fackenheim, himself a
Holocaust survivor, has become a part of the modern Jewish
belief system: "Thou shalt not grant Hitler a posthumous victory.
We Jews shall survive!" Jewish communities throughout the
world annually remember the Holocaust with a special day of
prayer and meditation. *Yom Ha Shoah,* the Day of the Holocaust,
has become an integral part of the Jewish liturgical experience.
It is observed on one Sunday each April. Some evangelical
churches have made *Yom Ha Shoah* a part of their official
church calendar. Many evangelicals wear a yellow Star of David
on their clothing on that Sunday when they attend church
services. The former "badge of shame" has now become a
symbol of heroism and solidarity with the Jewish people. It is
perhaps the most graphic symbol of the evangelical-Jewish
encounter. Even more important is the introduction of the
Holocaust into evangelical teaching materials. Christian educa-
tors are increasingly aware that the atrocious murder of the six
million Jews (and five million other innocent civilians) by the
German Nazis must be recalled in churches. It would be a
disservice to young evangelical men and women if they failed
to confront the Holocaust in their church schools. Christians
must not avoid facing the single greatest moral obscenity of this
century—perhaps of all time.

   An earlier European experience has also left its permanent
mark on evangelicals and Jews. Both communities were victims
when the state and the church became allied or united. The
Spanish Inquisition, the "star torture chambers" for "non-

believers," the religious tests for public office, the public persecution of evangelicals and Jews in several European nations,
and the terror that our peoples endured when attacked by the
established church in league with the state authorities are all
part of our collective histories. Hence, when evangelicals and
Jews came to America they were suspicious and indeed fearful
of attempts to link any religious group with the state. Evangelicals and Jews instinctively know they thrive best when there is a
clear and legal separation of religion and state, when religion
is allowed to express itself in a voluntary setting, free of state
interference and/or control. That is why evangelicals and Jews
have been at the forefront in advocating the principle of
church-state separation. We both know that the First Amendment to the U.S. Constitution must be vigorously defended
against those who would weaken or undermine its provisions
guaranteeing religious freedom and government non-inter-
ference. Jews and evangelicals have been allied in a host of
court cases involving this vital principle, and sometimes they
have stood almost alone in upholding the separationist principle. But if and when religion and politics become intertwined
both will suffer greatly. Religion will lose its prophetic stance, its
Nathan-like critique of government policies and actions. How
can Nathan, the prophet of today, point his finger of condemnation, saying, "Thou art the man," if in fact "the man" is
also Nathan, the political broker and the political ruler's chief
supporter and adherent? Despite the current temptations of
potential political influence, the dazzling and seductive allure
of political power, evangelicals and Jews are well-advised to
heed the clear warning from the Mishnah: "Be cautious with
the government, for they do not make advances to a man
except for their own need. They seem like friends in the hour
of their advantage, but they do not stand by a man in the hour
of his adversity" (Avot II:3).

On the domestic scene, the allegiance to human rights and
religious liberty has meant a parallel commitment to the concept of religious pluralism in America. Because we are two
religiously independent and diverse peoples, because we treasure our sense of uniqueness, and because we are champions of

the individual's role in religious life, we affirm religious pluralism as a positive good. Evangelicals and Jews are generally
suspicious of those who seek some kind of "super uniform
religion" in the United States, and we affirm the rich diversity
of authentic religious expressions in our midst. More study
needs to be undertaken in this area. Together we need to
examine religious pluralism from theological, cultural, political,
and individual perspectives. It is hoped that future evangelical-
Jewish meetings will address this question in a serious and
systematic way. However, for the first time in recent memory
there is present now in both the Jewish and Christian communities genuine concern that the tender plant of religious pluralism
is being severely challenged. Ironically, that challenge is coming
from what is called "The New Religious Right," an amalgam of
many single-issue groups that have recently coalesced in our
country. The rhetoric and programs of some of these "New
Right" religious leaders have the potential for undermining in
a de facto, if not de jure, way the carefully constructed and
hard-won foundations of American religious pluralism. Alarm
bells have sounded, and together as evangelicals and Jews we
must address this challenge to pluralism.

This overview of current evangelical-Jewish relations would
be incomplete without mentioning some existing problem
areas. The major problem centers on these themes: "Mission/
Witness/Conversion/Proselytization." Each term is value-laden
and emotionally charged for both communities. Several evangelical-Jewish conferences have already grappled with this
nexus, and some useful clarity and definitions have emerged.
Mission is a shared religious term that is interpreted in different
ways by each community. Jews have a religious mission to
spread the message of the one God to the entire world, to make
ethical monotheism operative everywhere: "On that day the
Lord shall be one and His name shall be one" (Zech. 14:9).
Isaiah commanded the Jewish people to be a "light to the
nations" (Isa. 42:6), but the Jewish mission has historically been
free of religious imperialism or triumphalism. The God-revering
person is required only to follow the seven classic Noachian
laws: the establishment of courts of justice, and prohibitions

against blasphemy, idolatry, incest, bloodshed, robbery, and eating flesh cut from a living animal.

Jews have generally experienced the "Christian mission" in negative ways. For centuries Jews were the victims of forced conversion, medieval "disputations," expulsions, and death at the hands of those Christians who sought to "bring the Jews to Christ." For over a thousand years "an oppressed minority within a Christianity which did not permit religious freedom as we accept it today, the Jews lived until the end of the Middle Ages in social, economic, and religious conditions that were humiliating and crushing." Even in modern times the Jewish people were confronted by coercive Christian missionaries who saw Jews only as candidates for conversion and saw Judaism as an incomplete religion. Because of that record of Christian contempt and hostility, *mission,* whatever its theological roots, is usually regarded by Jews as a hostile attack on a sacred history and an authentic and perfected religion. Tomes have been written about the child's (Christianity) hostility and hatred toward the parent (Judaism). Fortunately, an increasing number of Christian theologians are repudiating that dark and painful side of Christian history. They are genuinely repentant for Christianity's past injustices against the Jewish people, and today they emphasize the Jewish roots of Christianity. William S. LaSor, Professor of Old Testament at Fuller Theological Seminary in Pasadena, California, has written: "Just as I refuse to believe that God has rejected his people (Romans 11:1) and that there is no longer any place for Israel in God's redemptive work or in the messianic hope, so I refuse to believe that we who once were not his people, and who have become his people only through his grace, can learn nothing from those who from of old have been his people."

In 1973 Dr. Billy Graham publicly criticized the excesses of the Key 73 evangelistic campaign. Citing Romans 9–11, Graham declared: "I believe God has always had a special relationship with the Jewish people. . . . In my evangelistic efforts, I have never felt called to single out the Jews as Jews. . . . Just as Judaism frowns on proselytizing that is coercive, or that seeks to commit men against their will, so do I."

The concluding sentence of the 1972 Southern Baptist Convention resolution on anti-Semitism asserts in clear and unambiguous terms: "Southern Baptists covenant to work positively to replace all anti-Semitic bias with the Christian attitude and practice of love for the Jews, who along with all other men are equally beloved by God."

This powerful affirmation has led many evangelical leaders to see *mission* and *witness* in a different light. They make a distinction between the two, since mission may sometimes be insensitive and even coercive, while witness is the actual living out of one's faith without attempting to proselytize or convert another. Witness, by this definition, is what Jews and Christians do every day as they attempt faithfully to serve God. The quality of our family lives, the spiritual values we affirm, the prayer life found in our synagogues and churches, our active commitment to the moral issues of our time, the celebration of our place in God's universe, the integrity and authenticity of our religious communities—all of this and much more is witnessing. To witness to our faith means to translate our religious affirmations into ethical action in our homes, schools, shops, offices, and factories. As Jews and evangelicals, we can do this without seeking the conversion of the other; indeed, witness in this sense is free of hidden agendas and/or subliminal messages for our neighbor. Quite simply: "Ye are my witnesses, saith the Lord" (Isa. 43:12).

But such witnessing must be free of deception; it must be honest witnessing. One of the nagging and divisive problem areas between evangelicals and Jews is the myriad of Hebrew Christian groups that now dot our religious landscape. These groups combine the gospel message with cultural and ethnic aspects of Jewish life, such as the Hebrew language, Jewish humor, food, and holiday observance. They profess strong support of Israel and actively rally in behalf of Soviet Jewry. Hebrew Christians seek to assure prospective converts that they are not renouncing Judaism or the Jewish people if they accept Jesus as the messiah. They use sacred Jewish symbols, often in a distorted form, to get their message across. For example, the three matzot on the Passover Seder plate represent, for them, the Trinity; the broken "afikoman" is the crucified Jesus. The "shamash" or starter candle on the Hanukkah Menorah represents Jesus as the light to the world. One of the most widespread abuses is the Jewish Art Calendar that is distributed by a Hebrew Christian group, the American Board of Missions to the Jews. Outwardly it looks like the calendars so familiar to Jews, but closer examination reveals subtle proselytizing messages. One hundred thousand of these calendars are distributed annually. Each month features a conversionary message printed around Sabbath candle lighting times and the weekly Torah portion to be read in the synagogue.

Although such groups speak of "fulfilled Jews," the real intention and goal of one Hebrew Christian group, the Jews for Jesus, is clearly revealed in a document whose very title speaks volumes: "What Evangelical Christians Should Know about Jews for Jesus; a Confidential Report: Not to be Distributed to Non-Christians."

> We define ourselves as evangelical fundamentalists and we seek the cooperation of individuals and Christian bodies meeting this description. . . . We believe in affiliation with a local church and being accountable to the church for service and discipline. We will uphold the local church wherever we can.
>
> We consider ourselves an arm of the local church. We are primarily evangelists and we are always mindful that we should not usurp the authority of the local pastor. As we win and disciple (convert) Jewish people, we urge them either to take their place in a local evangelical church or establish a congregation and call their own minister. Our duty is to aid the church at large and we work as an arm of that body to gather in the Lost Sheep of the House of Israel.

It seems clear that the Jews for Jesus organization carefully changes its message to meet the specific needs of each audience, and as a result says certain things to Jews and exactly the opposite to Christians. The new believers in Jesus are not really "Jews for Jesus," but rather converts to Christianity, victims of deception.

What are the Christian community's reactions to the Hebrew

Christian phenomenon? Some official reactions of the Christian community are negative. Reverend Lawrence McCoombe, chairman of the Episcopal Church's Diocese of Long Island Commission on Christian-Jewish Relations, considers the activities of Hebrew Christians "distressing." He says: "It is upsetting to Jews because it impugns the integrity of Jewish belief. It is alarming to Christians because it misrepresents Christianity. It is disturbing to both Jews and Christians because it undermines the basis of mutual respect which it has taken so long for us to establish. We wish, therefore to make it clear that as Christians we acknowledge and affirm the integrity of Judaism and disavow completely the message and methods of these Jewish-Christian groups."

The board of governors of the Long Island Council of Churches has strongly condemned the Hebrew Christians.

> The Board . . . notes with alarm that certain groups are engaging in subterfuge and dishonesty in representing the claims of their faith groups . . . there is a confusion which results in mixing religious symbols in ways which distort their essential meaning. The Board also deplores the pressures which result when any faith group calls into question the right to continued existence of another faith group.

Yet the American Board of Missions to the Jews, the oldest and largest of the Hebrew Christian groups, claims it receives funds from three thousand churches and thirty thousand individual contributors, many of them evangelical Christians.

I fully recognize the religious imperatives of evangelical Christians to carry out the "Great Commission," to witness to their faith. However, I do not believe that deception, misrepresentation, and distortion are part of the "Great Commission." When an evangelical church or institution affords a Hebrew Christian group a platform, when otherwise well-intentioned evangelical Christians make financial contributions to such groups, or when evangelicals condone the duplicity of some Hebrew Christian and/or the Jews for Jesus groups—such actions compromise the integrity of the authentic dialogue now under way between our two faith communities. I urge the evangelical community to end any support it may be giving to the Hebrew Christian groups. There is such a thing as authentic Judaism and authentic Christianity, but the Hebrew Christian groups are neither.

With honest witnessing, we will be able to enter into a new and constructive evangelical-Jewish relationship. Gone will be the heavy, aggressive Christian proselytizers I encountered while growing up as a boy in Virginia. The Jewish people will no longer be singled out as a target group for Christian missionaries or as objects in some theological numbers game. Rather, every individual Jew and evangelical will be encouraged to live out his or her religious commitment to the fullest, drawing on the richness of our unique traditions. The affirmation of the other's cosmic worth is the necessary prelude to a fruitful and honest dialogue. In such a relationship, profound differences can be articulated and shared ideals confirmed. In such a relationship, individuals may, indeed, seek to change their religious identities; but it will take place in a climate free of coercion, pressure, or deception.

Clearly, Jews and evangelicals need to move together in this new moment that has been created. Such a moment of openness may not come to us again. Our teaching material must be purged of all stereotypes and caricatures; and, as peoples rooted in the message of the Hebrew Bible, we need to move energetically in the areas of social justice, human rights, and religious liberty. Our commitment to pluralism can free us from the dangers of religious triumphalism. Our enemies in this endeavor are bigotry, ignorance, prejudice, and suspicion. But if we truly believe we are people of God, repositories of moral and spiritual values, then it is our sacred obligation to overcome those enemies, so that future historians may say of our generation that we truly planted "mustard seeds" of reconciliation and mutual respect.

Part Two

Moral and Spiritual Challenges of the Eighties

3

The Concept of the Human Being in Jewish Thought
Some Ethical Implications

Marc H. Tanenbaum

Moral and Ethical Values and Ideals in Judaism

Neither the Bible nor rabbinic Judaism has a word for ethics. A small volume in the Mishnah, often referred to as the "Ethics of the Fathers" because it contains much ethical instruction, is titled in Hebrew merely "The Chapters of the Fathers." Ethics is not conceived apart from religion, so that it is included in whatever expression the Bible and the Talmud use for religion. Ethics is part and parcel of "the way of life" of Judaism. This conception is reflected in the following representative rabbinic statements:

> The beginning and the end of Torah is the performance of lovingkindness.

> Deeds of kindness weigh as much as all the commandments (Sotah 14 A).

> When one's deeds are greater than one's knowledge, knowledge is effective, but when one's knowledge is greater than one's deed, then knowledge is futile (Ethics of the Fathers 3:14).

That Jewish "way of life" has its origins in the experience of the divine presence in the midst of the decisive events of the

47

Exodus and of Sinai, events which have altered the entire course of human history. The children of Israel experienced the reality of the Lord of history through his involvement in their liberation from physical oppression, persecution, massacre, and injustices as "slaves unto Pharaoh in Egypt." To Pharaoh, who was worshiped as a divine emperor and who was the source of law, never its servant, the Israelite slaves were regarded as chattel, "the untouchables" of ancient Egypt.

At Sinai the Israelites had a transforming experience of divine revelation as moral will which was ratified by an everlasting covenant. Henceforth, the Israelites are perceived by God to be "a kingdom of priests and a holy nation." What an extraordinary divine-human scenario! Yesterday they were slaves, the outcasts of history; now an entire people are stamped with the dignity of priesthood and holiness and are set on the course of history with a messianic task of redemption in society and through history until the coming of the kingdom.

Israel's religion, Prof. David Flusser asserts, was a breakthrough in human consciousness. The God of Israel initiated a new era in the history of mankind, introducing a new concept of justice—which is the central message of his revelation—an uncompromising moral law, and an original social order to be established paradigmatically in the Holy Land of Palestine.[1] This postulate of individual and social justice was not to be limited to Israel only. The Creator of the universe postulates this justice for all his human creatures; it is incumbent on all the peoples of the world.

The concept of justice which emerges from the Hebrew Bible is not just the regimen of mighty men. The Bible does not identify God on the side of Pharaoh and his *imperium!* It stresses that God cares for the poor and unprotected, for the orphan, the widow, and the stranger. The basis of social justice is not to be external power and might, but the reverence of God and obedience to his moral will.

The Sacredness of Human Life

To understand the idea of justice in Israel, we must bear in mind the biblical teaching that the human being is created in the image of God, that each human life is sacred and of infinite worth. In consequence, a human being cannot be treated as a chattel or an object to be disposed of for someone's program or project or ideology, but must be treated as a personality. Every human being possesses the right to life, dignity, and honor, and the fruits of his or her labor.

Justice is respect for the personality of others and their inalienable rights, even as injustice is the most flagrant manifestation of disrespect for the personality of others. Judaism requires that human personality be respected in every human being—in the female prisoner of war, in the delinquent, even in the criminal condemned to death. The supreme importance of the human being in the economy of the universe is expressed in this rabbinic teaching:

> Man (the human being) was first created as a single individual to teach the lesson that whoever destroys one life, Scripture ascribes it to him as though he had destroyed a whole world; and whoever saves one life, Scripture ascribes it to him as though he had saved a whole world (Sanhedrin 4:5).

However, justice is more than mere abstention from injuring our fellow human beings. "The work of justice is peace, and the effect thereof quietness and confidence forever" (Isa. 32:17). It is a positive conception and includes economic well-being, intellectual and spiritual growth, philanthropy, and every endeavor that will enable human beings to realize the highest and best in their natures.

The conditions for that self-realization require active efforts to bring about the final disappearance of injustice and oppression, which, as represented in the Jewish High Holiday liturgy, is the goal of human history. "And may all wickedness be consumed as a flame and may evil rule be removed from the earth," declare the Rosh HaShanah prayers.

Moral Duties of *Tzedakah*

Nothing is more fundamental in biblical and rabbinic ethics than the moral obligation of *tzedakah*, a Hebrew term which

means both "charity" and "to do justice." The rabbinic sages of
the Talmud declared that "Almsgiving—i.e., aiding the poor
and feeding the hungry—weighs as heavily as all the other
commandments of the Torah" (Talmud Baba Batra 9A).

In proclaiming the Jubilee year, which like the Ten Commandments was ascribed to divinely inspired legislation revealed on Mount Sinai, the Bible ordained, "And if your brother
waxes poor, and his means fail with you, then you shall uphold
him; as a stranger and a settler shall he live with you" (Lev.
25:35). The rabbis observe that the expression, "your brother
may *live* with you," means that it is our personal and communal
duty to see to it that our fellow human beings do not die of
starvation. Though the person be a stranger or an alien settler,
he (or she) is to be included in the term *your brother* and is to be
treated in a brotherly and compassionate manner.

To underscore the supreme virtue of humanitarian aid to the
needy in the hierarchy of Jewish moral and spiritual values, the
rabbinic sages regarded such compassionate care of man as an
act worthy of association with divinity itself: "God says to Israel,
'My sons whenever you give sustenance to the poor, I impute it
to you as though you gave sustenance to me,' for it says, 'Command the children of Israel . . . *my* bread for *my* sacrifices . . .
shall ye observe unto *me*.' Does, then, God eat and drink? No,
but whenever you give food to the poor, God accounts it to you
as if you gave food to Him" (Numbers Rabbah XXVIII:2).

The virtue of such care for the poor and hungry is depicted
in Jewish tradition as the salient attribute of the founding
father of Judaism, the patriarch Abraham, who is called the
archetype of the "Pharisee of love." In a midrashic commentary
that begins with the phrases, "Let your house be open; let the
poor be members of your household. Let a man's house be
open to the north and to the south, and to the east and to the
west," the rabbis describe the humanitarianism of Abraham:
"He went out and wandered about, and when he found way-
farers, he brought them to his house, and he gave wheaten
bread to him whose wont it was *not* to eat wheaten bread, and
so with meat and wine. And not only this, but he built large
inns on the roads, and put food and drink within them, and all

came and ate and drank and blessed God. Therefore, quiet of spirit was granted to him, and all that the mouth of man can ask for was found in his house" (Abot de Rabbi Nathan, VII:17a, b). Elsewhere the Talmud admonishes, "He who has no pity upon his fellow creatures is assuredly not of the seed of Abraham our father" (Bezah 32b).

In Jewish communities from biblical times through the present, there was much free and generous giving of alms to all who asked. Even to deceivers! There was also much systematic and careful relief through established institutions. Each Jewish community had a *tamhui* (public kitchen) from which the poor received two meals daily. There was also the *kupah* (alms box) for the disbursement of benevolent funds on Sabbath eve to provide three meals for the Sabbath (Mishnah Peach VIII, 7). Additional care was exercised in respect to the itinerant poor who were provided with a loaf of bread which sufficed for two meals, and who were also entitled to the cost of lodging.

The biblical laws of charity in Palestine relating to "gleaning," the "forgotten sheaf," and "the corner of the field," implied the underlying idea that national territory belongs to the public as a whole. In accordance with Jewish law, landowners used to lay open fences surrounding their fields and vineyards, and during certain hours of the day the needy were allowed to eat from the produce of the harvest. There was also a three-yearly allocation of *Maaser Ani* (poor man's tithe) from the threshing floor.

Thus, there arose the charitable traditions and institutions of the Jewish people which have remained a religious-communal characteristic ever since. These customs of charity, which were foreign to the pagan frame of mind of the Greeks and Romans, also had an abiding impact on the nature of the Christian *caritas*.

Peace and War

And finally, the stability, as well as the happiness of a community, can be assured only when it rests on a foundation of peace. In the absence of peace there can be neither prosperity nor well-being. "Peace is equal in worth to everything," declare the rabbis (Sifra). And they add, "Beloved is peace since the

benedictions only conclude with the hope of peace," thus
teaching that the blessings even of the high priest are of no
avail unless accompanied by peace (Numbers Rabbah 11:7).

While the prophets of Israel and the rabbis believed that
God intended the nations to be at peace with one another, war
was not prohibited. Jewish ethics would admit the duty to defend
the higher values in human life by war if necessary. If Isaiah or
Jeremiah had thought that yielding to the foreign invader would
mean destruction to the religion or the people they valued,
they would have urged resistance with the same vigor that they
demanded constantly the practice of righteousness in obedience to God's will. All the facts of biblical and post-biblical
Judaism taken together lead to the conclusion that the ethical
judgment on war, according to Judaism, is that it must be eradi-
cated to make human life conform to the divine rule, that those
guilty of causing it commit a crime against humanity and a sin
against God. However, resistance is justified to defend the
higher values in human life. The justification would extend to a
nation's defense of its liberty. The spiritual values in the life of a
nation, which include its historic distinctiveness, may justify
defense when that nation is attacked and must engage in war to
save its independent existence. (See Dr. Israel Mattuck in his
study, *Jewish Ethics,* particularly his chapter on "The Judgment
on War.")

Some Implications of Moral Values
for the Current Human Condition

The deep concern for upholding and preserving the preciousness of human life and for building a just and peaceful
world community has at no time in human history been more
seriously threatened, in my judgment, than by the spread of
violence and terrorism throughout the world, accompanied by
the staggering increase in the international trade in arms and
the insane proliferation of nuclear weapons.

The first volume of a comprehensive work on psychoanalytic
theory written by the late Dr. Erich Fromm is titled, *The Anatomy
of Human Destructiveness* (Holt, Rinehart and Winston, 1973).

Dr. Fromm explains that he started with the study of aggression and destructiveness because, aside from being one of the fundamental theoretic problems in psychoanalysis, "the wave of destruction engulfing the world makes it also one of the most practically relevant ones." Noting that the preoccupation of professionals and the general public alike with the nature and causes of aggression is rather recent—dating in fact only to the middle of the 1960s—Dr. Fromm asserts that "one probable reason for this change was the fact that the level of violence and the fear of war had passed a certain threshold throughout the world."

As noted in a 1973 study of "Violence, Non-Violence and Struggle for Social Justice," prepared for the World Council of Churches, "violence today has become demonic in its hold on human life. In the life of some nations and among many severely oppressed peoples, it seems more like an addiction than like rational behavior."

Amnesty International, reporting on its worldwide study of the use of torture by individuals and governments, came to the conclusion that "torture can exist in any society," and indeed "the practice of torture is becoming internationalized." Although there are some exceptions, torture has been *standard* administrative practice in more than thirty countries and has occurred in more than sixty.

From the perspective of an economic historian in post-Vietnam, post-Watergate America, Robert L. Heilbroner, author of the book *An Inquiry Into the Human Prospect,* writes pessimistically of the "malaise of civilization." He states:

> There is a feeling that great troubles and changes loom for the future of civilization as we know it. Our age is one of profound turmoil, a time of deep change, and there is a widespread feeling that the world is coming apart at the seams.
>
> We have gone through "a drubbing of history," and a barrage of confidence-shaking events have filled us with a sense of unease and foreboding during the past decade or so. No doubt foremost among these has been the experience of the Vietnam War, an experience that has undermined every aspect of Ameri-

can life—our belief in our own invincible power, our trust in government, our estimate of our private level of morality.

But the Vietnam War was only one among many such confidence-shaking events. The explosion of violence in street crime, race riots, bombings, bizarre airplane hijackings, shocking assassinations have made a mockery of the TV image of middle class American gentility and brought home with terrible impact the recognition of a barbarism hidden behind the superficial amenities of life.

We switch on the evening TV and learn what's going to hit us next on the head—a hijacking, a murder, a rape, or some other daily terror. These things profoundly affect our outlook.

Social analysts report that ever since Hitler and the founding of the United Nations, more persons have been killed by massacre than by the traditional wars that have kept the world on edge. As Nathan Glazer has documented in his essay on "The Universalization of Ethnicity," (Encounter, London, Feb. 1975), "An epidemic of conflicts is taking place literally on every continent of the world in which race, religion, region and nationality are involved, frequently resulting in practices of torture, mass aggression, and in some cases, near-genocide."

Among informed observers of the international scene, a mood of pessimism, even despair, has emerged over the human prospect in the face of these assaults against human life. This *kulturpessimismus* is further compounded by a number of massive universal problems that show no signs of going away in the forseeable future.

1. There is the enormous world refugee problem. A total of 12.6 million people were refugees from their homelands or displaced from their homes within their native countries ("internally displaced peoples") at the beginning of 1981. While the world's attention has been focused on the plight of southeast Asians—the Vietnamese boat people, the Cambodians, the ethnic Chinese, among others—the most tragic, "life-threatening" refugee problems today are to be found among the 6.3 million refugees and displaced persons on the African continent.

According to the 1981 World Refugee Survey published by

the United States Committee for Refugees (on whose board of directors I am privileged to serve), the worldwide refugee total dropped 3.4 million over the last year, because of the improving situation in southeast Asia, where millions of Cambodians who were displaced by war and famine have returned to their farms. But in Africa, whose fifty-three countries are among the poorest in the world, the number of refugees and displaced persons jumped from 4 million to 6.3 million as a result of political turmoil, religious-ethnic-tribal conflicts, and a spreading catastrophic drought. Africa today has one refugee to every seventy-five people.

About a fourth of all Africa's refugees are in one country—Somalia. More than 1.5 million people have crossed the borders of this small country (with an original population of 3.6 million), seeking refuge from the war between Somalia and Ethiopia over possession of the arid Ogaden region. The land they are leaving, as well as other east African countries—Ethiopia, Djibouti, and Sudan—are all in the grip of a persistent drought which has forced thousands of people to move for survival.

In this barren region of northeast Africa, there are now some 3.9 million refugees, and they represent one of the world's largest concentrations of suffering peoples. Except for the major international relief agencies and the Christian and Jewish refugee agencies who are involved in seeking to bring relief to these tragic human beings, the plight of the Somalian and other African refugees is virtually unknown to most people. Tens of thousands will surely die before the world wakes up and responds adequately in time to save some lives.

In southeast Asia there are still 700,000 Cambodian refugees in camps in Thailand and on the Thai-Cambodian border. In addition, the flight of Indochinese to other Asian countries persisted through 1980 and 1981. More than 160,000 refugees escaped from Vietnam and Laos, among them an estimated 75,000 boat people. The flow from both countries continued at a rate exceeding 10,000 a month during the early months of 1981. (Since 1975, more than 1.6 million refugees survived their flight from Vietnam, Laos, and Cambodia. The number of those who died during the exodus is huge, probably several hundreds of thousands, although there is no valid way to count them.)

It should be here noted that the response of Catholic, protestant, evangelical, and Jewish leaders and institutions to the southeast Asian tragedy was one of the glorious chapters in the history of these religious bodies in this century. Since 1975, some 400,000 southeast Asians were resettled and rehabilitated in the United States alone, and 70 percent of these human beings were sponsored, resettled, and rehabilitated—restored to their human dignity—by groups such as Lutheran Relief Service, Catholic Relief Services, Church World Service, World Vision, and the American Jewish Joint Distribution Committee and the Hebrew Immigrant Aid Society.

These life-saving programs were a translation into human reality of the basic biblical affirmations of the dignity of human life and love of neighbor that is inspiring in itself. Equally important, however, is a paradigm for our future collaboration in seeking to humanize the conditions under which so many millions of fellow human beings are forced to exist, frequently through no fault of their own.

It should appropriately be acknowledged that Denmark, Norway, and Sweden are among the top contributors to the United Nations efforts to help refugees, when measured on a per capita basis. The United States accepted more refugees (677,000) than any other country but ranked fifth on a per capita basis. The United States also contributed more money than any other nation in refugee aid, but on a per capita basis ranked twelfth in its financial contributions. Israel accepted one refugee for every thirty-seven residents, and Malaysia, Australia, and Canada also accepted more refugees per capita than the United States.

In looking to our common work in this area of vital moral and human concern, we need to ponder our responsibilities for saving lives not only in Africa, but in Pakistan as well. Next to the Somalian refugees, the plight of 1.4 million Afghani refugees who fled to Pakistan after the brutal December 1979 Soviet intervention represents one of the great tragedies of our time. To complete the picture of human tragedy, we should know of the magnitude of the world refugee situation:

Asia and Oceania, 2 million
Africa, 6.3 million
Middle East, 3.5 million
Latin America, 240 thousand
Europe, 350 thousand

2. There is the world hunger and population problem, which is, of course, also part of the refugee complex of problems. Despite the recent heroic efforts to provide massive food supplies—in which Christian and Jewish institutions also played a leading role—some eight hundred million people in Asia, Africa, and Latin America continue to starve or suffer from severe malnutrition. It is estimated that in the developing countries several million people will die from hunger during the coming year.

The world's present economic condition, Robert Heilbroner writes, resembles an immense train, in which a few passengers, mainly in the advanced capitalist countries, ride in first-class coaches in conditions of comfort unimaginable to the enormously greater numbers crammed into cattle cars that make up the bulk of the train's carriages.

For Western civilization with its liberal, humanitarian ideals and for people with our unambiguous Jewish and Christian ethical heritages to temporize in the face of the greatest moral challenge in the last decades of the twentieth century is to risk the betrayal of everything morally meaningful that we profess to stand for. What is at stake in the way we respond during the coming months and years to this unparalleled world famine is our capacity to arrest the cycle of dehumanization and callousness to suffering that is abroad in the world, ultimately affecting all peoples. We need to set into motion forces of caring and compassion that are the singular qualities without which an emergent interdependent—and peaceful—world cannot be sustained.

The Christian and Jewish communities, I believe, in concert

with other cultural forces in our societies, can make a distinctive
contribution, namely, the definition and articulation of a new
"Ethic of Scarcity" for peoples in our Western (and other)
societies. The Western nations, in particular, have been blessed
since their founding with what appears to be almost limitless
natural resources and raw materials. We seem to have been
living in a set of unexamined assumptions that constitute an
"Ethic of Abundance" which has rationalized and justified end-
less consumption, self-indulgence, and permissive hedonism.
The waste at our business and social functions—conferences,
conventions, weddings, confirmations, bar mitzvahs, even fu-
neral wakes—has verged on the scandalous, especially when
seen against the background of the needs of the world's starving
masses. We have in fact entered a new experience of growing
scarcity of resources and energy supplies; and our nations
require a definition of values and human priorities that will
result in greater self-discipline, restraint, and a genuine motivation to share out of a more limited supply of the earth's goods.

3. There is the arms race and the nuclear weapons proliferation. Consider some representative data:

In each of the sixty military conflicts since the end of World
War II, imported weapons were used almost exclusively, and
those arms have brought not only violence and destruction but
death to more than 10 million people (The MIT Center for
International Studies).

In 1973, $240 billion were spent to train, equip, and maintain
armed forces. The international trade in nonnuclear arms now
tops $18 billion annually—up from a mere $300 million in 1952
and increasing 550% since 1950. In fiscal 1975 the United States
sold $9.5 million in military supplies to seventy-one countries;
$600 million worth more was sold through commercial chan-
nels and another $600 million worth was given away.

The Soviet Union is second in international arms sales—$39
billion since 1950, $5.5 billion in 1974. France is third with a
sale of $3 billion to eighty nations, and Britain follows with $1.5
billion.

In 1973 Third World nations imported $7.7 billion. Impover-
ished India has doled out $3 billion to the Soviet Union for

arms in the past three years. Pakistan, scrimping to find $250 million for a new fertilizer factory, spends at least that much on weapons annually.

Today there are 340 research reactors and 475 nuclear power plants in forty-six nations, a number of which would permit production of atomic bombs as well as electricity. Hans Grimm, deputy director of the IAEA, says, "Any really determined nation could now produce the bomb" (*Time* Magazine, June 22, 1981). The International Atomic Energy Agency in Vienna, according to the *New York Times* of November 2, 1975, predicts "the installation of 356 nuclear generating stations in the third world by 1990."

Poor nations can be expected to obtain nuclear weapons as a by-product of the atomic power plants that many of them are now building or contemplating, and it is quite conceivable that some may use these as instruments of blackmail to force the developed world to undertake a massive transfer of wealth to the poverty-stricken world.

Five arms control experts, writing in the Harvard magazine of November 1975, predict that some nuclear wars are likely to occur before this century's end as a direct result of bombs spreading around the world like an "epidemic disease." The proliferation of "peaceful" nuclear power only aggravates the danger because as MIT political scientist George Rathjens (formerly of the U. S. Arms Control and Disarmament Agency) writes, "By the end of the century there will be several thousand reactors around the world, each producing enough material to build a weapon a week."

The peril is compounded by the knowledge disclosed by Dr. Theodore Taylor in his study, "Nuclear Theft," that an atomic weapon would not be impossible for a guerilla-group to construct with just over thirteen pounds of plutonium. It is believed that more than four thousand pounds of plutonium were shipped in the United States last year and nobody knows exactly how much of that material was lost in transit or production.

I fully appreciate, and support in many ways, the argument made by Dr. Paul Nitze that "the United States take positive steps to maintain strategic stability and high-quality deterrence" to assure that the Soviet Union or some other enemy does not believe they could profit from seeking a nuclear-war-winning capability or effectively use pressure tactics to get their way in a crisis situation (*Foreign Affairs*, January 1976). Nor am I unmindful of the need and possibilities of controlling the defense budget through judicious pruning of waste (*Foreign Affairs*, January 1976, "Controlling the Defense Budget," by Barry M. Blechman and Edward R. Fried).

Given the absolutely catastrophic nature of nuclear war, we must ask whether or not our government and its allies have done enough to restrict their sales of nuclear reactors to unstable countries and to countries of uncertain persuasion. The late Sen. Hubert Humphrey introduced a bill calling for Congress to share systematically in shaping policies guiding arms exports. We sincerely trust that Congress will help America finally to develop a rational approach to arms sales as well as to the intensification of universal disarmament measures. The very survival of the human family depends on such measures taken vigorously here and in concert with other nations.

Some Implications for Christians and Jews

What are the implications of these facts for Christians and Jews today?

It is evident that we live in an age of violence and terror. There is not a continent on the globe that is not despoiled by terror and violence, by barbarism, by a growing callousness to human suffering and pain, and by threat to human existence. At the center of the human crisis is the fundamental depreciation of the meaning and value of human life. The biblical affirmation that each human being is created in the sacred image of God and is therefore of ultimate worth and preciousness is being battered from every side.

It is my conviction that this erosion in the belief in the sanctity of human life is one of the decisive black legacies bequeathed by Nazi Germany to mankind. The overwhelming majority of citizens of the Western world, and their dominant institutions have avoided confronting the magnitude of evil incarnate in the Nazi Holocaust, and have therefore failed to learn how to cope with forces and structures of dehumanization that are being replicated in many parts of the globe.

The Nazi campaign against the Jewish people was unique and in many ways unprecedented. Yet the Nazi trauma must not be seen as "a Jewish obsession," for the fateful meaning of the Holocaust is of ultimate importance to the future capacity of mankind to understand itself and to acquire the resources to cope with the challenges to its survival.[2]

Bleak as are the prospects for countering these forces of dehumanization in the world, "we need not complete the task," as Rabbi Tarphon admonished, "but neither are we free to desist therefrom." In concert, if we are to learn from the Nazi Holocaust and not be doomed to allow its repetition, we must attempt at the very least the following:

First, Christians and Jews should engage in a massive, concerted effort to establish a "new humanism" on a global basis. They should seek to restore the biblical value of the infinite worth of each human life, life that must be appreciated as an end in itself and never as an object of somebody else's project, program, ideology, or revolution.

Second, Christians and Jews must help engender a national and international attitude of scorn and contempt for those who use violence or who advocate the use of violence. We must work to deromanticize all appeals to use violence and terrorism as a means of liberation or of institutionalized oppression, since from a moral standpoint no ends can justify such anti-human means.

Third, Christians and Jews must work to curtail inflammatory propaganda, especially from international forums which have psychological impact on an international scale. As Prof. Gordon Allport of Harvard University demonstrated in his monumental study, "The Nature of Prejudice," there is an inevitable progression from "verbal aggression to violence, from rumor to riot, from gossip to genocide."

Fourth, Christians and Jews must work toward educational development and communication among peoples to reduce the abrasive effects of "differences." Differences, as we have learned in the pluralistic experiences of the Western world, can be a source of enrichment rather than a threat.

Fifth, Christians and Jews should engage in an urgent educational effort to elaborate a theology and ideology of pluralism which presupposes the right of each religious, racial, and ethnic group to define itself in its own terms and to be accepted unconditionally. Group narcissism, as Dr. Erich Fromm observes, arouses intense hostility between groups, and "is one of the most important sources of human aggression." In helping establish a pluralist world view, Christians and Jews have a decisive contribution to make to the building of the ideological foundations without which a stable world community cannot come into being.

Sixth, Christians and Jews should work toward making the economy of each nation as self-sufficient and stable as possible, not perpetually requiring relief support. Inextricably linked with such an effort is the control of the arms race on an international scale, and a rational reordering of priorities that allows for adequate defense and yet at the same time reallocates some of the billions wasted on arms for the crying needs of the hungry, the diseased, and the homeless.

Central in such efforts is the need to raise international human consciousness to halt the irrational proliferation of nuclear weaponry and to bring about serious action for universal simultaneous disarmament. There is no higher priority for human survival at this moment in human history.

Christians and Jews need to recognize the fundamental interdependence of all human rights and collaborate vigorously to assure that every nation implements fully the Universal Declaration on Human Rights. In particular, Christians and Jews should work for the completion of the judicial instrumentalities called for by Article 6 of the Genocide Convention in the form of an international penal tribunal for trying those who are accused of genocide attempts anywhere in the world.

"The salvation of mankind," Alexander Solzhenitzyn reminds us, "will depend on everyone becoming concerned about the welfare of everybody everywhere."

Notes

1. See *The Holy Year and Its Origins in the Jewish Jubilee Year*, by Flusser, published by the Vatican Office for the Holy Year, 1975, Vatican City.

2. See the discussion of Max Weber's "secularization, disenchantment of the world, and rationalization" as root causes for undermining all moral norms in a bureaucratized society in my "Religious Values in an Age of Violence," pp. 46–52.

4

Biblical Social Ethics
An Agenda for the Eighties

Timothy L. Smith

I speak tonight for what I believe is a moral minority. I can imagine no better time for representatives of that minority to ponder the moral agenda of the 1980s than in the second week of Advent and on the eighth day of Hanukkah, the Feast of Lights. In that week Christians remember John the Baptist laying the ax at the root of the tree of greed, oppression, and ethnic nationalism and calling on all humankind (including Roman soldiers) to repent and believe the Good News that the kingdom of God is at hand. And on that day, Jews everywhere commemorate the cleansing and rededication of the temple by Judas Maccabeus, in symbols of not only memory but hope. The hope is that the arm of the Almighty, whose mercy endures forever, will open the gates of righteousness (Ps. 118:1–4, 19). "And many nations shall be joined to the LORD in that day and shall be my people," Zechariah's prophecy declares, "Not by might, nor by power, but by my spirit, saith the LORD of hosts" (Zech. 2:11, 4:6, KJV).

No theme persists with more precision and intervity in the Hebrew and Christian Scriptures and in the teachings of Mishnah and Talmud than the right-making power of *Hesed,* that is, loyalty or ethical love to God and to one's fellow human beings. The definition of that "steadfast love," or faithfulness, is

64

rooted in the character of God that is revealed in both Testaments. In biblical terms, loving other persons as you love yourself is the moral expression of loving God with all your heart and soul and strength.

All else in biblical ethics flows from this. In the Book of Deuteronomy as in the teachings of Jesus, the only way to justify the possession of power (whether political, economic, cultural, or familial) is to exercise it on behalf of the oppressed. Wealth, including land, is not property owned, but held; and its stewardship is to be discharged in a community of mutual care. The congregation of the righteous, whether Jewish or Christian, exists by virtue of its mission to set wrongs right. In that congregation's incarnation of Torah all the nations of the world will be blessed.

Jesus of Nazareth meant precisely what he said in the words, "I have not come to destroy the law but to fulfill it." Like many rabbis of his time, he understood the law ethically, following the prophets Hosea and Micah, Jeremiah and Ezekiel, and both the first and second Isaiahs. All these spoke of God's judgment and faithfulness while the kingdoms of Israel and Judah were passing into captivity. A Jew from Tarsus shared that understanding fully when he declared, as both Moses and Jesus did, that love is the fulfilling of the law (Rom. 13:10). "Do not take revenge, my friends, but leave room for God's wrath," Paul wrote; "If your enemy is hungry, feed him" (Rom. 12:19–20, NIV, citing Lev. 19:18; Deut. 32:35; Prov. 25:21). A thousand rabbis were saying the same things in congregations of Jews scattered all over the Roman Empire.

What Jesus brought and Paul taught was not a new ethical standard but the promise of power from the Spirit of God to keep the old one. Paul's summary of his Epistle to the Romans was, I believe, what he also thought was a summary of the promise of the new age and the new covenant in the prophecies of Zechariah, Jeremiah, and Joel. The kingdom of God, Paul wrote, is righteousness, peace, and joy in the presence of the Lord, that is, in the "hallowing" or "right-making" Spirit.

John Wesley once wrote that when the Hebrew word *kōdhesh*, translated "holy" in the Scriptures, is applied to divinity, it has the force of an active verb. God's holiness, so far as we can know it, is expressed in setting the children of his covenant straight. That is what constitutes salvation, in both the Old and the New Testaments. The judgments of the Lord are true and right-making altogether. "Be ye holy for the Lord your God is holy," both prophets and apostles said—meaning by those words, be ethically righteous. Rudolph Otto's concept of what he called the numinous, the psychic and spiritual experience of the presence of God, is not in Hebrew or Christian faith a substitute but a foundation for ethics; our God is a consuming fire.

Christians and Jews, then, share a common heritage of law as ethical love. Alas, they also share a common history of temptation to substitute outward forms of legalism for the inner realities of loyalty. For Christians, that temptation has also included the inward substitute for loyalty proffered by an antinomian conception of grace. But the teachings of the New Testament will not allow it. The law is holy, just, and good, Paul wrote; and Peter chose the opening words of Moses' summary of the Ten Commandments in Leviticus for his text, "Be holy because I, the LORD your God, am holy" (Lev. 19:2; I Peter 1:16, NIV).

The social ethic of evangelical Protestants, reflected historically in moments of obedience as well as of what was acknowledged in retrospect as gross disobedience, has always rested on these Hebraic elements in New Testament religion. Consider, for example, the ethic of work. John Calvin did not invent it; and it is a libel on Jews, to say nothing of hard-working Orthodox Greeks and Polish Catholics, to call it "the Protestant work ethic." Calvin discovered honesty, industry, and self-restraint in the Bible—in the Book of the Proverbs and the Epistles of Paul. And like Calvinists since, he found ample warning against overdoing it in the account of the Feast of Tabernacles and the story of Mary and Martha.

The idea of a Christian commonwealth in Puritan England and colonial New England was likewise Hebraic to the core. The metaphors of exodus, pilgrimage, and promised land were pervasive. Chosenness, in Massachusetts Bay as in ancient Israel, implied mission, not privilege—or, perhaps I should say, the privilege of a mission destined to bless all humankind. John Winthrop's assumption that the magistrates were the Lord's anointed, responsible to protect the widows and the fatherless and to prevent the oppression of the poor, shaped the Puritan theocracy. The clergy, like their counterparts in ancient Israel, the priests and prophets, were advisors to the magistrates, who held power as stewards of the God of justice, peace, and love. In Pennsylvania a bit later, the communitarian idealism of Quakers, Mennonites, Brethren, and Moravians was rooted in the scriptural sensibility that had given the city of brotherly love its name. After 1730 the Evangelical Awakening spread across the Atlantic world, from New Brunswick and Northampton in America, and Halle and Herrnhut in Germany, to London and Bristol, and back again. Its leaders in both Europe and America—John Wesley, George Whitefield, Jonathan Edwards, and Count Zinzendorf—proclaimed in Hebraic terms the responsibility of Christians to place human society as well as their individual lives under the law of the Lord, and so to spread scriptural righteousness over the land.

True, the moral minority of committed believers in revolutionary America never thought the republic was at its outset a righteous one; but they wanted it to become so. Even in the confines of their Protestant perspective, however, that did not mean an English style of ethnocentric chosenness. During the half-century preceding the war for independence, churchmen in the colonies of New York, New Jersey, Pennsylvania, and Maryland caught the vision of a religiously plural society, even though a Protestant and Christian one. Whether Dutch Reformed, Scotch-Irish Presbyterian, German Lutheran, Welsh Quaker, English Methodist and Baptist, or Rhineland Mennonite and Brethren, the diverse settlers slowly became aware that they all defined goodness in biblical terms and shared similar biblical hopes for a just society.

Although each group survived in the American wilderness by developing a passion to win adult converts, and each in one way or another absorbed the evangelical idea that individuals should be born again by the power of the Spirit of God, the social and ethical goals of evangelism and Christian experience were Hebraic. Their vision was not a restoration of Nathan's Israel with an anointed David at its head, of course. That vision had long since faded away, even in New England. Rather, they saw themselves, and the new nation, called to become a people of Jeremiah's new covenant, a moral minority, a leaven in the lump. Jeremiah's ethics of exile, as I have called it, defined the colonists' duty to create a righteous society by personal example and spiritual leadership, without relying on the state to either sustain or restrain any form of religious commitment.

To be sure, the framers of the American Constitution, like the clergymen and the tiny group of rabbis of that day, were profoundly distrustful of human nature and convinced of the pervasiveness of original sin. But by the turning of Thomas Jefferson's century, the confidence was growing that a new age was dawning, especially in America, and that in the "last days" the Holy One of Israel would pour out his Spirit on all flesh.

This renewal of messianic and millennial visions of a world-wide kingdom of *shalom* shaped the moral aspirations of Victorian society on both sides of the Atlantic. We know, or at least I know, very little yet of the ways in which this biblical vision led Jews in America to share the optimism of the nineteenth century. But we all know its impact on leaders of every evangelical Protestant community in the young nation, from Francis Asbury and Lyman Beecher to Alexander Campbell and Charles G. Finney. All of these understood conversion to begin the process by which God would write his Torah in human hearts, and so bring about a real change in persons. And all of them affirmed both the necessity and the promise that that same law be incarnated in the customs, statutes, and institutions of society. Methodists, I believe, played a crucial role in helping evangelicals assimilate the biblical doctrine that law and love are one, and that the individual righteousness that flows from covenant faith is a redemptive force in society as well.

The combination of these hopes and convictions with the equally intense affirmation of liberty of conscience and freedom of religious choice kindled the midnineteenth-century movement for social reform in both the United States and Great Britain. I have chronicled its Protestant aspects in my book *Revivalism and Social Reform.* From that era to this, Christians and Jews in America have found both inspiration and guidance from their Scriptures to challenge the institutions of society that compounded the miseries of the poor, oppressed and enslaved Black people, restrained the creative powers of women, and denied justice to workers. In Woodrow Wilson's progressive era, the social gospel's renunciation of evil, as well as its call to spiritual commitment to the kingdom of God, drew not only on the words of Jesus but on the passages from Deuteronomy and the prophets in which they were rooted. The most radical of the Christian socialists, George D. Herron, focused every one of his college lectures on *The Social Meanings of Religious Experiences* on texts from the books of Moses.

The link between the social ethics of Judaism and Christianity is especially clear in the way Black ministers, converted in slavery or under the shadow of it, perceived Christian theology. White slaveowners and their wives, and white ministers, thought Black people possessed only a childlike intelligence, so they told them Bible stories. Spared the interminable logic by which both rabbis and clergymen often obscured the saving truths of Scripture, Black converts grasped the messages that lay in the stories themselves, as ancient Jews and early Christians had done. And the Blacks received those truths and embraced that faith in the justice and love of God from Christians who held them in slavery! Their masters told them the story of Moses and the law with obedience in mind. Listening Blacks understood obedience biblically; it was grounded in thankfulness for the goodness of the one who found his people slaves in Egypt and led them first to freedom and then into covenant with him. Slave ministers loved the story of Jonah because he declared, unwillingly, that God was gracious not only to Jews but also to the people of Nineveh and, therefore, to Black Africans and all the rest of humanity. They found in Job's sufferings a foreshadowing of theirs, and in his hold on a faith that transcended the tragedies of time a foundation for their hopes in both this world and the next. The stories of Mary and her baby and of a dying Son of God had no anti-Semitic overtones for Negro Christians at all; they bespoke rather a God whose suffering love would at last triumph in justice, on earth as in heaven.

The profundity of nineteenth-century Black preachers, as of Jewish theology since the Holocaust, lay in their deep wrestling with the actuality of incredible evil contrasted with the biblical declaration of the goodness of God. Black people never needed a social gospel. For in their first as in their latest encounter with the teachings of the Bible, whatever good news there was at all was social. It acknowledged the mystery of corporate sin and declared the wonder of an individual salvation which bound them, as it ought to bind all human beings, in forgiving and creative love.

In the face of such insight, I have in recent years found the traditional interpretations of the rise of the social gospel even less satisfactory than before. Liberal Christians and progressive historians have thought it stemmed from the new social sciences, the Marxist critique of capitalism, evolutionary thought, and historical criticism of the Bible. But the arguments by which such diverse Christian radicals as William Booth, Walter Rauschenbusch, and John A. Ryan condemned the existing order, as well as their proposals for its redemption were rooted in the ethical teachings of the Old and New Testaments. Solomon Schechter, founder of the Jewish Theological Seminary of America, understood this rooting very well. By contrast, Christian or Jewish modernists were never social radicals. Their position was, in fact, a model for twentieth-century culture religion; they made culture itself both source and standard for faith and ethics.

If the foregoing summary is correct, the moral confusions of what passes for biblical faith in the 1980s, whether among Jews or Christians, will be comprehensible only as you keep in mind what is new to the twentieth century and what is old. Religious modernism, of course, is new; so is its claim to have parented social idealism. New also to popular consciousness is the secularization of art and learning, of psychology and sociology. The long-term result was to undermine the ideals of fundamental law, individual virtue, and marital fidelity that have ordered public and private life for generations.

Widespread social despair is also new, as commentators upon it since the 1950s have said again and again. It was nurtured in the maddening acceleration of social change in the early part of the century and the tragedies of war and depression. Thereafter, it was fed by the rebirth of racist nationalism in Nazi Germany, the explosion of the Second World War, the horrors of the Holocaust, and the revelation at Hiroshima of the possibility of a worldwide holocaust that would decimate all peoples and contaminate all nature. The monster of death and despair, as Robert Lifton has shown in so many moving ways, has laid dark hands on all human hopes.

New religious developments in both evangelicalism and Judaism have contributed to the confused sense of hopelessness. Among these was the dispensational constriction of Christian hope that stemmed from both popular Jewish messianism and the spread among Protestants of the millenarian views of the Plymouth Brethren. Gershom Scholem has powerfully depicted the late medieval roots of the former. Tourists to Israel sometimes encounter its living vestiges in Mea Shearim or Safed. Both sets of ideas contributed to the rise of Zionism, but in ways that do not satisfy either the religious or the secular ideologies dominant in Israel today. Novel also, at least in its political application, was the spiritualizing of the idea of the religious congregation and the confinement of its social duty to sectarian boundaries. Equally enervating was the revival of an ancient preoccupation with the words rather than with the saving meanings of the Book to whose authority over faith and morals increasing thousands gave allegiance. The marriage of the dogma of individualism with the doctrine of the covenanted community, among both evangelical Fundamentalists and some elements of Orthodox and Hassidic Jewry, was one outcome of the effort to clothe that new dogma in the vestments of old time religion.

All these new factors sustained what I have concluded was the great sea-change in the religion of the twentieth as compared with the previous two centuries, namely, its pervasive antinomianism. The wholesale desertion of the idea of inward and radical obedience to Torah—the law of the Lord that Paul, following Jesus, had proclaimed to be holy, just and good—corrupted every Jewish and Christian tradition. The moral retreat took diverse paths, whether of externalized legalism or an internalized dogma of justification by faith alone; of a sacramental church or a ritually traditional synagogue; or of an unworldly and therefore, it was alleged, more godly spirituality. One symptom of moral declension was that the present generation of Christian scholars in Bible and theology received calmly and subsequently ignored the disclosure of the scandalous private life of two of the twentieth century's greatest theologians. Such a response betrays little commitment to the prophecies of either Zechariah or Zacharius. Both Amos and James the brother of Jesus would seem a moral minority here.

The primary agenda for the 1980s in both Jewish and evangelical social ethics, therefore, is the reconstruction of biblical faith and hope in a despairing age. Without it, the love which the authors of Psalms 113–118 and the first letter to the Corinthians say is eternal can have only limited temporal significance.

The ethical renewal which depends on that reconstruction is indeed urgent. Consider the following agenda for a biblical social morality which I think ought in the 1980s to claim the loyalty of those whose faith is being revived, whether they represent a majority or only a minority of morally concerned persons. I speak from an evangelical perspective, grounded in the history of the past two hundred years, to be sure. But I see no need at all to distinguish the moral commitments I think appropriate for Christians just now from those that many would identify as marks of faithfulness among Jews.

Like many others, I have been moved by certain moral preoccupations that became prominent in the 1970s: abortion, sexual licentiousness, the pollution of the environment, the oppression of women, the computerized bureaucratic assault on personhood, the theft of savings perpetrated by runaway inflation, and the financial corruption of the democratic process. I am persuaded, however, that any reasoned survey of the problems of the human race in a world that has become a neighborhood would rank the ethical significance of every one of these new issues somewhere below the old ones. The persisting moral challenges that the nineteenth-century Christians and Jews found central in the Scriptures, and which the Communist ideology in its original form professed to offer a cure, remain the critical ones: the distress of the poor, crying for bread, shelter and decent employment; the oppression of the weak by those who think power their right and privilege rather than an entrusted obligation; racial discrimination, especially racist nationalism, whether claiming to be justified by religion or not; and the violence which, in war as in private crime, attests the dehumanization of modern culture.

Much of the appeal of the new ethical issues is to the self-interest of the affluent populations of the industrial free world, especially the United States. Their advocacy turns our attention inward, on our own prosperity and privilege; and it provides a blanket of self-righteousness to insulate us from the depths of human suffering around the world. Much of that suffering seems to stem from as well as perpetuate our abundance. Our current preoccupation with survival, by which we too often mean the survival of our privileged status, ignores the fact that despite war, depression, and holocaust we have survived, with a success bordering on the obscene.

Meanwhile, helpless peoples in Africa and southern Asia fall victims of more desperate hunger, more inhumane violence, and more insolently racist warfare than Europe and America, which for a time seemed to make these evils a trademark, ever dreamed. A conscientious embrace of the notion of a common humanity forbids us to suppose that the victims in the barrios of Bogota and Rio, in the desert of the Ogaden, or in the jungles of Laos have somehow brought their fates on themselves. They did not *choose* to be born in cultures weak in progressive idealism and the commitment to equal justice that Hebrew and Christian faith have generally fostered. In us, God promised, they too are heirs of *shalom*—wholeness, righteousness, health, peace.

The moral minority of Jews and Christians, who have in the twentieth century sought to create a world order grounded in the righteousness intended for "the healing of the nations," must realize that the evils that have afflicted the whole world are deeply rooted in our own cultures. Judaism and Christianity both affirmed the dignity of toil, and the entitlement of the laborer—whether skilled or unskilled, professional, farmer or merchant prince—to a decent return for his or her work. Both affirmed that economic benefit is generally a product of individual and social righteousness. How easy it has been for us to forget that the wealth and property which flowed from the cultural heritage of Torah and atoning grace was in both Testaments forbidden fruit if eaten for our own pleasure or power. Neither Christians nor Jews should forget that when Jesus said, "The poor you always have with you," he was quoting the Book of Deuteronomy, in one of the Old Testament's sharpest delineations of the obligations of those who hold wealth to those who do not.

Nor should we forget that the oppressive use of political and military power is as intertwined with the history of Hebrew and Christian peoples as are the persistent denunciations of it by prophets and apostles. This evil has been pervasive in all times and all cultures, to be sure. But what Westerner can forget Commodore Perry's instruction of the Japanese in the use of force, or the example English troops first set for the peoples of China, India, and Arabia, whose current quest of nuclear weapons we deplore. President Richard Nixon and Secretary of State Henry Kissinger awakened Laotians to economic and political aspirations which that quiet people then sought to fulfill with archaic Communism. The resulting racial suicide we now witness with horror. And at this moment, all around the world, most notably in Latin America and the Near East, the sale of American arms to friends, and to both the friends and enemies of our earlier friends, has sown the dragon's teeth. The proliferation of the nuclear weapons we invented and first employed at Hiroshima and Nagasaki has now become, as President Jimmy Carter correctly put it, the gravest of many threats to human survival.

To speak of this is to remember also the Jewish and Christian contributions to the religiously sanctioned racism that now stokes the furnaces of militarist nationalism everywhere. Our collective heritage is to have known commonwealths that nur- tured justice and human dignity, to have recognized the God of creation as the Lord of our own natures, and to have seen out of both divine and human choosing a vision of universal peace and justice. Today, however, in Israel as in the United States, the covenant of servitude and accountability has been prostituted to privilege; and the alleged transcendent worth of national survival is used to justify oppression. Morroccan Jews in Israel, to say nothing of Israeli Arabs, know this quite as well as Black evangelicals in Mobile or Minneapolis.

Precisely because we are akin in the sin of having failed to keep the vision of justice clearly before us, I think, Jews and evangelicals need each other deeply just now. Only so can we effectively resist those who, in the name of morality in both Israel and the United States, are now wrapping a narrow and self-serving ethic in the flag of their nation and arguing that group survival is an ultimate human value.

I urge no cheap grace here, nor do I call for acquiescence in racist or nationalist terrorism that claims to promote justice for the oppressed. Much realistic moral thought, however, lay back of the earlier formulation of the ideology of the State of Israel Some of it stemmed from reflections on the Holocaust by psy- chiatrists, sociologists, political scientists, and theologians who were profoundly sensitive to the meanings, both immanent and transcendent, of Jewish culture and peoplehood in human history. I need not analyze that ethical ideology here in any detail. Its principal points were: to deal in radical justice with the peoples who in recent centuries had inhabited the land of Israel; to resist the clinically verified compulsion to adopt the ways of one's own oppressors in relationships with the weak; to make religious commitment an unfettered personal decision in an explicitly religious state, in the confidence (justified by later events) that secularized Jews would embrace one or another version of the faith of believing Jews when they returned to the land of their fathers; and finally, in a commitment to collective welfare that was more biblical than Marxist, to renounce eco- nomic oppression of not only fellow Jews but of Islamic and Christian neighbors.

No thoughtful evangelical can be ungrateful for the warnings issued recently by Jews such as Marc Tanenbaum against the potential danger of the movement that in recent months has claimed the name "Moral Majority." He and many others have done so knowing full well that some of the most uncompromising support for Israeli foreign policy comes from dispensational Fundamentalists in that self-styled majority. The latter have concluded in their biblically literal way, as some Jews have, that God's covenant with ethnic and political Israel is irrevocable, and that to support all the policies of its reconstituted government is surely to be on the right side at Armageddon. Sensitive Jews, however, have strong reasons to question the morality of the majorities of our time. I ask both Jews and evangelicals, then, to consider how the spirit of hard-lining nationalism—whether Israeli or American and pro-Israeli—is the same as that which, in Argentina and Iran now, and in Nicaragua and other places lately, yields oppressive and racist violence in God's name. It mocks the Third Commandment, I believe; and it reflects the same spirit that originally pervaded national socialism in Germany, when Adolf Hitler cast it as a Christian crusade against Communism.

Christians and Jews who share a deeply felt commitment to the ethics of the prophets have an obligation to bear witness to each other. Certainly I must do so here, appealing not only to Jesus and Paul, whom you Jews honor, but also to Micah, Isaiah, Jeremiah, the rabbis of the Diaspora, and the Essenes of Qumram, whom you may, understandably, honor more.

Without imposing on you the whole of Jeremiah's denial of the permanence of the covenant with the Kingdom of Judah and with David's royal line, I ask you to think afresh about that prophet's declaration that the survival of the Jewish nation and people was not dependent on the perpetuation of the throne of David on Mount Zion. He declared instead that Torah would only bring life, for Israel and for all humanity, if its truth were received in a covenant of the heart's intent and not simply the culture's compulsion. That Jeremiah stood on Micah's ground is evident from the successful use of the argument that he did, indeed, stand on Micah's ground by his defenders at the trial

for sedition that nearly cost his life. The second Isaiah also saw
the vision of a peaceable kingdom. When it came, all the
nations of the world and the islands of the sea would see the
light of the glory of the Lord risen on Israel; and the sound of
violence would no more be heard in the land. The same vision
is clear in a thousand Jewish readings of the history of the
prophets. America's religious liberty, grounded as it is in a deep
recognition of the right of individuals and groups to choose
their beliefs and moral commitments, stemmed directly from
the ethics of exile that Jeremiah proclaimed.

Why should this city be laid in ruins and these fields and
vineyards burned up, Jeremiah reasoned. He advised submission, even to the evil in the rule of the king of Babylon. He
believed that God meant it, as he did Joseph's enslavement, for
the good of his people, and that the Holy One of Israel does
not countenance injustice. Renew your hearts in repentance
for violating the principles of love and justice that permeate
the Torah, Jeremiah cried; for the hope of a renewed Israel,
own the new covenant of individual as well as of corporate
accountability.

I am not now asking you to consider either the modern
Jewish or the modern Christian understanding of the meaning
of Jeremiah's new covenant, but the understanding of it that
eventually prevailed among the congregations of exiles in the
four centuries following Jeremiah. That understanding shaped
Jewish relations with Gentile cultures in the great cities of the
Hellenistic world to which Jews migrated voluntarily by the tens
of thousands after Alexander the Great. And that understanding
was decisive in the definition of the Old Testament canon.

The ethic of that new covenant, I submit, is an ethic of
peace. Resistance without violence, submission without acquiescence sustained its strategy of hope. The deepest conviction
of the diaspora communities, from Jeremiah's day to the nineteenth century, was that the moral power of the righteousness
that the old covenant required and the new covenant promised
would prevail at last over the power of marching armies, and
bring *shalom* on earth.

I say all this in painful awareness that many deeply ethical

Jews think that in our time the strategy of submission may have helped in some small way to make Auschwitz possible. They have on that account decided to resist and take vengeance on any who would "kill Jewish children."

I say it also in honor of Dr. Herman Meyersburg, who with his no-nonsense wife and babies lived in our house in Charlottesville, Virginia, while he was a resident in psychiatry at the University of Virginia medical school in 1940–41. He taught me first what I suppose both he and I have often been troubled about since: that the only people in the world then practicing the ethics of Jesus' Sermon on the Mount—which I conceive to be the same as Jeremiah's ethic of exile—were the Jews of Nazi-occupied Europe. Neither he nor I could have then imagined the evil about to fall on that people. The Holocaust, like the covenant at Sinai or what Christians believe happened at Calvary, cannot be confined to some point in time, as defined by the Greek word *kairos*. Its evil is of such a magnitude that it seems to fill all of time and be an event of what the Greeks called *chronos*.

Not all Christians, I remind you, have been holders of power—not, certainly, those of the first century nor the brothers who followed St. Francis of Assisi; not the Mennonites of the Reformation Rhineland nor the Black Baptists of Mahalia Jackson's Chicago. The American evangelical community contains far larger proportions than many suppose of persons won from out-group families. Economically deprived white Americans were predominant in the charter membership of a score or more religious groups that are a part of the American evangelical mosaic, from the Salvation Army to the Churches of Christ, the Adventists, and the Black Pentecostals. For such persons, as for the Jews in their twenty-five hundred years of exile from the land of Israel, faith and hope are the grounds of steadfast love; and that love appears to us to be the source of both temporal and eternal *shalom*. My folks also said, "Blessed is the people whose God is the Lord; righteousness alone can exalt them, and only the reproach of sin should dismay them."

All of which brings me to the evil that I believe dominates the moral agenda for the eighties, and in which we who claim a biblical faith seem deeply involved, namely, the flowering of the ideology of violence. The moral affirmation by increasing numbers of Jews and evangelicals of making preparations to engage in nuclear warfare contradicts both their Bible and their history. For the threat of nuclear holocaust has become the evil that swallows up all others, making the solution of any social problem virtually impossible.

The endorsement by a seeming majority of voters in the last United States election of twin policies calling, first, for the maintenance of America's position of economic privilege and, second, for the nuclear superiority that some think is necessary to secure it, is ominous. The event exposes fully the mindless calculus of genocide, directed this time around at the whole human race, strangling every human hope. As in Nazi Germany forty years ago, educated, culturally refined, and pleasant men and women now seem determined to stand five missles against four to preserve peace on earth. The vast majority refuse to think about the likely result: not thirty but eighty million Soviet casualties some morning before breakfast, and an escalation from twenty-five to fifty million estimated American ones (making our side, as always, look best). Moreover, this moment of unimaginable human loss may not be triggered by either of these two powers but by a smaller nation whose use of nuclear weapons for its own purposes could lead the United States or the Soviet Union to think itself under attack by the other. Among those millions of dead or wounded on both sides will be probably 75 percent of the doctors and nurses, concentrated as they are in great population centers. Perhaps thirty million children, not in any way blameable for their fate, will die in the gargantuan gas ovens that their own homes and play-yards will become. There will be no heroic marching away of those children as at Buchenwald, singing a lament of memory, fear, or hope. The wounded children and adults who survive, horribly burned, will be a lifelong burden on the uninjured minority.

Could any moral argument justify the right of a person or group of persons on this earth to hold in readiness such destructive power? Is the survival of any nation, any people, worth this sharply escalating threat to all nations, all peoples?

Other issues that excite us just now may be moral opiates, deadening our awareness of the one that towers over all else of worth. A hundred Love Canals could not in a thousand years bear off the physical, psychic, and moral waste that would flow from one searing half-hour of nuclear war. Can you imagine that the capitalistic system of free enterprise would survive it? In such a holocaust what happens to the environment for which we profess to care? And what can I say for the dignity of womanhood, or for those unborn infants who, if the advocates of a constitutional amendment against abortion succeed, will be born to live for such a death?

Yet, if I am hearing correctly, for the first time in nearly two thousand years, persons who profess faith in the God of the Old and New Testaments are embracing the prospect of such hellish violence. They dignify it with the name *war* and justify it on the principle of group survival. Even the relatively unde-structive wars of medieval knights prompted the church, in holy outrage, to lay rigid rules on the conflicts (mostly among the elite classes) it was unable to prevent. Since Hiroshima, however, American military policy has been grounded on our supposed right to use nuclear weapons to destroy masses of ordinary people. Amidst such a mania, Julia Ward Howe's words about "truth marching on" as the Almighty tramples "out the vintage where grapes of wrath are stored" become the thunder of hell itself.

I am, please God, a human being first. I am a Christian, not simply by birth but by choice, because that faith, rooted as it was in the faith of Israel, promised to make human life true and righteous again. I ask you who are Jews to help save both Christians and Jews in America from the corruption of our historic commitment to the good of all mankind that presently flows from our besotted search for survival.

Asking that, however, I will not hold back my equal debt to warn you against what is happening in the citadel of your corporate soul, the holy city, Jerusalem. Only six years ago, when it was possible to speak of such things freely, I ended a faculty seminar on Israeli ethnic diversity at the Institute for the History of the Diaspora, Tel Aviv University, by sharing my thoughts on the *shalom* of Jerusalem. My wife, who was present, turned white. But my hosts listened as I spoke of the hundreds of years during which Jews, Moslems, and Christians of Eastern Orthodox, Roman Catholic and, later, Protestant persuasions had managed to keep relative peace in that sacred place.

Today, the world is Jerusalem. If peace is not kept everywhere it will probably not be kept anywhere. And the prophetic question is not what will the Almighty do, but what will we his people do in response to this moral challenge, and in the light of what he has already done.

Our own youngsters sense by their eighth birthday that they stand provisionally condemned to an Auschwitz that cannot be confined to a spot in East Germany, but will cover the whole world. They cry out in disbelief that we have brought them to life while endorsing the contingency of such a mass murder of our young, should it take that to preserve our affluence, power, and collective identity. Hear the cry of our own children in Israel and America, please, while you listen also to those who cry for peace and bread in Nicaragua and Bangladesh, in Chad and Laos.

No wonder Jeremiah and Ezekiel proclaimed that the new covenant had to be different from the old. They knew that *shalom* required more than the instruction of the sons by their fathers. *Shalom* required the purifying of the minds of God's people by the presence of his Spirit, writing Torah in their hearts. And so today, it requires the cleansing of our wills from the will to power, of our hearts from fear and hatred, and of our minds from the folly of calculating and acting only on our own national or ethnic advantage.

The right-making grace of God is still the only way to peace. No wonder a Jewish messianist, John the Baptist, was not content merely to call his people to repentance and faith but promised them, as Joel and Ezekiel had, a baptism in the Spirit of Yahweh's purity, justice, and love. And no wonder Saul of Tarsus, writing from Corinth, summarized his letter about the Good News to Jewish and Roman Christians with the words, "The kingdom of God is righteousness, peace, and joy in the Holy Spirit." The Spirit of him whom we own as Lord of all our covenants can set us right, when every temptation is to the wrong. He promises to share with us divine holiness, breathing into our souls the life of God. And the peace that the Spirit of God brings, every Jewish child of Paul's day knew, was not defined by the Greek word signifying the absence of violence, but by the rich meaning of the Hebrew *shalom:* health, completeness, righteousness; the holiness of loyalty to Torah; and a human community in which the hungry find food and the universal aspiration for love, fulfillment.

Peace comes by the Spirit of the Lord. His presence in the darkness of our days promises the blossoming of the moral and physical desert Isaiah prophesied, if we will dare to believe it. The fullness of his joy can flow only from the right-making justice, the renewing and hallowing love of the all-blessed creator who is our redeemer.

In a day when the whole human race has come to the crossroads called survival, ethical choices can be made only in the power of the presence of the Lord. In his presence, the psalmist said, is fullness of joy, and at his right hand are pleasures forevermore. Holiness, virtue, justice, righteousness— they are all Torah: they all bespeak atoning grace.

Part Three

The Bible and Biblical Interpretation

5

A Jewish View of the New Testament

Ellis Rivkin

As the title of my paper suggests, the views which I share with you are the views of a single Jew. They are not the views of either the Jewish people as a whole or any fraction thereof. For all I know, these views may be singular, shared by no other Jew. They are nonetheless the views of a Jew who is deeply committed to Judaism and who has for more than a generation been teaching the history of Jews and Judaism to rabbinic students at the Hebrew Union College and to Christian graduate students as well. Nonetheless, what I shall share with you is the outcome of a highly personal odyssey which reaches back to my early life in Judaism when I was, as to the law a Pharisee, as to righteousness under the law, blameless, and as to the writings of the New Testament both ignorant and rejective. My odyssey extends to this very moment when I stand before you unbound by the law, highly insecure as to my righteousness, knowledgeable of the teachings of the New Testament, and confessing that my Jewish spirit has been enriched by them.

How, I ask myself, could I, of all people, be speaking to you here today of a book which, until my university years, I never dared to read, lest its false teachings contaminate my soul nurtured on the purity of God's authentic revelations? I was born and raised in an ultra-Orthodox home. I learned to read Hebrew before English and the Torah before Little Red Riding Hood. I went to Heder, the Hebrew school, several hours each day; began the study of the Talmud before I was bar mitzvah; was trained to read from the scroll of the Torah on the Sabbath and festivals; trekked miles to attend daily morning services in the synagogue and only when the services were over did I board the street car to a distant high school; and gained for myself a reputation for righteousness and piety that filled the hearts of my parents with pride and my fantasies with messianic ambition. If ever there was a life predestined for the glory of God, seemingly it was mine. I had been singled out so it seemed to me, by God the Father to tend his vineyard and keep it free of alien and blighting growths.

But as it turned out, neither I nor my parents nor my teachers had read the signs aright. To be sure, I was pious, and I was law-abiding, and I was confident that my piety and righteousness would assure for me eternal life and resurrection. Yet when I was feeling most pleased with myself and most confident of my salvation, I had a terrifying experience on the road to the synagogue. I was sixteen years old at the time, and at the height of my piety and righteousness and confidence. I was more and more visualizing myself as the intrepid champion of the law and defender of the faith. With these goals in the forefront of my mind, I had been reading R. Travers Herford's highly appealing and sympathetic reappraisal of the Pharisees, and was deeply impressed with his efforts to convey to Christian readers the inner joy which a believing Jew feels when he is yoked to the law. Herford also exposed me to Paul for the first time, and I was appalled that anyone who had been so loyal a son of the law could have been so out of his mind that he could have thrown over the law for a false Messiah, Jesus.

I could not help but feel a glow of pride and satisfaction that, unlike Paul, my faith and loyalty were sturdy and impregnable. Exultant, I trudged off to the synagogue for study and for the afternoon and evening prayers which would follow. It was the Sabbath, around four o'clock in the afternoon, and a baseball game was in progress on the sandlot diamond which I had to pass enroute. The day was sunny and pleasant and as I paused to watch the game for a moment or two, I was flooded with pre-bar-mitzvah memories of joys and ambitions that had had nothing to do with the law. Indeed the law had been in the way, for it forbade playing of ball on the Sabbath, the very day which, for a young boy, should have been set aside for sporting events. This, it seemed to me, was asking too much. The law may have been given by God, and it may have prohibited the playing of ball on the Sabbath, yet God's command, "Thou shalt not play ball," was countermanded by an even more powerful command deep within me which proclaimed, "Thou shalt play ball, even on the Sabbath." And play ball I did, even though this meant sneaking off to some neighborhood far from my father's prying eyes.

Suddenly I was jolted out of my reverie by a terrifying thought. "What if Paul was right?" "What if the law was not binding?" "What if behind the law, sin lurked, ready to provoke some untamed impulse to defy the law and the God who had revealed it?" I broke out in a cold sweat and began to run, not walk, toward the synagogue. But I had great difficulty. The thought would not go away. I became more and more terrified. I was on the edge of paralysis when, by a sheer exertion of will, I marshaled my religious defenses, calmed down, and made my way to the synagogue where my spirits and confidence were revived. Buoyed by the return of my senses, I "forgot" the incident and resumed my lawful ways.

Though I "forgot" what had occurred, the episode itself was a portent far more prophetic than the resumption of my pious and righteous life under the law. For it was to be only a few years later that I was to diverge from the road I had been following. At The Johns Hopkins University I studied under brilliant scholars who compelled me to rethink and reevaluate all that I had taken for granted, and I was persuaded that the key to understanding both Judaism and Christianity was to be found in a critical rethinking and restructuring of the history and religion of the people of Israel. And it was in the process of carrying through this task that the New Testament was transformed for me from a book of revulsion into a book of revelation. For what I was more and more forced to acknowledge was the fact that the New Testament records not so much an irreparable break from Judaism, as a mutation of Judaism, a mutation which was not recognized as such at the time because Judaism had never been thought of as a developmental religion, or Israel as a developmental people, or God as a Being, so infinite and beyond human understanding, that his fullness needed more than one revelation for its disclosure.

Ironically, the more I drifted away from the law and the more I shed the unquestioning faith of my early life in Judaism, the more I was able to deepen my faith by discovering that God had given multiple revelations to Israel. The orthodox Judaism on which I had been nurtured was not the pristine form of Judaism, but rather a form of Judaism that had not been known to Moses or Isaiah or Ezekiel. It was not the religion of Israel as set forth in the Pentateuch. Rather it was a mutational form of Judaism. Far from having been given on Sinai, the oral law had been born in the crucible of the Hasmonean Revolt against Antiochus and his Jewish supporters. The belief in eternal life and resurrection which went hand in hand with the oral law had not been spelled out in the Pentateuch. The Scribes/ Pharisees who had legitimitized this mutation had themselves exercised an authority which had no Pentateuchal warrant. The proof-texting manner in which Scriptures were now read by the Scribes/Pharisees was at odds with the way Scriptures had previously been read. The institutions which were to become bywords, the *Beth Din ha-Gadol* and the synagogue, were nowhere provided for in the Pentateuch. The daily reciting of the Shema and mandatory prayers were not called for by Pentateuchal law. The Sadducees who insisted, with justice, that God had given only the written law and that the rewards and punishments spelled out by the written law were to be exclusively this world's rewards and punishments—these Sadducees were denounced by the Scribes/Pharisees and condemned to eternal damnation. Far from being the only revelation, the twofold law of my early life in Judaism was a mutational form of Judaism which had displaced the Judaism which, for several centuries, had been grounded in a literal reading of the Pentateuch.

Further study revealed more complications. The Pentateuchal form of Judaism itself had been preceded by a form which had been radically different. It was a form whose hallmark was prophecy. God talked to prophets and revealed his will to them. They, the prophets, and not the priests, were the ultimate authorities. Pentateuchal Judaism thus showed itself to have been a mutational form of Judaism. Its triumph had sealed the lips of the prophets by limiting God's revelation to the immutable laws given to Moses on Sinai and written down once and for all.

It thus became evident to me that the development of the religion of Israel was no simple replicating process, but had been punctuated by the bursting out of unanticipated mutations. The prophets had never anticipated a day when prophecy would end. The Aaronide priesthood had never anticipated a day when the Scribes/Pharisees would sit in Moses' seat and God's revelation on Sinai would have been of a twofold law, written and oral, and not the written law alone. Yet the unanticipated not only occurred, but became a normative form of Judaism. If normative, then God must have had the power to reveal again and again. Otherwise how could the written law displace prophecy, and the oral law gain ascendency over the written?

And to compound the complexity, I discovered that there had arisen in Alexandria a Hellenistic form of Judaism which was mutational in its own right. It was mutational because it dissolved the highly personal anthropomorphic God of the Pentateuch into the God of the philosophers, and the simple stories of Genesis and Exodus into sophisticated allegories. Yet it was this transmuted Judaism that was the Judaism of Philo even though it had not been the Judaism of the prophets or of the literal Pentateuch or of the twofold law of the Scribes/Pharisees.

With these three mutations spread before me I concluded that each of these mutations must have been bona fide revelation for those Jews who altered their beliefs and restructured their mode of life. For otherwise, that form of Judaism which to this day is regarded as normative by most Jews, namely rabbinic Judaism, would have had no historical legitimacy.

If then I acknowledged that mutations had occurred in Judaism before the rise of Christianity, and that these mutations had come to be regarded as revelations by large numbers of Jews, then I was bound to read the New Testament with an eye to the possibility that the Gospels, Acts, the Letters of Paul, and the other books of the New Testament were recording the breakout of a fourth mutation, a mutation which had been no less a revelation than the three mutations which had preceded it.

It is with this possibility in mind that I invite you to take a look with me at the New Testament. What is so striking at first glance is that we find ourselves, despite the Greek, within the framework of Judaism. The synoptic Gospels are cast in literary forms evocative of the historical books of the Bible; the proof-texting which abounds is none other than the proof-texting we find in the Mishnah; the controversies between Jesus and the Scribes/Pharisees have no referent outside the community of Israel; Jesus' preaching of the coming of the kingdom could have had meaning only for Jews; the synagogues in which Jesus reads from the prophets, heals the sick, and forgives sins are Jewish houses of worship for believing Jews and not un-converted Gentiles; terms such as *Son of man, Messiah,* and *David's scion* were emotion-laden for the descendents of Abra-ham, Isaac, and Jacob, but for no others; and Jesus' last words on the cross are from a psalm, not from some alien litany.

The Book of Acts is no less Jewish than are the Synoptics. An outsider would be at a loss to find his way in this Jewish world until he had become an insider. One has only to recall the tussle that broke out between the Pharisees and the Sadducees when Paul cried out that he was being harried because of his teaching of the resurrection, to appreciate how bewildering these doctrinal differences were bound to be to unbriefed Gentiles.

Even the Gospel of John does not extricate itself from the matrix of Judaism. The Gospel is addressed to Gentiles; it is rejective of the Jews as the people of God; it mounts a harsh and bitter polemic against the entire Jewish people for having crucified the Christ: yet it is a Gospel that underscores the fact that the people of Israel were the people of Christ in the flesh; they were the people to whom God the Father had sent the light; they were the people who had, by failing to see the light while Christ was among them and by failing to see the Christ when he was crucified, had lost their right to be the people of God to those Gentiles who had seen the light through the resurrection. But the postresurrection people of God are not cut off from the Israel to whom Christ had been sent in the flesh. Far from it. The Gospel of John, like the synoptic Gospels, feels compelled to proof-text claims from Scripture with the implication that if scriptural proof were lacking, claims that the Christians were the true people of God would be worthless. The fact that in John's time the true Israel consisted over-whelmingly of Gentiles was beside the point, if indeed it was a fact that the God of Israel had sent his son to his people in the flesh and they had rejected him. There was, after all, good biblical and Pharisaic precedent for God's casting off those of his people Israel, like the Sadducees, who had violated the covenant and, though born to Israel of the flesh, were cast out of Israel of the spirit.

Now it is true, of course, that the Gospel of John raises some very sticky questions, not so much in principle as in practice. In the past, however large the number of Jews who had been deemed outcasts, and however large the number of Gentiles who had converted to Judaism, the majority of the Jewish people consisted of Jews who had been born into the faith and nur-tured on it. Not so however with the Christian community to which the Gospel of John speaks. This community consisted predominately of Gentiles who laid claim to being the true Israel because they had come to believe in the risen Christ while the Jews had not. Though in principle this should have made no difference, in fact it made a great deal of difference, because it meant that the constituents of this new Israel had had no experience belonging to the Israel which was being displaced. All that they knew was that Jesus had been rejected by his people and had been accepted by them. The Jesus of the Synoptics, who had come to bring the Good News of the coming of the kingdom of God to his people, the Jesus who fits so tightly into the contours of real time and real space, one who heals the sick, exorcises the demon-haunted, and comforts the poor: a charismatic of flesh and blood even though he was to become more than he seemed to have been—this Jesus is dissolved in the Gospel of John into the divine light which should have been seen by the Jews but was not. It was the Jesus who had lived so that he might die and reveal the divine self that he had always been, through the medium of the resurrection. And since the Jews had failed to recognize the divine light while Jesus had been alive and had failed to recognize the divine light when he had been resurrected, what need was there for believing Gentiles to have any knowledge of the historical Jewish Jesus at all? A Christian community could thus lay claim to being the true Israel, could call on Scriptures to justify these claims, and yet could have no knowledge of what it was to have been born and raised as a Jew.

A community such as John's audience which needed nothing but the resurrection was an anomaly indeed. But its anomalous status does not extricate it from its rootage. It does not cease to be a mutation of Israel simply because it is a community consisting almost exclusively of Gentiles. This I think will become evident when we turn to Paul.

With Paul we are on more secure ground. By his own testimony, he had been born a Jew, and a precocious one at that. He had been, as to law a Pharisee and as to righteousness under the law, blameless. Indeed, he had prided himself on having been more advanced in Judaism than others his own age, so zealous had he been for the traditions of the Fathers. This precociousness and zeal had gone hand in hand with Paul's violent persecution of the church.

How then did Paul, the zealous champion of the twofold law, come to Christ? He came to Christ because he saw Jesus Christ risen from the dead, not because he wanted to see him risen, but because he could not help seeing him resurrected and alive. What Paul had thought was a blasphemous claim had been transformed for him into an undeniable fact. He had been wrong, grievously so. Having witnessed with his own eyes the risen Christ, Paul had to bring his conception of Judaism into line with this astonishing fact.

Paul's conception of Judaism had been that conception which had been taught by the Scribes/Pharisees. It was the Judaism of the twofold law, and it was the Judaism that preached eternal life for the soul and the resurrection of the body. It was a form of Judaism which rejected the Judaism of the Sadducees as spurious and heretical, and it was a form of Judaism which was incongruent with the Hellenistic form of Judaism flourishing in Philo's Alexandria. It was a form of Judaism whose leaders were teachers and not prophets. It was, in fact, a form of Judaism which was mutational, even though for Paul and the Scribes/Pharisees it was believed to have been designed at Sinai. When, therefore, Paul was zealously persecuting the followers of Jesus for claiming that Jesus had risen from the dead and was the Christ, he was persecuting them, not as a Sadducee or as a Philonic philosopher or as a prophet, but as a follower of the Pharisees and as a preacher of the Good News of eternal life and resurrection, beliefs which were in Paul's day still being denounced as heretical by the Sadducees. As a teacher of the twofold law and as a preacher of eternal life and resurrection, Paul was absolutely convinced that the resurrection of the dead was not only possible, but inevitable for those who adhered to the twofold law and who listened to the teachings of the Scribes/Pharisees. For Paul then the issue had never been whether Jesus could have been resurrected, as it would have been for a Sadducee, but whether he had been resurrected. When therefore Paul persecuted those who were preaching the risen Christ, he was not persecuting them because they believed that there would be a resurrection, but because they claimed that Jesus had been resurrected and that this resurrection was proof positive that Jesus must be the Christ.

For Paul this was an impossibility, since Jesus had during his lifetime challenged the Scribes/Pharisees and had refused to knuckle under to their authority. How then could Jesus have been resurrected when a precondition for resurrection was the acknowledgment of the authority of the Scribes/Pharisees to determine what was right law and what was right doctrine? Since the answer to this question was that Jesus could not have been resurrected, Paul acted accordingly and sought to root out the preachers of this blasphemous heresy. But when he himself saw the risen Christ, he was forced to face the implications of this fact—and face them he did.

Since, Paul reasoned, Jesus had risen from the dead even though Jesus had challenged the Scribes/Pharisees during his lifetime, the teachings of the Pharisees must be seriously flawed. Adherence to the twofold law could not in and of itself guarantee eternal life and resurrection, since Jesus had risen from the dead even though he had defied the authoritative teachers of the twofold law. The road to resurrection therefore could not be the road of the law, but a road marked out by the resurrection of Jesus and its meaning.

For Paul this meaning was to be found in a weakness inherent, not in the law itself, but in the human condition. The law is indeed divine and good, but the individual is a slave of sin. The law may temporarily dam up the impulse to sin, but sooner or later sin will have its way. Indeed, the law lends itself to manipulation by sin, since the "Thou shalt nots" of the law only goad our sinful impulses to respond defiantly with "Thou shalt." The law thus serves as an *agent provocateur* of sin. To look to the law for salvation is to be put off guard, since it diverts us from focusing on sin and its power and on our human condition and its helplessness.

This then must be the meaning of the resurrection. God, knowing of man's helplessness in the face of sin, sent Jesus Christ so that, through his death and through his resurrection, man might dissolve his sinful impulses in response to Christ's unconditional love. Whereas the law provokes sin, Christ's love dissolves it.

It is here, in Paul's radical critique of the law, that Jews and Christians have tended to see the parting of the ways. And with good reason. For if the law is the essence of Judaism, then it would follow that Paul's rejection of the law would ipso facto be a rejection of Judaism.

But, is the law the essence of Judaism? This is the root question, to which we must now seek an answer.

At first glance, the answer would seem to be obvious enough. Paul stresses in both Philippians and Galatians his precocious relationship to the law. In Romans 7 he clearly identifies the law as having been essential to Judaism prior to the resurrection of Jesus. But a more penetrating analysis does not yield so clear-cut a conclusion. For though it is indeed true that for the Scribes/Pharisees adherence to the twofold law was essential for salvation, and for the Sadducees the adherence to the literal commands of the Pentateuch was a *sine qua non*, it had not been at all true for such prophets as Amos, Hosea, Micah, and Isaiah. These prophets regarded not the law but righteousness, justice, and lovingkindness as the essence of God's covenant with Israel. Not a single one of these prophets even mentions Sinai. Not a single one of these prophets recalls Moses as a lawgiver. Not a single one of these prophets regarded sacrifices as mandatory: "I hate your Sabbaths, I despise your feasts, and I reject your sacrifices, but let justice roll down like water and righteousness like an everlasting stream," is the leitmotif first enunciated by Amos. For prophets such as these, the Sabbath, the festivals, and the cultus were allowable so long as they did not deflect the people from what was essential to the covenant: namely God's singularity, God's attributes (justice, mercy, and lovingkindness), and Israel's commitment to this God and to his attributes.

The teachings of these grand prophets thus preclude the law as being essential to the covenant, however important the law became for subsequent forms of Judaism. But is this not also evident from the fact that the written law, the Pentateuch, is a radically different law than the twofold law proclaimed by the Scribes/Pharisees? One has only to flip through the titles of the tractates of the Mishnah to become aware that this repository of the oral law deals with categories of law, such as *Berakhot* (blessings), *Ketuboth* (marriage contracts), *Yedayim* (uncleanness of hands), *Erubin* (Sabbath limits) which are not even mentioned in the Pentateuch. After all there would have been no point for Paul to have prided himself on having been "as to the law a Pharisee," if there was only one law to which all Jews adhered. Thus not only do prophets such as Amos testify to the fact that the essence of the covenant was not law, but the fact that there could be such a cleavage as to what the law was (a cleavage which during the reign of Alexander Janneus pitted the Pharisees and Sadducees against one another in a savage civil war), clearly reveals that the law was a superimposition, not an essence. Both before the law and beyond the law, the essence of Judaism continued to be as it was for the prophets: God's singularity and his attributes of justice, mercy, and lovingkindness.

But it is not only retrospectively that we discern a form of Judaism, namely the prophetic, which did not acknowledge the law as the essence of the religion of Israel, but in the existence of a form of Judaism in our own day which likewise does not regard the law as the essence of Judaism. This form of Judaism is flourishing, and its seminary, the Hebrew Union College-Jewish Institute of Religion, trains rabbis for Reform congregations both in the United States and abroad. There can be no question that this seminary is a seminary devoted to the teaching and the perpetuation of Judaism. It may be denounced as a seedbed of heresy by the ultra-Orthodox, it may even be viewed by them as worse than a Christian seminary, but it is regarded by friend and foe alike as a Jewish institution. Yet Reform Judaism does not recognize the binding character of either the written or oral law, nor the Orthodox claims that God had revealed his total revelation to Moses on Sinai. Instead, Reform Judaism affirms that God's revelation is ongoing, and that the essence of Judaism is to be found in the singularity of God and in his attributes of justice, mercy, and lovingkindness.

Reform Judaism thus bears witness to the fact that Pharisaism was not the last mutation-revelation in Judaism. For Reform Judaism is as legitimate a mutation-revelation for Jews who acknowledge it as such, as were the Pentateuchal and Pharisaic mutation-revelations for those Jews who adopted these mutation-revelations as normative. If then Reform Judaism can be Judaism without the law, the law cannot be the essence of Judaism for those who have adopted Reform Judaism as normative. And if there can be a Judaism unrooted in the law in our own day, by what right can I as a Reform Jew read Paul out of Judaism merely because in his day Jews believed that the law was the essence of Judaism? So long as Paul insisted, as he did, that the Christ was sent by the one God of Israel to redeem humankind from the bondage of sin, and so long as he justified his revelation of Christ by an appeal to Scriptures, and so long as he proclaimed that the followers of Christ were the Israel of the spirit, I see no way of denying to Paul's teachings the right to be categorized as a mutation-revelation of Judaism for all those Jews or Gentiles who accept these teachings as normative, without at the same time denying, not only the right of Reform Judaism to be categorized as a mutation-revelation, but of Orthodox Judaism as well—a form of Judaism which owes its own legitimacy to a mutation-revelation. And as for Gentiles, there is in principle no way to exclude the possibility that a community of Israel could emerge consisting of a majority who were either converts themselves or the children of converts, unless there is some quota or cut-off point for new converts. In principle, even the most extreme Orthodox rabbi cannot countenance such a quota or cut-off so long as the convert fulfills all the legal requirements. The fact then that Pauline Christianity spread almost exclusively among Gentiles does not in and of itself derogate from Pauline Christianity's right to be regarded as a mutation-revelation within Judaism, so long as the community affirms that it is the Israel of the spirit. Hence, when we read the Gospel of John and recognize that it is a Gospel that is speaking to a Christian community consisting of Gentiles, we are confronted by an anomaly, but not by a new religion. John may be addressing Gentiles, and he may be rejecting Jews, but he is not rejecting either the God of Israel or the authority of Scriptures. He is affirming that Jesus was a Jew in the flesh, that he was sent by God, the Father, to the Jews who failed to recognize him, and became the Christ for all those who did so recognize him either during his earthly sojourn or after his resurrection. The Jews were not cut off from Christ; they cut themselves off. Christ did not come only for the Gentiles but for all humankind. The fact that Gentiles and not Jews acknowledged him as the Christ was simply a fact, not a destiny.

If then I read the New Testament as the record of a mutation-revelation within the framework of Judaism, what do I do with the hostility which suffuses the Gospels and the Epistles of Paul? What do I do with Matthew 23 and its condemnation of the Scribes/Pharisees as whitewashed tombs, vipers, and sons

of hell? How do I react to the trial and crucifixion of Jesus and
the harsh judgment leveled against the Jews for their complicity?

I answer these questions by facing them head on. What,
after all, is one to expect? Genteel polemic and serene travail
when a charismatic of charismatics challenges the authority of
the Scribes/Pharisees; exposes the Jews to Roman wrath by
preaching the coming of God's kingdom and not the continuity
of Caesar's kingdom; attracts crowds who could go beserk;
causes a rumpus in the temple area in the midst of maddening
crowds; evokes shouts of "Long live the King of Jews," "Long
live the Son of David, Hosanna in the highest"; and neither
affirms or denies that he is the King of the Jews?

These were harsh and unruly times. Judea had proved to be
ungovernable. There was not a day without violence, a week
without demonstrations, a year without insurrection. The Roman emperors did not know how to keep the peace; the procu-
rators did not know how to keep the peace; the high priest and
his privy council did not know how to keep the peace. Repression did not work, permissiveness did not work, muddle did not
work. When John the Baptist had preached repentance and
baptism, he had been put to death, not because of his teachings,
but because he attracted crowds, and crowds were unpredictably
dangerous. Even those religious leaders, who, as in the case of
John, may have been sympathetic to his religious revivalism,
were frightened lest a naive charismatic unintentionally spark
an insurrection which would lead to devasting reprisals on the
entire people. Hence it is not surprising that everyone did what
they did, because nobody knew what else to do.

In this maelstrom of violence and anarchy, no charismatic
was likely to come out alive, least of all a gentle charismatic with
no political ambitions, only a prophetic impulse to awaken his
people to the coming of God's kingdom. To the degree that his
teachings found a hearing and to the degree that his preachings
attracted crowds of listeners and to the degree that his wonder-
working aroused awe, to that degree was he bound to attract
the attention of the high priest and arouse his concern. All that
was needed was some incident that spelled potential danger,
and his fate was sealed.

For Jesus' disciples this fate was intolerable. Here was their gentle teacher being arrested by the orders of the high priest, tried by the high priest's council, and crucified by Pontius Pilate acting on the judgment of the high priest and his council; and they, his disciples, were to be unmoved? Seeing their teacher brutally crucified, were they to remain unbitter? Or were they to cry out in their pain and anguish and hit out at all those who had been in any way party to this gruesome deed?

And was not their bitterness compounded when bruised, stunned, and bewildered by the seeming death of their beloved teacher, they saw Jesus risen from the dead, proclaimed the Good News, and found themselves rebuked and hounded from the synagogue by the very Scribes/Pharisees who had taught them to believe in the resurrection of the dead? How then can I be surprised if I find the Gospels full of bitterness, recrimination, and anathemas? After all if Jesus' disciples were human beings of flesh and blood, am I to expect them to respond to pain, anguish, and harassment with divine transcendence? Not at all. I would expect them to be angry, bitter, and vengeful as indeed the Gospels portray them as having been.

But their bitterness, their anger, and vengefulness has nothing to do with anti-Semitism. Rather it was the normal by-product of mutation-revelation in Judaism, and in Christianity as well. We have evidence enough of this in the struggle between the Pharisees and the Sadducees. Not only did the Pharisees and Sadducees denounce each other as heretics, but they slugged it out in a bloody, generation-long civil war. And when the Pharisees regained power, they wreaked vengeance on Diogenes and others who had counseled Alexander Janneus to crucify eight hundred followers of the Pharisees.

In subsequent epochs, Rabbinates and Karaites, Maimanists and anti-Maimanists, Hasidim and Mitnagdim hurled vituperation at each other, read each other out of the faith, and would have translated their harsh words into violent deeds if this option had been open to them.

And when we turn to the history of Christianity, is it not marked by violent confrontations between the followers of Christ? Is there any diatribe in the New Testament against the

Scribe/Pharisees which has not been outdone by Luther? Is there any act of harassment by the Scribes/Pharisees against the followers of Jesus more harassing than the decades of religious wars that followed the Protestant Reformation? Yet such intense collisions are looked upon as intra-Christian struggles, and not as interreligious struggles. So why should we not look on the collisions recorded in the New Testament as intra-Jewish collisions and not the collision of two separate religions?

When, therefore, I look at the New Testament I see a precious record of the birth of Judaism's fourth mutation-revelation, with all the travail that attends such a birth. And like the mutation-revelations which preceded it and the mutation-revelations which followed it, the New Testament seems to me to display two levels, divine light and the human prism. For like all previous revelations, I see this revelation too as being refracted through human prisms. As a consequence, the divine light is not simply reflected, but is fractured. What I find in the New Testament is a commingling of light and shadow; and it is this commingling which explains for me the ease with which anti-Semites have exploited the bitter, harsh, and vengeful sayings in the New Testament to justify the harassment and the persecution of the Jews through the centuries. Focusing on the Gospel accounts of the trial and crucifixion of Jesus, anti-Semites have been able to whip up the passions of the mob by accusing the Jews of being Christ killers, host desecraters, ritual murderers, well-poisoners, and children of Satan. Confronted by such animus and hostility, proof-texted as they were from the New Testament, there could be no way that Jews could see any divine light emanating from a Christ imprisoned within texts bursting with hostility and vengefulness. Little wonder then that when I was growing up, Christ was an anathema and not a redeemer, the New Testament a blasphemy and not a revelation.

Despite these barriers, however, I found it possible through a deeper understanding of how God reveals himself to Israel through mutation-revelations, each one a commingling of divine light and human shadow, to vault over barriers and find, snuggling behind the hostility and vengefulness, a Christ of compassion, graciousness, and love. This Christ bore no resemblance to the Christ of hatred and vengeance. It was a Christ who forgave the Jews because they did not know what they were doing. It was this Christ that in some way may have been reaching out to me when, puffed with pride and righteousness, I was terrified by the unwilled thought, "What if Paul was right," and was confronted with the haunting possibility that deep within me was an impulse to defy the law which might prove to be more powerful than the impulse to obey it.

But I did not become a Christian even when I did part from the law, and even when I concluded that the New Testament was a mutation-revelation within Judaism, and that Paul's radical critique of the law and his proclamation that the true Israel was the Israel of the spirit and not of the flesh, were as legitimate an expression of Judaism's quest for the fullness of God as the Pharisaic proclamation that God had given two laws, not one. I did not become a Christian because to have done so would have deprived me of the revelations which had preceded the rise of Christianity and the revelations which were to follow. I would have cut myself off from a divine odyssey which reaches back to the patriarchs and which reaches forward to the messianic age, an odyssey of a people ever searching for the fullness of God. It is an odyssey which a people of flesh and spirit undergo, and it is this odyssey that is for Jews, such as myself, the ultimate revelation. For what we find spread before us is a record of continuous revelation, to and through the Jews—revelations through prophets, through books, through Scribes/Pharisees, through philosophers, through Christ Jesus, through rationalists, through Kabbalists, through charismatics, through reformers, and even through Jewish secularists and nationalists.

And all to what end? To make manifest through the history of a people God's faith in humankind's capacity for shaping a world which God can pronounce as good, very good indeed. If we open our Bibles to the first verses of Genesis, we read that God created heaven and earth and all that is therein and that he capped his creation with a single individual, formed in his image and after his likeness, an individual whom God entrusted with his goodly creation. God looked on the whole world he had created as good and not just some special land or territory or place. He had also created a single individual, male and female, and not a multitude of people. And this individual was not an Egyptian or a Babylonian or a Frenchman or an American or a Jew. He was just an individual, like God was an individual, but what an individual, created as he was in the image of God! God's commitment was thus not to a race or nation or class or mob, but to the individual.

And God put this individual into a paradise which the individual had not earned but which would provide him with every good, without effort, provided that he foreswore knowledge and responsibility for making religious, moral, and ethical choices. This the individual was unable to do. Therefore, God cast him out of Paradise and plunged him into history, where he might strive to regain Paradise by refining his religious, moral, and ethical choices.

But when it became evident that human beings were not choosing at all wisely, God, as a decision of last resort, decided to experiment with a single people and chose Abraham to father a nation which would keep alive the belief in the one God who had created a goodly universe, who had capped his creation with an individual in his own image and after his own likeness, and who had given this individual and his descendants the power to discriminate between good and evil.

This people, which Abraham fathered, was thus launched by God on an odyssey which could not come to an end until humankind had so refined its religious sensitivities that it would freely choose good over evil and regain for itself a paradise which this time it had earned through pain, suffering, anguish, and knowledge. Throughout the centuries this people of God clung to their faith and they clung to their hopes, however tempestuous the waters and however crushing the breakers. This they were able to do because they were continuously being buoyed up by revelations which assured them that God still cared and that God would not totally abandon them, even when they seemed to be abandoning him.

Among the revelations along the way was the revelation which has come down to us in the New Testament. It was a divine revelation, a revelation which vividly personified God's loving compassion for every individual, but it was a revelation which, because few Jews were able to see it as such, found its home among the Gentiles. For the first time in all of Israel's history, a revelation of God to his people had brought life and light to Gentiles who had known him not, but who knew him now—and another people of God were launched on their odyssey with their own unique and special destiny.

But the Jews persisted in their own uniqueness and continued to spawn revelations, revelations which sustained their faith and their hope even when, as a tiny minority among Christians and Moslems (who in affirming Islam, were in their own unique way, bearing witness to still another mutation), continuously being mocked for their stubbornness and persecuted for their stiff-neckedness. They gave the lie, however, to their detractors by continuing to bear spiritual fruit: two Talmuds, Midrash, commentaries without end, ethical treatises, mystical probings, philosophic forays, liturgical gems, and poetic flights.

The Jewish people were sustained by revelations in the modern age as well, as gifted religious leaders, teachers, and philosophers searched for more of God. They did not fall prey to secularism, nor were they stripped of their religious questing by the triumphs of Jewish nationalism—a nationalism whose own claims to nationhood are gleaned from God-saturated Scriptures and whose enduring national heritage from the past are spiritual and not political triumphs. So sturdy indeed is this people of God that not even the Holocaust could burn out their spirit.

The Jewish people are thus very much alive today, for, it seems to me, that their divine odyssey is not yet at an end. Humankind has still not recognized that God is one, that his universe is a goodly one, and that every individual is created in his image and after his likeness. The end of days, which the prophets preached, is still far off. The meaning of the Jewish odyssey has yet to be assimilated. Paradise has not yet been regained. A regenesis still eludes us. The need of Israel for multiple revelations is still manifest to those Jews, like myself, who see and feel this need.

This then explains how I, a Jew, can look at the New Testament and read it as a record of a revelation-mutation and yet not become a Christian. For whereas a true Christian is totally fulfilled in Christ and needs no other revelation, I cannot be so fulfilled. I cannot be so fulfilled because I have become convinced that so long as God reveals himself through human instruments, every revelation is partial. Therefore, I feel the need for all the revelations that were given to Israel in the past, all the revelations which are being given to Israel in the present, and all the revelations which may be given to Israel in the future, until the ushering in of the messianic age give us, at long last, the fullness of God. Convinced that until that end of days the divine light will always be refracted through human prisms, and convinced at the same time that the divine light will always be straining to break through, I do not wish to have the light streaming toward me and yet see it not.

6

An Evangelical Christian View of the Hebrew Scriptures

Bruce K. Waltke

When Dr. Marvin Wilson contacted me by phone regarding the topic of this paper, he instructed me that he had in mind that I address myself to the topic "The Hermeneutics of Evangelicals." I gathered from his comments that I should emphasize the principles and processes followed by evangelicals in their interpretation of the Old Testament, and that I should represent both the agreements and disagreements among evangelicals in their reading of Scripture. My approach, therefore, will be broad and wide ranging, my concern will be on method, and my presentation will be both descriptive or real and prescriptive or ideal.[1]

Since the term *evangelical* today is very imprecise and has been so historically—for example, most who claim the label evangelical will not be pleased to concede Schleiermacher's claim that his theology is evangelical[2]—and since the term *hermeneutics* is used in several different ways, it is necessary that I first define these two crucial terms in the topic. By defining evangelical we shall also begin to lay the foundations for a systematic presentation of the rules and methods by which evangelicals interpret the older testament.

The Term *Evangelical*

The term *evangelical* has both theological and historical antecedents. C. Pinnock wrote: "Classical (conservative, orthodox) theology is characterized by concentration upon fidelity and continuity with the historic Christian belief system set forth in Scripture and reproduced in creed and confession, with what C. S. Lewis called 'mere Christianity.'"[3]

Defined theologically, an evangelical is above all one who considers himself a steward of the gospel (Greek, *euaggelion*), attested authoritatively in the Holy Scriptures. Friedrick[4] observed that two passages seem to give a brief summary of Paul's evangelical message: "Paul, a servant of Christ Jesus . . . set apart for the *gospel* of God—the *gospel* he promised beforehand through his prophets in the Holy Scriptures regarding his Son, who as to his human nature was a descendant of David, and who through the Spirit of holiness was declared with power to be the Son of God by his resurrection from the dead: Jesus Christ our Lord" (Rom. 1:1–4). "Now, brothers, I want to remind you of the *gospel* I preached to you. . . . By this *gospel* you are saved. . . . that Christ died for our sins according to the Scriptures, that he was buried, that he was raised on the third day according to the Scriptures, and that he appeared to Peter, and then to the Twelve. After that, he appeared to more than five hundred of the brothers at the same time, most of whom are still living, though some have fallen asleep. Then he appeared to James, then to all the apostles, and last of all he appeared to me also, as to one abnormally born" (I Cor. 15:1–7).

In sum, an evangelical is one who proclaims that Jesus of Nazareth is the preexisting Son of God, the expected Messiah of the line of David, who died for sin, is raised from the dead, and is exalted as the Lord over all. Response to this Good News entails a decision to trust Jesus as Savior and Lord and to accept God's free gift of salvation through him.

When used in this theological sense, Bloesch notes that "evangelical" crosses sectarian lines. He cites as evangelicals among the fathers of the Roman Catholic Church: Ambrose, Augustine, Bernard of Clairvaux, Thomas Aquinas, and Pascal;

and among moderns of that tradition: Jerome Haber, Louis Bouyer, and Ralph Martin.[5]

Defined historically, evangelical has come to refer to that kind of religion espoused by the Protestant Reformation with its emphasis on *sola Scriptura* ("Scripture alone"), *sola gratia* ("grace alone"), and *sola fide* ("faith alone"). Besides its Reformation moorings, evangelicalism is also indissolubly linked with the tradition of evangelical revivalism, which includes Anabaptists, the Pietists, and Puritanism. "All these movements stressed the necessity for the new birth, the experience of the heart and the reality of regeneration which served as a complement to the Reformation emphasis on justification." "Evangelicalism numbers among its forefathers not only Luther, Calvin, Zwingli, and Knox but also Menno Simons, Philip Spener, Richard Baxter, John Owen, John Wesley, Count Zinzendorf and Jonathan Edwards."[6] Bloesch further noted that evangelicalism is at odds with traditional Roman Catholicism because the latter tends to obscure and distort the gospel message by its church dogma and intricacies of ritual, and that it is at war with liberalism because in that movement "the gospel appears to be either reduced to ethics or translated into ontology or dissolved into mysticism."[7] These theological and historical antecedents strongly influence the way evangelicals read the Hebrew Scriptures.

The Term *Hermeneutics*

By *hermeneutics* I have in mind that discipline which takes as its goal to discover, establish, and systematically set forth the proper rules for the interpretation of the Bible. The interpretive process normally requires only common sense and does not regularly demand any special theoretical reflection or practical skill. But in the case of the Hebrew Scriptures evangelicals recognize the need for such rules because a gap exists between the Scriptures and themselves; therefore, they must set up rules to bridge that gap. They are separated from the Bible by its theological profundity and its presentation in foreign literary forms, languages, and culture. Moreover, Scriptures demand a spiritual enlightenment to be understood.

But as we shall see, evangelicals are acutely aware that hermeneutics is both an art and a science. Ramm noted: "It is a science in that it can reduce interpretation within limits to a set of rules; it is an art in that not infrequently elements in the text escape easy treatment by rules."[8] This statement should be underscored. My observation is that evangelicals agree about the rules, but they sometimes come to widely different readings of the Hebrew Scriptures because they apply the rules differently.

The content of Scripture originated in at least three distinct levels: (1) the *historical* level in which God revealed himself in word and deed in the life of Israel; (2) the *authorial* level in which he inspired a writer to inscripturate and further the historical revelation; (3) the *canonical* level in which the individual inspired literary works were given a wider frame of reference as the canon expanded. The three levels require their own rules of interpretation. Finally, there is the *application* level where the interpreter attempts to apply the total revelation to his own historical situation, and it too requires rules of interpretation. I will content myself in this paper with attempting to set forth the rules evangelicals employ, or which I think they should employ, in three of these levels: (1) the authorial level, traditionally referred to as "principles and practice of exegesis"; (2) the canonical level with special attention being given to the rules governing the relationship of the Old Testament to the New Testament; and (3) the level of application, to be treated more briefly.

But before setting forth the rules for each of these levels, we need first to lay bare the theological convictions that give rise to these rules.

Theological Inheritance from the Reformation Informing Evangelical Hermeneutics

The evangelical's rules for interpreting the Bible cannot be disassociated from the following convictions drawn from the Bible itself and from the Reformation. (Since evangelicals draw their rules for reading the Bible from the Bible, they admit that they are caught to some extent in circular reasoning for the way in which they read the Bible in the first place also determines to some extent the rules they draw from it for its proper reading. This problem confronts the reader of all sorts of literature. One attempts to escape the dilemma by dialoguing with the text as much as possible—that is by allowing the text to correct one at every turn.)

Sola Scriptura.

The evangelical is convinced that the Scriptures, the traditional canon of both testaments consisting of thirty-nine books in the Old Testament and twenty-seven in the New Testament, are the Word of God written and the only authority for faith and practice. These Scriptures are the one and only foundation of Christian theology because they alone are the inspired works of God. Jesus said, for example, "The Scripture cannot be broken" (John 10:35); Paul said, "All scripture is God-breathed" (II Tim. 3:16). Calvin wrote: "By His Word God rendered faith unambiguous forever, a faith superior to all opinion . . . no one can get even the slightest test of right and sound doctrine unless he be a pupil of Scripture . . . now daily oracles are not sent from heaven, for it pleased the Lord to hallow his truth to everlasting remembrance in the Scriptures alone. Hence the Scriptures obtain full authority among believers only when men regard them as having sprung from heaven, as if there the living Word of God were heard."[9] In an eloquent paragraph patterned on the Westminster Confession, the New Hampshire Confession stated: "We believe that the Holy Bible was written by men divinely inspired and is a perfect treasure for heavenly instruction; that it has God for its author, salvation for its end, and truth without any mixture of error for its matter; that it reveals the principles by which God will judge us, and therefore is, and shall remain to the end of the world, the true center of Christian union, and the supreme standard by which all human conduct, creeds and opinions should be tried" (Article 1).

This conviction about the source, nature, and aim of the Bible entails the following evangelical convictions regarding its interpretation.

1. Evangelicals do not adopt the stance of standing as

authoritative critics of Scripture, but they stand under it allowing it to critique, shape, and judge their thoughts. Accordingly, they reject that aspect of historical criticism which replaces the Bible's supernaturalism with a naturalistic interpretation of history. Moreover, they do not feel free to interpret the sacred text in accordance with modern self-understanding or to impose contemporary modes of thinking on it. Scripture is the norm, not Bultmann's existentialism or the ethical idealism of liberalism.

2. Because Scripture stands over man's opinion, the evangelical gives primacy to the Word over tradition, to the text over commentary. His final appeal is Scripture, not church dogmas, church fathers, or rabbis.

3. Because Scripture has as its aim man's salvation, the evangelical does not treat the Bible principally as a sourcebook of data on Israel's religion (as Wellhausen alleges) but as a revelation from God to make man wise unto salvation. Genesis 1 ought not to be used as a sourcebook for matters pertaining to science, but unfortunately not all evangelicals realize this implication. When Felix the Manichean claimed that the Holy Spirit had revealed to Manicheus the orbits of the heavenly bodies, Augustine replied that God intended us to become Christians and not astronomers. The Westminster divines applauded scientific investigation and did not confound that object of study and its appropriate methods of investigation with divine matters.

4. When he confesses that the Scriptures are inspired of God, the evangelical means that God spoke through men without denying their personality or rationality. Therefore, the evangelical engages in the grammatico-historical method of interpretation. F. F. Bruce noted: "The Alexandrians understood biblical inspiration in the sense of utterance in a state of ecstatic possession. It was fitting therefore that words so imparted should be interpreted mystically if their inner significance was to be laid bare. Theodore and the Antiochenes thought of inspiration rather as a divinely given quickening of the writers' awareness and understanding, in which their individuality was unimpaired and their intellectual activity remained under their control. It was important therefore in interpreting them to have

regard to their particular usage, aims, and methods. The literal sense was primary, and it was from it that moral lessons should be drawn; the typological and allegorical senses, while not excluded, were secondary."[10]

Analogia fidei *("the analogy of faith").*

Because the Bible in all its parts is the Word of God, it is unified and consistent with itself. The conviction in the Bible's inspiration and its inferred unity, a unity affirmed by Jesus himself (John 10:35), led the Reformers to the rule that Scripture is its own intepreter *(Scriptura sacra sui ipsius interpres).* Ramm interprets this rule, which continues to undergird evangelical hermeneutics, as follows: "Obviously the word 'Scripture' is used in two senses in this catch phrase. What it means is that the *whole* of Scripture interprets the parts of Scripture and thus no part of Scripture can be so interpreted as to deform the teaching of the whole of Scripture. Thus incidental references in Scripture cannot be made pillars of truth. One of the most familiar traits of a sect is that it carries on this very sort of exegesis."[11]

This doctrine of the analogy of faith is not to be confused with the rule of faith. According to this latter belief, the church's traditions (the rule of faith) are consistent with Scripture, and this Christian oral tradition sets the larger context in which individual portions of Scripture must be understood. Appeal to this rule tended to drown out the Scriptures even as in an earlier period the rabbinical interpretations tended to make void both Moses and the prophets. Jesus answered his accusers: "You nullify the word of God for the sake of your tradition" (Matt. 15:6). In practice evangelicals read Scripture through the glasses of their confessions, convinced that their creeds are consistent with Scripture, but in principle they deny the rule of faith; their denominational creeds and confessions are in theory not equal to Scripture.

The clarity of Scripture and private interpretation.

At the Diet of Worms (1521) Luther replied to Johann von Eck's demand that he recant his alleged error: "Unless I am

convinced by the testimonies of the sacred scriptures or manifest reason. . . . I am bound by the scriptures which I have
adduced. My conscience has been taken captive by the Word of
God, and I neither can nor will recant, since it is neither safe
nor right to act against conscience."

This confession entailed the conviction that the Scriptures
were perspicuous and that it was necessary for the individual to
judge the church's tradition and to follow his own understanding of Scriptures. In his first interview with Mary, Queen of
Scots, John Knox expounded the same doctrine: "The Word of
God is plain in itself; and if there appear any obscurity in any
one place, the Holy Ghost, who is never contrary to Himself,
explains the same more clearly in other places; so that there can
remain no doubt; but to such as are obstinately ignorant."

According to the Reformers and their spiritual heirs, the
evangelicals, the God who revealed divine matters by inspiring
the writers of Scripture through his Spirit, and who convinced
men of their inspiration by the same Holy Spirit, also illumi-
nates by that selfsame Spirit the mind of believers about what
these Scriptures mean. This last ministry of the Spirit, in effect,
completes the circle of revelation. Zwingli put it this way: "But
eventually I came to the point where led by the Word and Spirit
of God I saw the need to set aside all things and to learn the
doctrine of God directly from his own Word. Then I began to
ask God for light and Scriptures became far clearer to me—even
though I read nothing else—then if I had studied many commentators and expositors."

But the Reformers' naive optimism about the Scripture's clarity has been replaced among learned evangelicals by both a
chastened spirit and a sophisticated awareness of Scripture's
complexities. Evangelicals, for example, are divided as to what
the Scriptures teach about Israel's future. They confess that in
part their differences are due to carnal pride and in part to the
complexity of Scripture or to the attempt to infer from the
Scriptures more than they reveal. As a scientist distinguishes
laws from theories from hypotheses, evangelicals are learning
to distinguish dogma from systems from hypotheses. Dr. Vernon
Grounds has helpfully distinguished dogmatic doctrine, based

on explicit statements of Scripture, which neither need nor permit debate, from debatable doctrine occasioned by the profound, complex, and sometimes paradoxical statements of Scripture. With respect to this latter category he notes that even Peter (II Peter 3:16) recognized that in Paul's writings there are "things hard to be understood and vulnerable to distortion by the unlearned." Grounds also noted that our imperfect understanding is due to our sinful disobedience. "Although the Holy Ghost has come to lead us into all truth, we as sinners refuse to surrender our minds completely to Him, and the penalty is a measure of spiritual ignorance."[12] The evangelical's creed regarding the perspicuousness of Scripture ought to be "in dogmatic statements, unity; in debatable systems, liberty; and in all things, charity."

This compound of difficult truth and sinful obedience ought not lead evangelicals to skepticism or to defensiveness, but challenge us to greater discipline of mind and a more complete surrender of our spirits "until we all reach unity in the faith and in the knowledge of the Son of God" (Eph. 4:13). Moreover, were the rules of interpretation about to be set forth rigorously and intelligently applied I think there would be more progress in our understanding of Scripture and more unity in our convictions.

The literal method of interpretation.

Since Scripture is sufficient and authoritative in matters pertaining to man's salvation, written not to obscure but to make plain these truths and intended for every man to read, the Reformers recognized that there must be a clear understanding of the principles by which it ought to be read. Chief among them was an insistence on the plain, literal meaning. Luther wrote: "We must keep to the simple, pure and natural sense of the words, as demanded by grammar and the usage of language created by God among men."

This conviction implies that one approaches the Bible not from the perspective of an *a priori* but from that of an *a posteriori*. Although evangelicals recognize that one does not approach the text without being preconditioned by one's culture, yet they insist that one must come to the Scriptures with an open heart desirous to hear the Word of God in such a way as to correct the misconceptions each may have brought to the text. Krabbendam makes the point forcefully: "The hermeneut does not 'construe' the meaning of a word or passage, or attach a sense to it from the perspective of a subjective conviction. He may only recognize its meaning and pass on its sense. In short, he does not creatively construct. He receptively recognizes. He is not an originator. He is an intermediary. He is not a critic. He is a discerner. He is not a judge. He receives a verdict. He is not in control of the passage, the passage controls him. He is not its master; he is its servant. He does not assume an independent stance toward the text; he is bound by its content. The text has the first and final word."[13] Evangelicals regard Bultmann's attempt to interpret the Bible in an existential manner as an illegitimate method because his meaning must be "read into the text." Only by the allegorical method—imposing a doctrine not derived in the first place from the Scripture but from a perspective shaped by forces outside the text—can the Scriptures be read as promising not the triumphant reign of a personal Messiah but of the victory of ethical idealism.

By the "literal method" of interpretation the evangelical does not mean a "wooden literalism" or "literalistically." The evangelical means instead that the Bible must be read as literature. We now turn to the principles employed to bring this about.

Principles of Exegesis

Since the Hebrew Scriptures have both an objective dimension, the text itself, and a spiritual dimension, the mind of God, the evangelical recognizes the need to employ at one and the same time a scientific procedure to handle the objective text and a spiritual dimension to apprehend the divine meaning. He rejects the Kantian polarity between the attempt to achieve mastery over the realm of nature, in this case the text, by explaining it, and the attempt "to understand" the realm of freedom by the inward, psychic life experience of becoming "contemporary" with the author beyond the language of the text. In place of this dialectic the evangelical tends to see the text as the point of departure for knowing the subject matter. For the evangelical the difficulty in knowing the subject is not due to the philosophical problem that the text and its subject matter are by their nature of very different orders, but due to the spiritual darkness of the unregenerated mind.

Spiritual illumination.

As indicated, the Reformers inferred that since the Word of God is spiritual, it could only be perceived spiritually. Scripture itself supports this conviction: "The man without the Spirit does not accept the things that come from the Spirit of God, for they are foolishness to him, and he cannot understand them, because they are spiritually discerned" (I Cor. 2:14). Bloesch wrote: "Historical criticism must give way to spiritual discernment, which must ultimately be given to the critic by the divine author of Scripture (cf. Luke 24:45). The text is no longer the interpreted object but now the dynamic interpreter (Bengel)."[14]

Accordingly evangelicals contend that a man must be regenerated by God's Spirit in order to be taught of God. Moreover, the regenerated man must cooperate fully with the Spirit through obedience, prayer, and meditation. John Owen expressed in practical terms the application of being "spiritually" taught: "As unto them whom the Spirit of God undertakes to instruct he requires that they be *meek* and *humble,* that they give themselves unto *continual prayer, meditation* and study . . . *day and night;* above all that they endeavor a conformity in their souls and lives unto the truths that he instructs them in. These are hard conditions unto *flesh and blood;* few there are who like them, and therefore few they are who apply themselves unto the *school of God.*" Owen is obviously drinking from the same spiritual fountain as the psalmist: "Blessed is the man [whose] . . . delight is in the law of the LORD, and on his law he meditates day and night" (Ps. 1:1–2). Likewise Lady Wisdom proclaimed to fools: "If you had responded to my rebuke, I would have poured out my heart to you and made my thoughts known to you" (Prov. 1:23). In short, it is our "pride, our carnal confidence, love of honor and praise, a tight adherence to corrupt traditions, spiritual sloth"[15] that blinds our eyes to God's truth.

The literary sciences.

However, relying on the Spirit is no substitute for learning. The Word of God became incarnate in specific times and places, and, therefore, to grasp its meaning evangelicals avail themselves of those technical windows that permit the ancient text to shine its light into their hearts. In their reading of the Old Testament evangelicals study attentively textual variants, the text's literary form, language, historical situation, figures of speech, and context. In this paper I must limit myself to those concepts I deem salient in connection with each of these sciences.

1. *Textual criticism.* The starting point for the evangelical hermeneut is that of establishing the correct text from the witness of the Hebrew MSS and the ancient versions. Most evangelicals assume there is an original autographa. For some this means the text as it came from the hand of Moses or an inspired prophet. Others may recognize the possibility of inspired editors and tradents. In either case evangelicals reckon with a text produced by God's Spirit, the autographa, in contradistinction to a text produced merely by scribal activity. Through the canons of textual criticism the evangelical aims to restore the inspired text. In general the textual witnesses point to an original text, though the line between the inspired text and that of the scribes is blurred in the case of Jeremiah. We cannot deal with that problem here, however.

We need to note further that the evangelical is persuaded that the original text is essentially preserved and the textual variants do not leave in doubt the essential doctrines for becoming wise to salvation. He also believes that all translations, except those written from a sectarian bias, are trustworthy and will not lead their readers into wrong doctrine or behavior.

Evangelicals do disagree, however, regarding the degree to which priority should be given to the Masoretic Text over the LXX. Both the New International Version and the New American Standard Bible were produced by evangelicals. A comparison of these two translations will show that the latter stands much closer to the Jewish text than the former. For example NASB renders Psalm 73:7, "Their *eye* bulges from fatness" (reading *cên* with MT), but NIV reads, "From their callous hearts comes *iniquity*" (reading *cawōn* with LXX and interpreting "fat" as a metaphor for callousness). The NIV also puts the MT reading in the footnote because following the LXX reading demanded emending the consonantal text from *'yn* to *'wn*, a common textual corruption. Thus both give priority to MT, and the issue is only one of degree. The NASB also adheres to the Masoretic vocalization more conservatively than NIV. For example in Psalm 2:9 NASB follows MT vocalization and renders it: "Thou shalt *break* them" (reading *terōcēm*), but NIV has: "You will rule them" (reading with LXX *tircēm*). In this case NIV offers no footnotes because the new reading depends solely on the vocalization and not on the consonants.

2. *Literary genre.* A second stage in understanding the text involves the identification of its literary genre. Regrettably, however, it must be admitted that evangelical theologians have not been as sensitive to this area as they should have been. As a result, for example, instead of reading Genesis 1 as *Torah*, many have treated it as a scientific treatise. Moreover, they have all too frequently read the poetic literature rich with evocative figures of speech as prose; the symbols of the apocalyptic have gone by unrecognized; the psalms are read with no awareness of Gunkel's research into their forms or of Mowinckel's research into their cult-functional use.

3. *Philology.* A third stage in understanding consists in philology—the meaning of words (lexicography), the values of morphemes and their syntax (grammar), and linguistics. A reference work frequently used to introduce seminarians to the tools for this discipline is F. F. Danker, *Multipurpose Tools for Bible Study* (1970). Evangelical seminaries usually demand several years in the study of the original languages in their aim to find the literal meaning of the text, by which they mean the normal, natural, customary sense of words *in situ*. Many younger evangelicals will be found in the major universities of the world,

hoping to advance their linguistic skills in the interpretation of the Hebrew Scriptures.

It is neither possible nor necessary to discuss the philology of the biblical languages in detail at this point. It may be of interest to the readers of this paper, however, to note that Calvin was fiercely attacked for denying that the plural form of God, *'elōhîm,* in Genesis 1:1 and elsewhere pointed to the persons of the Trinity. This illustrates the evangelical's commitment not only to reject the allegorical method of interpretation but also the time-honored method of defending the Christian faith by finding proof-texts in the Old Testament.

4. *Backgrounds.* A fourth stage in understanding concerns itself with the text's background: geography, historical causes influencing an event, the culture shaping it, etc. In a work I cosponsored with my former colleagues at Dallas Theological Seminary, titled *Bibliography for Old Testament Exposition* (1979), we devoted pages to introduce expositors of Hebrew Scriptures to the literature, helping them to re-create in their minds the historical situation in which God's revelatory act took shape and in which it was recorded.

Unfortunately, evangelicals sometimes ignore this material and perhaps unwittingly use the Old Testament to proof-text the Christian doctrine. For example, evangelical theologians frequently appeal to the line, "You are my Son, today I have become your Father" (Ps. 2:7) to prove the "eternal generation" of the Messiah (v. 2), failing to realize both that the term "son of God" was used of the historic David and the successors to his throne (cf. I Chron. 22:10; 28:6; Ps. 89:26) and that the psalm functioned as a part of the coronation liturgy in Israel's cultus.

In determining a text's historical background, the evangelical must be involved in historical criticism (literary sources, oral tradition, redaction criticism, etc.). However, according to E. J. Young, a former leading evangelical Old Testament scholar at Westminster Theological Seminary, "A man may practice the principles of criticism or he may be a believer in evangelical Christianity. One thing, however, is clear: if he is consistent, he cannot possibly espouse both."[16] But many younger evangelicals think this assessment is too extreme. I. H. Marshall, an evangelical New Testament scholar and senior lecturer in New Testament exegesis, University of Aberdeen, concluded: "But in reality the Christian cannot deny the *legitimacy of historical criticism.*" F. F. Bruce quipped: "Doubt comes in at the window, when Inquiry is denied at the door."[17] But all evangelicals reject those conclusions of historical criticism drawn from its out-of-hand denial of the supernatural. Historical criticism is often associated with a naturalistic philosophy or world view that denies *a priori* the very possibility of supernatural intervention into human history. To allow supernatural explanations, it is argued, would be to abandon the ordinary principle of natural cause and effect in history and to allow a place to the irrational. In addition, scholars of this persuasion point out that in precritical cultures the supernatural is everywhere. Therefore, the historian in exegeting the Old Testament ought to treat the reports of the supernatural in Scriptures as he would in any document from antiquity that reported a supernatural event. Against this line of reasoning, however, I. H. Marshall responded: "The conservative scholar accepts the possibility, and indeed the probability, of the supernatural."[18] Ramm explained the position: "The evangelical Christian believes that there is a radical difference between the report of the supernatural in Scripture and in other literature. There is a sober rationale for the supernatural in Scripture based upon the Biblical structure of revelation and redemption which is completely lacking in precritical cultures. Part of God's revelatory and redemptive work in humanity and cosmos darkened by sin is the employment of the supernatural. Therefore when the evangelical expositor is confronted with the supernatural in the text he does not rule it out *ex hypothesi,* but accepts it as an important element of the Biblical revelation."[19]

Finally, most evangelicals reject the allegorical method of *eisegesis* for in this method history is not taken seriously.

5. *Figures of Speech.* A fifth stage in understanding pertains to the recognition, identification, and interpretation of figurative language found in the Hebrew Scriptures. Evangelicals of all persuasion confess that the Bible contains figures of speech,

but many have neither a rule nor canon for their identification and interpretation. To be sure, evangelicals (Berkhof, Michelsen, Terry, Ramm, Bullinger, et al.) have worked in this discipline to assure a proper reading of the Old Testament, but in spite of their efforts all too often simplistic rules such as "literal wherever possible" (H. Bonar) or "literal unless absurd" (Govett) have carried the day. A popular rule is that the text be given a *normal* meaning. Regrettably, little attention has been given to the fact that this is a highly relative term—what is normal to the scientific, twentieth-century, Occidental mind may not be normal to the imaginative, ancient, Oriental mode of thinking.

I would like to propose in place of these simplistic rules the canon that one can usually recognize figurative language by noting whether the poet has juxtaposed or transferred his words into a foreign semantic field of thought. For example, in the sentence, "The LORD is my shepherd" (Ps. 23:1), the word "shepherd," which belongs to the semantic realm of animal husbandry, is juxtaposed into the thought pertaining to a transcendent, spiritual being. When David prays, "Cause me to hear joy and gladness" he juxtaposes words describing an emotional state as the object of a verb denoting physical activity. Elsewhere the poet says "the mountain clapped" whereby he transferred a verb describing a human activity to an inanimate subject. A juxtaposition of semantic realms also takes place when Elijah taunts the prophets of Baal, "Cry louder, for he is a God," for he grants existence to Baal in the very context where he is proving his nonexistence. In all these examples—metaphor, metonymy, personification, and irony respectively—the poets artfully and evocatively communicated their thought by transference.

Moreover, whole lines and even paragraphs may be transferred into a foreign context. For example in Isaiah 42:1–4 the poet asserts three times that the servant of the LORD will bring justice to the nations (vv. 1, 3, 4). Into this clear context he throws the line "a bruised reed he will not break, and a smoldering wick he will not snuff out" (v. 3). Thus he places inanimate objects (reed and wick) into the context of salvation history of the nations. In this context the broken and spent objects represent the nations that will be "repaired" and "rekindled" through the Servant's spiritual ministry.

In a similar context Isaiah prophesied that the "stump of Jesse" with the Spirit of the Lord upon him would both judge the needy and poor of the earth and slay the wicked (Isa. 11:1–5). He follows these clear predictions with the unexpected lines "the wolf will be the guest of [Heb. *gûr*] the lamb" (v. 6). Is it not likely that this last statement ought not to be interpreted in a pedestrian way as a reference to "Messiah's reign in the yet future millenial kingdom, which will be characterized by harmony in the whole creation" (Rom. 8:18–22),[20] but rather as a picturesque portrayal of the harmony that will exist among men when the tyrant turns to the meek for salvation?

This last passage also illustrates the principle of embellishment in figurative language. Isaiah continued: "The leopard will lie down with the goat, the calf and the lion and the yearling together; and a little child will lead them. The cow will feed with the bear . . ." (Isa. 11:6b–7). No attempt should be made to relate these species of animals with specific types of people; that would subject the text to allegorizing. The amplification serves to evoke the full extent of harmony that will exist during Messiah's righteous rule. The poet concludes by safeguarding his text against literalism: "The earth will be full of the knowledge of the LORD as the waters cover the sea" (Isa. 11:9). Since animals cannot know God, it becomes absolutely clear that mankind is in view.

A similar embellishment of language is found in Joel's famous prophecy about the coming of God's Spirit on his people in the last days. After predicting, "Your sons and daughters will prophesy, your old men will dream dreams, your young men will see visions," he adds, "I will show wonders in the heavens and on the earth, blood and fire and billows of smoke. The sun will be turned to darkness and the moon to blood before the coming of the great and dreadful day of the LORD" (Joel 2:28–31). Centuries later Peter said of the coming of the Spirit on the day of Pentecost: "This is what was spoken by the prophet Joel" and proceeded to quote the passage cited above. But the cosmic phenomena, so common in Jewish apocalyptic for end times, did not literalistically take place. No, but something of cosmic import did occur—the Spirit of God founded God's church, and the world has never been the same since then. It was turned upside down as Joel prophesied.

I think that it is fair to say that premillennialists, who believe in a future Jewish kingdom on this earth, tend to minimize figures of speech in the prophetic literature. Moreover, they tend to ignore the symbolism in apocalyptic literature. James Dunn, in an essay with which I am not in full agreement otherwise, wrote: "Certainly the language of apocalyptic is not to be interpreted literally or pedantically, as is clear from the apocalyptists' use of symbol and cipher."[21] All will agree that the four great beasts of Daniel 7:1–7, the horns of verses 8ff., and "the rock cut out of a mountain, but not by human hands" (Dan. 2:45), are symbolic along with the cipher 666 in Revelation 13:18. But elsewhere premillennialists often interpret the text far too literalistically. Indeed, the premillennialists' conviction that the Jewish kingdom will last precisely one thousand years is based on one passage in apocalyptic (Rev. 20:1–6), notorious for its symbolic use of numbers, and in spite of the fact that elsewhere one thousand is used for an indefinite extended period of time (cf. Exod. 20:6; Deut. 1:11).

Some scholars discuss typology in connection with figures of speech, but in this essay I have opted to face that subject elsewhere.

6. *Context.* Another stage in understanding involves interpreting a word or text within its context. Thistleton made the point with respect to words by calling attention to Sausurre's work. Sausurre wrote: "Language is a system of interdependent terms (*les termes sont solidaires*) in which the value (*la valeur*) of each term results solely from the simultaneous presence of the others."[22] Sausurre illustrates his point from chess: "The 'value' of a given piece depends on its place within the whole system. Depending on the state of the whole board when one piece is moved, resulting changes of value will be either nil, very serious, or of average importance. A certain move can revolutionize the whole game, i.e. radically affect the value of all the other pieces."[23] Exactly the same holds for languages.

"Righteousness" in Paul means one thing; but "righteousness" in the Psalms, for example, has a very different value. In the Psalms it means that those in covenant relationship do what is "right" by each other. It is with that sense that David prays "Lead me, O LORD, in your righteousness because of my enemies" (Ps. 5:8) and confidently sings: "He guides me in the paths of righteousness for his name's sake" (Ps. 23:3).

Evangelicals not only concern themselves with the context of words but also that of whole verses. For example, the proverb "The wealth of the rich is their fortified city, but poverty is the ruin of the poor" (Prov. 10:15) seems at first reading to instruct Israel's youth to amass a fortune to provide themselves with security in the day of financial calamity. But read in the context of the entire book it turns out to have an altogether different meaning. Other proverbs read: "Wealth is worthless in the day of wrath" (Prov. 11:4); "Whoever trusts in his riches will fall" (Prov. 11:28); "The wealth of the rich is their fortified city; they imagine it an unscalable wall" (Prov. 18:11). One of the thirty sayings of the wise admonishes: "Do not wear yourself out to get rich; have the wisdom to show restraint. Cast but a glance at riches, and they are gone, for they will surely sprout wings and fly off to the sky like an eagle" (Prov. 23:4–5); and Agur prayed that he might have neither poverty nor riches: "Give me neither poverty nor riches, but give me only my daily bread. Otherwise, I may have too much and disown you and say, 'Who is the LORD?'" (Prov. 30:8–9). The sage admonishes Israel's youth to trust the Lord (Prov. 3:5; 22:19), not money. In the light of the book's full context it is clear that Proverbs 10:15 aims to warn the youth that the rich man's wealth is his false security. Both he and the poor will come to ruin in the day of calamity.

This rule of interpreting a text within its context leads the evangelical at length to the most complex and profound level in the interpretation of Hebrew Scriptures; namely, what is the context of the full canon of Scripture, including the New Testament, within which any given book of the Old Testament must be interpreted. To go back to Sausurre's analogy of the chess board, the answer to that question is the decisive move that can revolutionize the value of all the other pieces on the board. In a word, systematic theology provides the final and decisive move in the interpretation of the Old Testament.

It may seem strange to refer to systematic theology as a scientific discipline, but in fact it may be properly understood as such. A scientist in the physical sciences works from his mass of data to erect a model by which he can better understand the data, and then turns around to test the validity of his model by applying it to the data, to correct his model as necessary. So also the systematic theologian creates a model for understanding the mass of undifferentiated biblical material and then applies that model to the biblical text to correct it as necessary. Scientists, however, tend to distinguish law from theory from hypothesis, and tend to show a readiness to correct their models. But evangelical theologians foolishly absolutize their systems and then defend them by canonizing them in confessional statements. This is part of the reason why evangelicals are divided in their interpretation of the Hebrew Scriptures and find themselves entrenched within fixed parameters of thought.

The interpretation of the Old Testament within the context of a canon including the New Testament is so complex that it demands its own section.

Rules for Interpreting the Old Testament Within the New Testament

In this section I will try the impossible: to systematically set forth the rules that evangelicals employ in relating the Testaments, their agreement and disagreement in the application of these rules, and the most significant diverse systems that emerge from their diverse application. Obviously we are once again trapped in a logical circle, for the data determines the system and the system turns around and determines the interpretation of the data. The circle, however, need not be a vicious one if evangelicals would keep an open mind and heart to dialogue with the text and with each other so that knowledge of both the biblical material and developing system might be gradually built, developed, and refined, and left unresolved where necessary.

For the sake of lending clarity to the discussion I shall begin by setting forth the most popular models or systems, and then I will turn to the rules and their application.

The systems.

First of all, let it be said clearly that all evangelicals agree that the gospel of Jesus Christ constitutes the unifying center of the Bible; it all points to him and finds its clear focus when he is granted his rightful position of Lord of all. The Old Testament is incomplete without the New Testament; it is a torso without a head, a stem without a blossom, a promise without fulfillment, a start without a finish, a tragedy without relief. God promised the first couple that they would have a seed that would destroy Satan (Gen. 3:15). He swore to the faithful Abraham that he would have a seed that would bring salvation to all the families of the earth (Gen. 22:15–18). He covenanted with his servant David that his house and throne and kingdom would endure forever (II Sam. 7:8–16). David foresaw a son greater than himself that would sit at God's right hand and exercise universal dominion over the earth (Ps. 2, 72, 110). He promised his people, Israel, a final rest through the Servant of the Lord in a land free from attack and anxiety (Isa. 40–66). The tabernacle Moses built was intended only as an earthly model of the heavenly temple. The blood of bulls and goats, which could never take away sin, served as an earnest of a sacrifice that would remove sin forever. Israel's exodus out of Egypt and Babylon gave promise of a final exodus from sin and death. All these pictures and prophecies and many more find their fulfillment in Jesus Christ. On this point of doctrine there is no disagreement; it is a law, a dogma. Moreover, they are agreed that God will hold men accountable who despise this great salvation offered in Jesus Christ. The writer of the Book of Hebrews asks: "For if the message spoken by angels was binding, and every violation and disobedience received its just punishment, how shall we escape if we ignore such a great salvation?" (Heb. 2:2–3). In proportion to the magnitude of these truths our differences are minor.

Since I cannot set forth all the systems that evangelicals adhere to in the interpretation of the Old Testament, I must limit myself to the major one: the dispensational system versus the covenantal system. As we shall see, the dispensational evangelical must also be a premillennialist, but a covenantal theologian may be an amillennialist, postmillennialist, or historic premillennialist.[24] But the decisive issue in the way an evangelical reads the Old Testament is whether he adopts the dispensational system or the covenantal system.

1. *The dispensational system.* J. N. Darby (first half of the nineteenth century) was the first to set this system forth systematically. (Many of the patristic fathers were premillennialist, but it cannot be said that they were dispensationalist.) Dispensationalism was popularized within the evangelical community all through the *Scofield Reference Bible.* Dallas Theological Seminary has been the most influential in training men in it,[25] and Hal Lindsey, a graduate of Dallas, has popularized it far beyond the confines of the church through his book *The Late Great Planet Earth.*

According to this system of interpretation God has a distinct program for the Jews, an earthly people, and another for the church, the heavenly people. L. S. Chafer, the founder of Dallas Theological Seminary, wrote: "The dispensationalist believes that throughout the ages God is pursuing two distinct purposes: one related to the earth with earthly people and earthly objectives involved which is Judaism, while the other is related to heaven with heavenly people and heavenly objectives involved which is Christianity."[26] "The covenants and destinies of Israel are all earthly, the covenants and destinies of the Church are all heavenly."[27] Ryrie, Chairman of the Department of Systematic Theology at Dallas, wrote: "The dispensationalist believes that God has two purposes—one for Israel and one for the Church."[28]

Moreover, the church is a parenthesis, an intercalation, in God's salvation history. When the Jews rejected Jesus as their Messiah, God temporarily "stopped the clock" in his program for Israel, and in their stead he began his new program with the church. God's program for the church has no relationship with his program for Israel and only temporarily interrupts it. Chafer wrote: "The new, hitherto unrevealed purpose of God in the outcalling of a heavenly people from Jews and Gentiles is so divergent with respect to the divine purpose toward Israel, which purpose preceded it and will yet follow it, that the term parenthetical, commonly employed to describe the new age-purpose, is inaccurate. A parenthetical portion sustains some direct or indirect relation to that which goes before or that which follows after; but the present age-purpose is not thus related and therefore is more properly termed an intercalation."[29] The church began not at the death of Jesus on the cross but more precisely about fifty days later at Pentecost when the Spirit baptised the first Christian disciples into the body of Christ. The church will end its earthly sojourn at the rapture (I Thess. 4:13–18). After the Lord has come to catch his church away from the earth God will return once again to his earthly program for Israel. The restoration of the political state of Israel is universally regarded by dispensationalists as the first sign that God is about to return to this earthly program.

His future program for Israel includes among other things a time of terrible tribulation for seven years ("The Great Tribulation") after which Israel will repent, call upon the Lord Jesus, and be saved. This salvation will include the return of Christ to this earth with the resurrected church saints and the establishment of the Jewish kingdom according to the Scriptures for one thousand years. Dispensationalists differ regarding the exact place of the church saints at this time. Ryrie says, "The Church will reign with Him on earth,"[30] but J. D. Pentecost thinks: "From that heavenly city (the holy city hovering over the earth) she will reign with him."[31]

Furthermore, the church is a "mystery," that is, God did not reveal in the Old Testament his unique program for the church. It was hidden from the eyes of Moses and prophets alike. The Old Testament reveals only God's program for the Jews; it has no direct revelation for or regarding the church.

According to Darby, the distinction between the church and Israel is the "hinge upon which the subject and the understanding of Scripture turns."[32] The Old Testament is interpreted as essentially "Jewish," the Gospels pertain to the announcement of the Davidic kingdom; the Epistles are "Christian." The

Hebrew Scriptures pertain to the Jews, not the church. "The Bible student must recognize the difference between a primary and a secondary application of the Word of God. Only those portions of Scripture which are directly addressed to the child of God under grace are to be given a personal application. . . . It does not follow that the Christian is appointed by God to conform to those governing principles which were the will of God for people of other dispensations."[33] To confound these dispensations, to take the principle of action revealed to one and apply it indiscriminately to another, to ignore the classes of persons and the peculiar aims of each dispensation is to produce confusion, contradiction, and lay foundations for that disharmony which reigns all too manifestly today among Christian expositors. . . . We have no right to take truth from one class and give it to another. . . . Whole sections, chapters, and passages have been taken bodily from the Jews and transferred without compunction to the Church and Christians."[34]

According to the dispensationalists the covenants belong to Israel alone, the Mosaic legislation has been abrogated and has no place in the administration of the present dispensation. The prophetic threats and promises pertain exclusively to Israel. "In prophecy, when the Jewish nation . . . is concerned, i.e., when the address is directed to the Jews, there we may look for a plain and direct testimony, because earthly things were the Jews' proper portion."[35] Certainly one cannot say the New Testament Church is national Israel fulfilling promises given to that nation."[36]

Dispensationalists find in the Hebrew Scriptures truths about their unchanging God, about man and the world, and principles that when applied in a secondary manner modify their behavior.

2. *The covenantal system.* Bullinger (first half of the sixteenth century) was the first to present systematically the covenantal system of interpretation in order to defend infant baptism. Calvin virtually agreed; and it reached its final, classic expression in the Westminster Confession. At present, a theology of the covenants still has to be written; there are too many conflicting opinions, too many loose ends. But the classic covenantal system found expression principally in the Presbyterian,

Congregationalist, and Calvinistic Baptist churches. Though there is much diversity of opinion today, the classic formulation still influences this mode of interpreting the Old Testament. Krabbendam at Covenant Theological Seminary succinctly summarized the history of this system of interpreting the Old Testament, and I shall précis his summary here in order to set forth its classic expression.

> Bullinger wrote the first major treatise on the subject . . . *Brief Exposition Concerning the One and Eternal Testament or Covenant of God*. . . . It can be summarized in the words of Gen. 17:1, "I am God Almighty, walk before me and be perfect. . . ." The covenant in the bud becomes progressively the covenant in full bloom. Hence the later covenants are called covenant renewals. The covenant . . . is made between God on the one hand and Abraham and his children, on the other hand. Furthermore, it contains both promises and conditions or stipulations. . . . When he is faced with the question how he can maintain the unity of the covenant in view of Jer. 31 and Gal. 4 which seem to indicate that there are at least two covenants—the old mediated by Moses and the new mediated by Christ, his answer is as follows, The substance of the covenant remains the same. This determines its unity. . . . However, there is a progression of the external forms in the one covenant history. This determines that there are two administrations.
>
> Calvin's views are virtually identical to those of Bullinger. . . . The unity is rooted in its substance, which is Christ foreshadowed in the old and having come in the new covenant. The difference between the old and new covenants is a matter of the form and mode of administration. The term abrogation with regard to the old covenant pertains to the latter. The law as a perpetual condemnation of sin is not abolished. But the law as ceremonial and the old covenant economy as preparatory to the full glory of Christ was abolished, when the substance that was promised finally came.
>
> Regrettably, however, as covenant theology continued to be developed, strands begin to appear and become soon solidified that seem more imposed upon Scripture than gleaned from it.
>
> It soon became the majority opinion that the covenant was made with the elect and that, therefore, it is unconditional. . . . The demands are called obligations and in no way impinge on the gratuitous, unconditional character of the covenant.

In addition to this development the concept of the covenant of works was introduced. God promises eternal life to Adam before the fall upon the condition of good works. When man fails to meet the condition, the covenant of grace takes its place, in which eternal life is promised upon faith on the part of the sinner. . . . The good works envisioned in the covenant of works are identical to the sum and substance of the ten command- ments, at that time written in the heart. . . . Facing the impossi- bility of keeping the commandments the sinner would recognize that the covenant of works is no longer a possible avenue to God and turn to the covenant of grace.

Eventually the concept of the covenant of redemption, also called the *pactum salutis,* was added to the lists of covenants. This was a pact between the Father and the Son, fully two-sided, in which the Father gave the elect to the Son, and the Son promised to secure their eternal salvation. . . . The name of Coccejus is connected with this theology.

It is interesting to note that the development of the theology of the covenant is reflected in the creeds of the Reformed Churches. . . . In the later creeds, culminating in the Westminster Confession, the covenant had become somewhat like the or- ganizing principle of the Scripture teachings."

According to the covenantal system, the church participates in the Old Testament covenants (Abrahamic, Mosaic, Davidic, New). The substance of the Mosaic legislation applies directly to the church. But Christ is foreshadowed in the old and has come in the new. The difference between the old and new covenants is a matter of form and mode of administration. The ceremonial part of the covenant was done away with once Jesus came and replaced it with its antitypical reality.

The prophetic vision of Israel's glorious future is being pres- ently realized in part in the church on whom the end of the ages has come. Isaiah's prophecy that the Messiah will rule on the throne of David and rule from sea to sea is presently being realized in Jesus' ascension into heaven where he sits on his throne at God's right hand in the heavenly Mt. Zion (Heb. 12:22ff). From here he exercises authority over all creatures in heaven and on earth.

A few covenant theologians are also premillennialist. They

tend to interpret the prophecies about Israel's glorious future literally in terms of a restored political state. Otherwise they interpret the OT as stated above.

3. *Conclusion.* For myself I cannot accept either system in its entirety. My own convictions regarding some of the essential points raised in this description of the two systems are:

1. We should reckon only with the historic covenants of the Old Testament and not construct abstract, theological covenants such as a covenant of grace or redemption and confound them with the historic covenants (Noahic, Abrahamic, Mosaic, Davidic, New).
2. We ought to recognize the distinctiveness of the Old Testament covenants and not confound them as parts of one eternal covenant.
3. We need to distinguish the conditional covenants from the unconditional covenants.
4. We need to emphasize that the church has been grafted into the covenants of promises (Abrahamic, Davidic, New). Thus we ought not to radically separate the church from "spiritual" Israel.
5. The new covenant, which pertains to the believing seed, contains the substance of the Mosaic legislation. Christ fulfilled the righteousness demanded in the old covenant and its ceremonial provisions. Many of its provisions are symbolic of antitypical spiritual realities.
6. The prophetic vision of Messiah's reign is being fulfilled in the church and will be consummated in the eternal state.
7. We ought not to think of the Old Testament saints as Jews or belonging to Judaism. The common practice of calling Abraham Jewish is both anachronistic and obscures the reality that Abraham was related more closely with Christ and the church, his spiritual seed, than with his physical seed which rejected Jesus.
8. The Jewish people, Abraham's physical seed in unbelief, will one day repent, call upon the Lord Jesus, and be saved. The present reunification of Israel in a common homeland may be preparatory to their spiritual salvation.

9. There will not be a millennium nor a future Jewish kingdom under Messiah before the eternal state. There is but
one holy tree, not two, and we both together look with
Abraham for the eternal city of God.

10. The Old Testament has direct relevance to the church as
part of the people of God. The church yearns for the day
when the physical seed will once again participate in its
true spiritual heritage.

All evangelicals will agree with Krabbendam's analysis of the
fourfold purpose of the older covenant: 1) God wishes to convey
the essence of life. That is obedience to the law (Deut. 32:47).
2) He wishes to expose the essence of death. That is disobedience to the law (Rom. 3:20). 3) He wishes to disclose the
transition from death to life. That is grace (Rom. 3:21b). 4) He
wishes to display the way he deals with his people and the way
in which they should and should not respond to him (Rom.
15:4; I Cor. 10:11; I Tim. 3:16). I would like to add to these that
he wishes to point us to the Messiah who satisfies the demands
of the law.

The rules.

We now turn to the rules for relating the two testaments to
one another.

1. *A recognition of the unity of the two testaments.* To judge from
Longenecker's list of Old Testament quotations in the New
Testament, there are approximately 250 clearly marked as such;
another 200 not prefaced by any formula; 950 Old Testament
passages referred to in the New Testament; and at least 1000
that allude to, paraphrase, summarize, or reflect Old Testament
verses. These numerous citations demonstrate in the final
analysis the unity, contiguity, and progress of the Scriptures.
The New Testament considers itself as a part and a continuation
of the Old Testament.

2. *The progress of revelation.* The doctrine of progressive revelation is based on the conviction that revelation and salvation
history move along a historical line united by the activity of

God in both. This concept has several important ramifications for hermeneutics.

The revelation and form of salvation history take shape in changing historical situations. God meets man where he is and his revelation becomes incarnate in such a way that empirical contact between God and man can take place. God met Abraham under trees, according to the prevailing religious customs of Abraham's age. He dwelt with Israel in the portable tent appropriate to the wilderness and later in a temple of stone when they found stability with the monarchy. Today he dwells with his universal, spiritual body in his Spirit wherever it convenes. It follows, therefore, that the changing historical husks within which the revelation takes place are not normative for faith and practice; it is the unchanging spiritual kernel that constitutes the essence to be apprehended by faith and allowed to determine the believer's practices.

Progressive revelation also means that the later revelation has priority over the earlier. Although the testaments are unified there is not uniformity of importance in them. This means that if there is any tension between them, the old must give way to the new; the old must be interpreted in the light of the new. "The locus of a text in the corpus of revelation determines the mode of its exegesis and the theological weight that can be assessed to it."[37] In the New Testament are recorded the incarnation of God, the life of the incarnate Son, the saving events of the cross, the resurrection of Messiah from the dead and his exaltation to God's right hand as lord of all, and the interpretation of his person and work. This revelation of God in Jesus Christ constitutes the fulfillment and climax of the Old Testament revelation, and thus it must be granted priority.

Earlier revelation must be interpreted in the light of later revelation. In theological exegesis the original meaning of an earlier revelation is both fulfilled and transcended in the later revelation. The earlier, inspired writer only partially grasped what the Spirit later revealed in the progress of salvation history (cf. I Peter 1:10–11). Thus we must not only ask what a biblical writer had in mind at the time of the original revelation, but we must go on to ask what the text came to mean in the light of further revelation. As the literary context of earlier passages expanded with the addition of more canonical books, the full meaning of the original text became more clear.

As suggested at the beginning of this paper there are at least three distinct stages in the progressive clarification of Old Testament texts: (1) the meaning of the text at the time of composition; (2) its meaning at the time the Old Testament canon closed; (3) its meaning with the addition of the New Testament. Thus, for example, Psalm 2:7, "You are my Son" in its original setting had primary reference to Israel's historic kings; and "son" would appropriately be translated with a small "s." But when the Old Testament canon closed there was no king sitting on David's throne, and in retrospect it was clear that none of David's historic sons satisfied the poetic vision of an ideal king. In this context the psalm is prophetic of a future king, a Messiah who would fulfill the ideal. In the New Testament it is revealed that the Lord Jesus Christ is the expected king. Furthermore, he is God incarnate, the preexisting Son, born of a virgin. Within this context it is necessary to render "son" in Psalm 2:7 with a capital "S."[38]

The Old Testament is prophetic.

God inspired the writers of the Old Testament to predict the future messianic age both by pictures and by explicit statements. Moses predicted a seed of the woman that would destroy the serpent (Gen. 3:15; fulfilled in Jesus Christ and his church, Rom. 16:20). Isaiah heard in a vision: "The voice of him that crieth in the wilderness, Prepare ye the way of the LORD, make straight in the desert a highway for our God" (Isa. 40:3, KJV; fulfilled in John the Baptist preparing the way for Jesus, Luke 3:3–6). Malachi predicted: "Behold, I will send you Elijah the prophet before the coming of the great and dreadful day of the LORD" (Mal. 4:5, KJV; fulfilled in John the Baptist who came in the spirit and power of Elijah, Matt. 11:13ff; 17:10–13). Isaiah reported the rejection of the Servant of the LORD and his offering up of his soul as a trespass offering (Isa. 52:13–53:12) and Zechariah predicted that Israel would look upon God "whom they have pierced" (Zech. 12:10, KJV; fulfilled in Jesus, John 19:37).

God not only predicted the life and work of Messiah, he also pictured it. Even as writing evolved from pictures to abstract symbols, so also God gave Israel in its infancy pictures of the later spiritual realities. For example, Israel's cultus with its tabernacle, priesthood, and sacrifices is a picture, a shadow, of the heavenly temple where Christ ministers as the church's high priest and offers his body as an eternal sacrifice for the sins of all people (Heb. 9–10). In brief, the form of God's kingdom in the Old Testament is a type of the church, the antitype. (As noted above, however, dispensationalists would dispute this statement.)

The prophets predicted the future age in terms appropriate to the earthly form of the kingdom of God as they knew it. In what other terms could they speak? But this historic presentation of things to come in an earthly garb is but a representation of the later glorious age which the apostles said had come: "Indeed, all the prophets from Samuel on, as many as have spoken, have foretold these days" (Peter, Acts 3:24). "Unto whom [the prophets] it was revealed, that not unto themselves, but unto us they did minister the things, which are now reported unto you by them that have preached the gospel unto you with the Holy Ghost sent down from heaven; which things the angels desire to look into" (I Peter 1:12, KJV). Their prophecies could be fulfilled very literalistically with regard to the birth and earthly life of Messiah, but they could not be fulfilled in the same way once Messiah began his heavenly ministry over his spiritual body. The New Testament writers do not predict a restoration of Israel as a carnal kingdom back in the Promised Land prior to the eternal state. Dispensationalists, as noted however, insist that the literal reading of the Old Testament must have priority in interpretation.

Rules for Applying the Hebrew Scriptures to Today

Having set forth the rules by which evangelicals interpret the intention of the authors of the Hebrew Scriptures, and the rules by which they interpret the text as the canon expanded to include the New Testament, it now remains to set forth briefly the rules by which they apply the older testament to today. In this section we note that they interpret the text dialogically, dialectically, suprahistorically, and philosophically.

Approach the text dialogically.

Evangelicals are convinced that God aims to speak to the entire community of faith throughout space and time. God's Spirit continues to speak through the Scriptures for doctrine, reproof, correction, and instruction in righteousness. Mickelsen expresses this conviction on the part of evangelicals: "What should a man know about what God has done or revealed? The answer is found in *doctrine.* How should a man *respond* to God whom he knows by virtue of his experience of salvation? This is the concern of *devotion.* What should a man *do* in the existential situations of life? Here we face the problem of conduct."[39]

Approach the text dialectically.

Evangelicals are learning to hold the truths of Scripture that are in tension with the same weight at the same time. For example, in the first creation account (Gen. 1:1–2:3) God is presented as the transcendent, sovereign God, whereas in the second account (Gen. 2:4–25) he is presented as the immanent God who has handed over to man responsibility for governing the earth. In Genesis 1 God exists before history and beyond his creation; in Genesis 2 he walks on the earth and works with his hands "forming" (*ysr*) the man and "building" (*bnh*) the woman. In Genesis 1 he calls as a master architect the earth into existence; in Genesis 2 he brings the animals to the man "to see what he would call them." In Genesis 1 he commands the man to subdue the earth; in Genesis 2 he commands him to work it and take care of it. These truths about God and man are not contradictory but lie beyond rational comprehension. They must be held in tension.

Other paradoxes include "God loves the world" but "he hates Esau"; "the earth is the LORD's" (Ps. 24:1) but "the earth he has given to man" (Ps. 115:16). These truths and many more must be presented with equal weight. If we minimize one aspect of the polarity we distort truth by presenting half truths.

So likewise evangelicals believe that the Old Testament predicts both a reigning and suffering Messiah. The tension runs throughout the Old Testament. "I will put enmity between you and the woman, and between your offspring and hers; he will crush your head, and you will strike his heel" (Gen. 3:15). "Ask of me [my son/Son], and I will make the nations your inheritance, the ends of the earth your possession" (Ps. 2:8) and "My God, my God, why have you forsaken me?" (Ps. 22:1).[40] "See, my servant will act wisely;he will be raised and lifted up and highly exalted" (Isa. 52:13) and "By oppression and judgment, he was taken away. And who can speak of his descendants? For he was cut off from the land of the living; for the transgression of my people he was stricken" (Isa. 53:8).

Approach the text suprahistorically.

Evangelicals discriminate between the passing, temporal form in which the revelation came and its eternal verity. They ask themselves how the passage helps to concretize their expressions of love for God and love for others. They ask how it involves them personally.

Approach the text philosophically.

Finally, the evangelical recognizes that many issues confronting modern man did not confront the biblical writers. He also recognizes that if he asks the ancient text wrong questions, he will get wrong answers. Instead of using the text to provide proof-texts for answering these new issues, he rather allows it to shape his personal outlook, his *Weltanschauung,* and with that perspective he attempts to address himself to the modern world. (This presentation has been prescriptive rather than descriptive.)

Notes

All Scripture references are taken from the New International Version, unless otherwise noted.

138 The Bible and Biblical Interpretation

1. Standard reference works on this topic and employed by evangelicals include: Fairbairn, FauIck, *Hermeneutical Manual* (1858); Terry, Milton, *Biblical Hermeneutics* (1883); Beecher, W. J., *The Prophets and the Promise* (1905); Berkhof, L., *Principles of Biblical Interpretation* (1952); Brown, R. E., *The Sensus Plenior of Sacred Scripture* (1955); Ramm, Bernard, *Protestant Biblical Interpretation* (1956); Dodd, C. H., *According to the Scriptures* (1952); Ellis, E., *Paul's Use of the Old Testament* (1957); Von Hoffman, J. C. K., *Interpreting the Bible* (Eng. tr., 1959); Mickelsen, A. Berkeley, *Interpreting the Bible* (1963); Smart, James, *The Interpretation of Scripture* (1961); Farrar, F. W., *History of Interpretation* (1886, reprint 1961); Ramm, B. and others, *Hermeneutics* (1974); Marshall, I. H. (ed.), *New Testament Interpretation* (1979). I found much help in the preparation of this paper in a syllabus by Henry Krabbendam (Covenant College), *Toward a Biblical Hermeneutic* (unpublished, no date). I have not yet read the widely acclaimed, Thistleton, A., *The Two Horizons* (1980).

2. F. Schleiermacher, *The Christian Faith* (Fortress Press, 1976), p. vii.

3. Clark H. Pinnock, "Evangelical Theology—Conservative and Contemporary," *Theological Bulletin McMaster Divinity College*, Vol. 4 (May 1978).

4. Friedrick, *Theological Dictionary of the New Testament*, ed. by G. Kittel, trans. and ed. by G. W. Bromiley, II (1974⁶):726.

5. Donald G. Bloesch, *Essentials of Evangelical Theology*, I (1978):8.

6. *Ibid.*, p. 11.

7. *Ibid.*, p. 13.

8. B. Ramm, "Biblical Hermeneutics," *Hermeneutics* (1974), p. 10.

9. J. Calvin, *Institutes of the Christian Religion*, Book I, ch. 6–7.

10. F. F. Bruce, "The History of New Testament Study," *New Testament Interpretation*, p. 26.

11. Ramm, p. 25.

12. Vernon Grounds, "Evangelicalism and Education, "Seminary Study Series" (*Conservative Baptist Theological Seminary*, n.d.).

13. Henry Krabbendam, "Toward a Biblical Hermeneutic."

14. Bloesch, p. 71.

15. Krabbendam, 6:6.

16. E. J. Young, *Thy Word Is Truth* (1957), p. 219.

17. Bruce, p. 44.

18. I. H. Marshall, "Historical Criticism," *Hermeneutics*, p. 134.

19. Ramm, p. 26.

20. *The Ryrie Study Bible* (1978).

21. James D. G. Dunn, "Demythologizing—The Problem of Myth in the New Testament," *Hermeneutics*, p. 293.

22. A. C. Thistleton, "Semantics and New Testament Interpretation," *meneutics*, p. 82.

23. *Ibid.*, p. 80.

24. For a convenient summary of these views see Robert G. Clouse (ed.), *The Meaning of the Millennium* (Inter-Varsity, 1977).

25. I received both my Th.M. and Th.D. from this institution and had the distinct privilege of serving on its faculty for eighteen years. I reluctantly left that position in order to be able to think more objectively about some of the essential distinctives of the school.

26. L. S. Chafer, *Dispensationalism* (1936), p. 107.

27. L. S. Chafer, *The Kingdom in History and Prophecy*, p. 84.

28. C. C. Ryrie, *Dispensationalism Today* (1975[10]), p. 95.

29. Chafer, *Systematic Theology*, IV (1948):41.

30. Ryrie, p. 93.

31. J. D. Pentecost, *Things to Come* (1958), pp. 577f.

32. J. H. Darby, "Reflections Upon the Prophetic Inquiry," *Col. Writ.*, I:27.

33. L. S. Chafer, *Major Bible Themes*, pp. 97f.

34. I. M. Haldeman, *How to Study the Bible* (1907), pp. 7, 3.

35. Darby, "On 'Days' Signifying 'Years' in Prophetic Language," *Col. Writ.*, I:53f.

36. Ryrie, p. 143.

37. Ramm, p. 24.

38. This approach, which may be called "the canonical process approach, offers a way out of the crux whether the text has a single meaning (W. Kaiser) or multiple meanings, a *sensus plenior.*

39. Mickelsen, p. 356.

40. For defense of an extensive royal interpretation of the Psalms, see John Eaton, *Kingship and the Psalms* (1976).

7

Jerusalem in Biblical and Theological Tradition

A Jewish Perspective

Asher Finkel

Jerusalem—Zion—occupies a significant place in the
historical, prophetic, and psalmic works of the Hebrew Bible.[1]
After all, the city of God's temple is the experiential setting of
"*hagios topos*" (holy place) and the spatial configuration of a
socio-religious reality for the biblical writers, from the prophets
and the psalmists to the redactors and scribes. As such, Jerusalem becomes a powerful literary image in the formation of
prophetic thought and in the expression of psalmic prayer. It
serves as a symbol, capturing meaning on different levels, and
it portrays an idea that lends to various parabolic forms. The
Hebrew Bible links Jerusalem affectively with basic theological
concepts of creation, revelation, and salvation. These notions
of biblical faith are determined in the highest sense by the
human encounter with God's presence in the temple.[2] Jerusalem as a cultic place for God's enthronement and manifestation affects deeply the one who prays, producing awe and
fascination.

Standing before God in humility and dependence is the
condition and attitude of the worshiper. Standing implies a
"place" orientation; one's thoughts and feelings in prayer are
directed to God in a place. Through the events of pollution and

destruction, purification and restoration, the temple of Jerusalem produces a setting for biblical prayer, to express lament and yearning, to relate despair and joy, and to reflect pain and peacefulness. The worshiper relates to God in the direction of the temple,[3] already reflected in the prayer of Solomon (I Kings 8:30) and in the practice of Daniel (Dan. 6:13). Thus, Jerusalem remains the visible symbol of faith in Jewish prayer throughout the ages.

Likewise, Jerusalem affects the prophets' protest concerning evil, as well as their response to sinfulness and catastrophe. Moreover, it determines the prophetic vision of messianic renewal and universal redemption. The offshoot of prophecy is apocalypticism,[4] which has shaped significantly the eschatological vision and orientation of both Judaism and Christianity. Clearly apocalyptic thought is affected by the crisis in Jerusalem and the hope for Zion. Moreover, Jerusalem and temple emerge on a dual plane as the earthly place of God's indwelling and their counterpart in heaven, the realm of apocalypticist's ascent.[5] This correspondence bespeaks a biblical orientation, that God remains durative and abiding in the religious experience of his transcendental presence, while on earth he is manifested in history punctually and elusively. The earthly Jerusalem relates affectively to its heavenly counterpart, and they coalesce meaningfully in the end of time when God's presence will be enjoyed universally.

Jerusalem in Rabbinic Thought

The frequent mention of Jerusalem (over two thousand references) in the Hebrew Bible is noted by the rabbis; and in Midrash Canticles Zuta, a list of seventy names, including metaphors and allusions, is given.[6] This betrays a significant hermeneutical approach, analogous to the exegetical method employed by Justin in his Dialogue with Trypho,[7] the rabbi. Justin offers a list of scriptural titles for Jesus, as a christological guide to the interpretation of the Hebrew Bible. Jerusalem, therefore, is a dominant theological feature in homiletic thought and peroration of the rabbis. This is definitely related to its centrality in the hope and prayer of the synagogal community, for scriptural preaching was addressed to the liturgically oriented audience, affecting both faith and praxis.

In the above Midrash, the city is linked with the seventy names of God, of Torah, and of Israel, similar expressions being interchangeable. This indicates how far Jerusalem has penetrated the theological construct of an organic trilogy,[8] that "God, Torah and Israel are one." Israel's historical conscious-ness of a continuous relationship with God through Torah, his living words, is determined by a "place" orientation. This effec-tive linkage of God's people with God's place is clearly mani-fested in the Pentateuch, the authoritative Torah. For Jerusalem and temple are inextricable and both serve as the quintessence of the land. The land dominates the Pentateuchal account of salvation in history.[9] Accordingly, the place with Yahweh is cen-tral to biblical faith, and the Hebrew canon relates the story of God's people with God's land. So it began with the patriarchs and was later experienced by their descendants. It is characteris-tic of the history of the Jewish people to be dynamically related to the human spirit on the move, as M. Buber indicates,[10] from epochs of *"Behausung,"* to be at home in the universe, and epochs of *"Hauslosigkeit,"* to feel homeless and to be regarded problematically.

Place as land, city, and temple is so central a motif to the biblical witness, that in New Testament times, the "place" already coalesced with God's name.[11] Matthew (5:35; 23:21) pre-serves the teaching of Jesus that Jerusalem is the city of the great King (Ps. 48:2) and the temple is the place of God's indwelling (Ps. 74:2). Neither is to be used in oath-taking for this violates the third commandment on not taking God's name in vain. In the early rabbinic period, the "place" (*maqom*) was used as a divine title, and R. Yohanan of the third century indicates (Babylonian Talmud Baba Bathra 75b) that Jerusalem and the Messiah both receive the divine name in prophetic writings (Ezek. 48:35; Jer. 23:6). For the manifestation of God's kingdom was closely associated in the early Palestinian liturgy with the coming of the Son of David and the restoration of

Jerusalem. Such an association dominates also the early Christian liturgy[12] as recorded in Didache 10:5-6, and it becomes a distinctive feature in the tradition and redaction of the Gospels.[13]

Jerusalem in Contemporary Discussion

It is surprising that only in recent times has some attention been paid to the motif, land, and temple in biblical theology. This appears to be related, on one hand to a contemporary concern of the industrialized world and its agony of rootlessness, as well as with the aspiration of the Third-World people for a land which will assure survival and give hope of freedom, as pointed out by W. Brueggemann.[14] On the other hand, the interest in Jewish and Christian circles is also marked by the establishment of the state of Israel and the restoration of Jerusalem. These recent historical events offer a confirmation of biblical hope, when Jews and Christians feel that solidarity with Israel and Jerusalem is an inseparable part of their faith. Yet the contemporary theological discussion seems to be following dogmatic lines. The recent work of W. D. Davies on *The Gospel and the Land*[15] offers a dichotomy of land orientation in Judaism and "disenlandizement" in Christianity, a shift to Christ as the holy place. Such an erudite presentation, which conforms to his line of research, seems to be concerned with the process of Christian departure from Judaism. He further concludes that "Jesus paid little attention to the relationship between God, Israel and the land."[16] Interestingly, Jesus himself is interpreted as being in tension with Judaism. This reminds one of the similar quest in the early part of this century,[17] which came to promote a theologically biased contrast between Jesus and the rabbis to the detriment of the latter. In the case of Jerusalem, the Christian exegetical approach comes either to spiritualize and transcendentalize the city or to see in the destruction and restoration of Jerusalem the prophetic judgment and promise as prelude to Jesus' coming. The Jewish response, as in the earlier work of A. Heschel,[18] seems to focus on the significance of time or event in the Bible and Judaism, while space remains secondary. This emphasis on Israel as a people of time goes back to Hegel. One should be cautious with a philosophical interpretation; for in Old Testament thought both time and place are equally important, as is so brilliantly argued by J. Barr.[19]

New Approaches in Biblical Theology

The theological meaning of Jerusalem-temple must be judged afresh in light of the recent development in biblical criticism and theological overtures, as well as in light of the sociological, structural, and phenomenological investigations.[20] The two major presentations, which dominate biblical studies today, have been challenged. On one hand, these are the results of "myth and ritual" research and on the other, there is a *Heilsgeschichte* interpretation. The latter offers an option that sees theology reflected in the biblical recital of redemptive events, the *Magnalia Dei*. The biblical works present a theological historiography which stressed the ideology of covenant.[21] This approach is questioned by S. Terrien,[22] who sees the basic focus of biblical theology as on God's presence. He writes: "The religion of the Hebrews, of Israel, of post-exilic Judaism and of early Christians [and the rabbis][23] is permeated by the experience, the cultic recollection, and the proleptically appropriated expectation of the presence of God in human history."[24]

The covenant is not to be reduced to the form of ancient Near Eastern Suzerain treaty, with its demands on the covenanted vassal people. In contrast, the prophetic thought utilizes matrimonial symbolism[25] to express anthropopathically the dynamic relationship between God and Israel. The eschatological time of covenant renewal corresponds to the historical time of the initial encounter between God and his people. The dynamic religious history of Israel between these two temporal poles, then, reflects the true dialectic of the covenant. It is an interplay of closeness and distance, of excitement and weariness, of "*da'at*" (intimate knowledge) and unfaithfulness. The prophets link effectively the remembered past of encounter with the prospect of renewal in the future. The new covenant will be sealed perpetually in the commitments of justice and righteousness, of love and faithfulness. The city itself and the land provide the place[26] for the collective translation of such commitments, transforming the society and attracting universal attention, due to a *da'at* of God. Only then will the trans-personal relationship reflect a mutual declaration like that of the nuptial vow: "You are my people" and "you are my God" (Hos. 2:23). Thus, the midrashic interpretation of Canticles, similarly employed by Origen,[27] shares in the prophetic hiero-gamic understanding. The Midrash views the temple as the canopy[28] under which Israel meets God in an agapic encounter. This reflects the passionate attitude of the returnees and later the pilgrims in their coming to Jerusalem. It is already expressed in Isaiah 62:5, "As a young man husbands a young woman, so will your children husband you." The prophet is describing the affective meaning of the promise of return to Jerusalem and the land after the period of Babylonian exile. He links this human response parabolically to God's response in the encounter. "As the bridegroom rejoices over the bride, so shall your God rejoice over you." Israel and Jerusalem coalesce through the experience of encounter. Zion[29] in rabbinic thought stands for both the place and for the people. God is encountered as in a marital covenant, when the parties experience life together through a "home" setting.

A theology of presence does incorporate the prophetic hermeneutics itself, whereas the religious phenomenon governing such a collective involvement with the temple can be examined as a liminal experience.[30] Attention is therefore directed not toward events or acts of God in history but rather toward religio-historical processes affecting the worshiping community. They are first reflected in the biblical tradition and then they reemerge in a dialogue with God's presence through Scriptures. The recent stress by B. Childs on canonical interpretation[31] properly relates biblical theology itself to the formation of biblical canon. The initial midrashic dialogue with Scriptures through a community of faith governed by a canonical consciousness reveals the key hermeneutical forms in early biblical theology. Such a development can be traced from *Urtext* to the

Massoretic text through the stages of accepted and received texts,[32] i.e. from Persian time to the New Testament period. Only this approach dynamically complements the investigation of how the Scriptures were experienced by a liturgical community through reading and preaching, faith and praxis.

This leads us to the second option, that of the history of religion school and its comparative exploration of myth and ritual. Temple is viewed as *axis mundi*,[33] similar to the Omphalos myth[34] of a central place in mythopoeic thought. Thus, the contemporary theological method seeks to demythologize the earlier religious expression of the biblical writers and instead to offer an existential understanding of faith as it addresses us today. It limits the biblical themes to their mythological frames without recognizing the experiential setting that deepens religious consciousness and ethical behavior. There is a close relationship between the worshiping community and its temple. The temple was central not only to the cultic but also to the political, economic, and social organization of national life. The recent emphasis on sociological interpretation of religions indicates that there is a close link between theological vision and sociological organization.[35]

Responses to God's Presence in the Temple

A phenomenological understanding of the basic determinents in a socio-religious setting reveals how the worshiping community relates to God's presence in a place and how it comes to translate a particular religious consciousness. Neither the physical nor the functional reality of Jerusalem and temple exhaust their meaning for Israel. For temple and Messiah, closely associated in eschatological hope, also were believed to be preexistent.[36] Both were viewed in relation to God's presence, whose transcendental existence was the foundation of their faith. The theistic faith of Israel maintained that God exists perpetually in a heavenly realm, where he transcends both time and space. On earth God is encountered in an act of his presence or in the act of his removal (*silluq*).[37] Such experience is described in connection with the temple in prophetic (Ezek.

8–11) and rabbinic writings. Likewise in the Gospels, the Messiah is depicted in terms of God's presence and his removal. This experiential response to Jesus affects the evangelical vocabulary of movement. Scripture scholarship[38] that does not pay attention to this underlying meaning in redactional theological work fails to recognize the intent of the gospel writers.

Biblically oriented Judaism always viewed God as the ground of all existence, and space itself cannot contain him.[39] Early Christian polemics, usually explained in light of Stephen's speech (Acts 7:48) or John's gospel (2:21; 4:21), could not have misinterpreted this faith position in Judaism. For the biblically oriented community encountered God's presence in the temple only through its faith in a transcendental reality. Nothing but the Wholly Other can affect the creature's feelings in the event of *mysterium tremendum et fascinans* (the overwhelming yet fascinating mystery: Rudolf Otto, *The Idea of the Holy*). In no way was God limited to an earthly place, and the statement about the temple by Jesus and early Christians was similar to the Essene criticism. Both questioned that the polluted temple of Herod could offer an opportunity for the pilgrims to encounter the Holy. It was criticized as a temple built by human hands, betraying the intention of human arrogance and self-aggrandizement, antithetical to God's presence. At the same time, both Christians and Essenes as well as the rabbis spoke of a heavenly reality of God's presence envisioned as a counterpart to temple and Jerusalem. It was established as the divine throne before all existence to serve as a divine "pattern" (*tabhnit*) for its earthly abode.[40]

The Essenes prepared themselves, therefore, for a final cosmic battle which would lead to the restoration of the temple in its purified glory, as described in the War Scroll. In the interim period, the community in the desert becomes the temple in waiting.[41] The holy community does not, however, replace the rejected spatial abode, as argued by B. Gärtner[42] and followed by J. Neusner.[43] The Temple Scroll, recently published by Y. Yadin, appears to belong to proto-Essenic time.[44] It offers a blueprint for the ideal temple in Jerusalem with a fixed liturgical calendar of a solar year determined from Wednesday, the day when the luminaries were created. The Scroll relates: "'They shall be unto me a people and I will be unto them forever'—the nuptial vow—'I shall dwell among them forever'—the biblical promise of presence. 'And I shall sanctify the Temple with my glory'—the earthly Temple sanctified by God's presence. 'For I will cause my glory to dwell upon it until the day of blessing (i.e. the end time) when I will create my Temple to be established all the days, according to the covenant I made with Jacob at Beth-El' (29:7–10). This undoubtedly refers to the heavenly Temple as Jacob experienced it in the vision of the Ladder (Gen. 28:10–22)."

The early Christian community also viewed themselves as the temple awaiting the Parousia. They anticipated the ingathering of the dispersed *ecclesia* to the call of the Shofar and the establishment of the twelve seats of judgment in the presence of the Son of David. All these will occur with the descent of the heavenly Jerusalem. Such eschatology[45] corresponds to the basic hope expression of the eschatological petitions of the synagogue. However, in the Jewish Christian work of Revelation, this new Jerusalem is without a temple. For "the Lord, God of hosts and the lamb are the Temple" (Rev. 21:22; 22:3). This corresponds to the Markan explanation: "I will raise another Temple that is not made with human hands" (Mark 14:58). These depictions come to emphasize that God's presence through Jesus will be the central experience of pilgrims to Jerusalem in the end of time. For long before the days of Jesus, Jerusalem and temple have been invested with extraordinary significance in the expression of theistic faith. They have a role not only for Israel in history but for the whole world in its ultimate acknowledgment of God's reign. J. Jeremias[46] correctly argues that Jesus looked forward to an eschatological pilgrimage of Gentiles to the mountain of God in Zion. There they will celebrate the great feast at the redemption of Israel. The Gentiles would be guaranteed a share in the revelation vouchsafed to Israel and inclusion in God's redeemed community at the time of the last judgment.

Pilgrimage and the Temple

The significance of Jerusalem-Zion for Israel and the early church lies in the pilgrimage event. It is the pilgrimage to the temple[47] as an encounter with God's presence in his place, which deepened the attachment to the city. Jerusalem became the unique setting for all people from near and far in this dispersion to come together in fellowship before God's presence. It provided the opportunity for the biblically oriented community to experience a covenantal relationship with God. The city demanded a human response of love and compassion, of welcome and hospitality, of brotherhood and common purpose. The early rabbinic tradition[48] preserves accounts and customs of the above responses, which were peculiar to Jerusalem. The rabbis explain[49] one does not come to the city on a pilgrimage in order to enjoy its food or its baths but mainly for the sake of heaven. Jerusalem offered the pilgrims an experiential setting to express their theistic faith and to enjoy a sense of atonement and closeness to God.[50]

This religious intention is already reflected in the early cultic song and prayer in the Pentateuch. The song at the Red Sea (Exod. 15:17) and the Deuteronomic confession of the farmers (Deut. 26:9) both relate the redemptive process in history, leading from bondage and threat of annihilation to the entry into the land, for the purpose of "coming to the place," i.e. "the established abode made by God's hands." Only there will God's kingdom[51] be proclaimed: "God will reign forever." The early agrarian ritual decalogue (Exod. 23:17, 18) and the prayer of Solomon (I Kings 8:23ff.) refer to a pilgrimage experience in visiting the temple in the act of prayer before God's presence. Jerusalem becomes then the focus of the canonical Hebrew Bible. As the Scribes' Midrash of Israelite history, Chronicles is the last item in the list of authoritative books of the Hagiographa (Babylonian Talmud Baba Bathra 14b). It ends with the appeal: "Whoever is among you of all his people, may Yahweh his God be with him, let him go up" (II Chron. 36:23), a call to pilgrimage to Jerusalem. Such a stress is canonically introduced

at the beginning of the diaries of Ezra-Nehemiah. These
became biblical works that relate the effective realization of
such an appeal with its impact on the second temple period
through the renewal of the covenant in Jerusalem. The Chris-
tion canon ends with the Book of Revelation, which describes
Jerusalem as the site for universal pilgrimage to a heavenly
reality in the end of time. Thus, the city as a center of eschatological hope remained in Judaism also on the earthly plane,
whereas in Christianity it was exclusive to the heavenly plane.
For Jerusalem holds the prospect from the remembered past,
when the community before God was judged, and will be
renewed by its setting. Jerusalem does not become simply a site
invested with mythological meaning of the Canaanite type,[52]
with the motifs of a divine mountain, paradisical river, and
conquest of chaos. The eschatological expectation flows from a
present religious reality that is charged by the historical experience of the past.

What holds the promise for the biblically oriented community
of Jews and Christians is its rootedness in the *anamnesis*
(remembrance) of the ultimate expression of faith in God.
Jerusalem was the same site (Gen. 22:2; II Chron. 3:1) where
Abraham displayed his total commitment to God through the
sacrifice (*Akedah*) of his beloved son Isaac on Mount Moriah.
As such it affected the Jewish appeal of *anamnesis* in praying for
divine atonement. This midrashic frame in liturgical life was
conclusively argued by G. Vermes[53] to have affected the meaning of the crucifixion in Jerusalem of Jesus, the beloved Son, as
the atoning sacrifice for the many.

Corresponding to worship is the ethical behavior, which, for
the pilgrim in Jerusalem seeking atonement, is assumed by
walking in the way of Abraham. It is the way of altruistic love
which is described as the act of *imitatio Dei*. Abraham is chosen
to charge his descendants, according to Midrash Genesis 18:19[54]
to teach "them to keep the way of the Lord," i.e. acts of love and
"righteousness," acts of charity and "justice." This way (*odos* =
halakhah) was demanded from the pilgrims in Psalms 15 and 24.
The way to God's presence in the temple is paved by the
demands of love, righteousness, and justice in the realm of

interpersonal relationship. Jerusalem captured the ideal social order, which is to serve as the model for the theocratic state based on "Torah, Service and Acts of Love" before its fall and for a theocratic community based on "Justice, Truth and Peace" after its fall, according to Mishnah Abot 1:2 (Simon the Righteous) and 18 (Simon the Patriarch). For such a community the catastrophe that befell Jerusalem was explained as judgment for sins committed toward fellow human beings, the motivational act of ill feeling and the corporal act of blood shedding.[55]

The remnant community, as in the period after the first temple, redefines its historical role as the people of God due to a pilgrimage consciousness. It judges its relationship with Jerusalem by the past violations of its socio-religious order. Therefore, it pursues in exile its model: temple as synagogue and altar as table, while being guided by the rule of *"homonia"* and "surety,"[56] philanthropy and Torah life. The return to Jerusalem becomes confirmation of pilgrimage consciousness, which shaped the hope of the oppressed in exile. For the biblically oriented, life in Diaspora becomes possible through the annual dramatization of pilgrimage events in Zion with its liturgical calendar. The holiday periods were collectively celebrated with joy in Jerusalem, and they now help the community in exile to reexperience covenant love in God's presence. The synagogal liturgy,[57] therefore, preserves the *anamnesis* of Zion and its pilgrimage service in the daily prayer and following the prophetic reading, at mealtime and at rites of passage (circumcision, marriage, and death), during the holidays and fast days. Thus, the eschatological hope in the restoration of Jerusalem is deeply rooted in the worshiping community that continues to experience exile as a pilgrim on the way back to Zion.

The Liminal Experience

Pilgrimage itself is a religious phenomena[58] that charges individual participants through a collective experience in the removal from the secular in order to enter the sacred. This movement involves separation and reaggregation through the decisive phase of liminality. During this period of transition and transformation, as in the rites of passage, the participants are stripped of status and authority, removed from a social structure maintained and sanctioned by power and force, and leveled to a homogenous social state through discipline and ordeal. Pilgrimage promotes comradeship and sense of equality, all are sharing in the awe before God and in the *pathos* of love. It combines the qualities of lowliness and sacredness, to be charged by God's presence and to be moved by creative feelings. It produces a *communitas*, which is marked by the absence of property and by simplicity of dress, by the acceptance of suffering and hardship as well as by the elated feeling of joy and celebration.

The fifteen "psalms of ascent" (120–134) reflect these determinants of liminal experience for the pilgrims. They relate the yearning for peace, the sense of providence, the experience of fellowship, the attitude of humility before God, the purity of intention, the feeling of joy, and the blessing of brotherhood. The joy of the pilgrims, gathering in Jerusalem as the *ecclesia* of Israel (so 11Q Ps., Col. 3:9) to offer thanks to the name of God, holds the apocalyptic promise for the throne of David and the seats of judgment (Ps. 110:5, see Matt. 19:28 and Luke 22:30). The liminal stage toward a new world construction is manifested in apocalyptic thought as "between the times" consciousness. It reflects a collective movement toward a historical end, and perfection will be obtained in the new order. Apocalypticism[59] offers an alienated protest to the present order and produces in individuals a transforming awareness, which promotes a spirited vitality of life through total commitment to God's justice. Apocalyptic thought sees the human being on a pilgrimage in an earthly plane arriving at a temple on a heavenly plane. The visionary experience a journey into the third heaven. In Christian tradition the ministry of Jesus is an earthly pilgrimage to Jerusalem, where he ascends into the heavenly temple. His followers encounter Jesus in apocalyptic vision as the exalted one in the heavenly temple. On earth the apostles assume a pilgrim's attitude in taking no gold, no silver, and no extra garments but entering towns with the intention of service and peace.

Two movements of post-biblical Judaism reflect a deep attachment to Jerusalem even though they had rejected its temple.
They are the Essenes who left for the wilderness of Judea and
the nations to prepare the way for return to Zion, and they are
the early Christians who remained in Jerusalem awaiting the
Parousia at the time of the destruction of the temple. The Essene
scroll of Psalms[60] preserves an apostrophe to Zion. In the
alphabetical arrangement of the hymn, it relates a love for Zion
that bespeaks a love for God (11QPsa). "I remember thee for
blessing, O Zion; with all my might have I loved thee." This
agapic feeling is motivated by a deep hope, a longing for its
salvation. "The generation of Hasideans" (the Hebrew name
for Essenes) also expresses a yearning even in voluntary exile.
The same hope expression is associated with the prophetess
Anna in the temple according to Luke 2:38. Her own widow-
hood comes to dramatize the fate of the polluted temple since
Pompey's invasion in 63 b.c.e. According to Josephus the historian, the decisive event that led to the destruction also produced a Pharisaic hymnic response in hope for Davidic Messiah
and the restoration of Zion in the kingdom of God (Psalms of
Solomon). Thus Anna lived almost a jubilee of years in constant
vigil of fasting and prayer in the temple. After its destruction,
this was also the practice of the "mourners of Zion."[61] Their
constant vigil in mourning for Zion was like mourning for the
death of a beloved person.

The Christian tradition (Matt. 23:37–39; Luke 13:34–35),
reacting to the same polluted temple, preserves God's lament
for Jerusalem attributed to Jesus. "O Jerusalem, O Jerusalem . . .
how often would I have gathered your children together"; as in
time of pilgrimage so the dispersed of Israel will be gathered
(see Isa. 49:25; 60:9). "As a hen gathers her brood under her
wings"; the depiction of a relationship with God's presence
through the pilgrims' "*homonia*," which is destined by God
(compare Lamentation Rabbati, proem 20 on Ps. 102:8), "Behold your house [the temple] is forsaken and desolate. Therefore I tell you—God is speaking—you will not see me again. . . ."
The occasion of pilgrimage provides the opportunity to see and
to be seen by God's presence (Exod. 23:17, the dual reading

"*yera'eh*," "*yir'eh*"). "Until you say [the pilgrim's salutation]: Blessed is he who comes in the name of the Lord" (Ps. 129:8).

Such is also the love expression and the lament form found in the Rabbinic Midrash to Lamentation, proem 20. The reference to God's lament reflects dramatically the deep pain for the destruction of the temple, which was coupled with a prayerful hope for joy in the return to Jerusalem. The city generated concrete memories of God's presence among people, affecting a relationship in altruistic love. It served, therefore, as the basis for messianic faith, as the Midrash[62] to Ps. 43 relates:

> Israel says: Please send to this generation two saviors, like Moses and Aaron. "Send thy light and thy truth, let them guide and bring me to your holy mountain, to your place of indwelling" (v. 3).
>
> God replies: I will send to you Elijah the prophet, as promised, "Behold I send Elijah the prophet before the coming of the great awesome day" (Mal. 3:23), "and the second one (I will send) who is my servant with whom I am well pleased" (Isa. 42:1).

The purposed coming of the beloved servant and his forerunner is to bring the community back to Zion. This messianic faith affects the early Christian interpreters of Jesus' historical coming. The evangelical intent is to relate that the universal church is on a pilgrimage to Jerusalem at the time of the heavenly advent of Jesus. The physical city remains a center that generates hope in the biblically oriented community. An authentic Christian theology must then relate such a hope with its messianic understanding. Jerusalem—I mean the city between the walls—must be allowed to link its fate with the people, who long ago and ever since lived and offered to others, those who share in the prophetic faith, a purposeful life because of her. A denial to these people of the Bible, the Jews in Israel today, to translate their existential and historical hope in a return to Zion is also a denial of one's own messianic faith, which is deeply rooted in the biblical notion of pilgrimage to Jerusalem.

Notes

1. On the historical significance, see S. Talmon, "The Biblical Concept of Jerusalem" in *Jerusalem,* ed. J. Oesterreicher and A. Sinai (New York: John Day, 1974), ch. 14.

2. On God's presence in the temple, see S. Terrien, *The Elusive Presence* (New York: Harper and Row, 1978), ch. 4. Both the hypothetical enthronement psalms and incubation oracles at the temple (see L. Sabourin, *The Psalms,* New York: Abba House, 1970, pp. 117ff., 217) reflect, however, in post-exilic times a religious consciousness affected by God's presence in the temple. See A. Finkel, *Responses to God's Presence and Withdrawal* (So. Orange, N.J.: Institute of Judeao-Christian Studies, 1981).

3. Mishnah Berakhot 4:5, 6 and Tosefta 3:15, 16. Such orientation is reflected in the architectural plan of the synagogues excavated in recent times. See H. Shanks, *Judaism in Stone* (New York: Harper and Row, 1979), pp. 51–52.

4. Refer to P. Hanson, *The Dawn of Apocalyptic* (Philadelphia: Fortress, 1975) and see the discussion in D. S. Russell, *The Method and Message of Jewish Apocalyptic* (Philadelphia: Westminster, 1964).

5. On ascent into the heavenly palaces, see H. Odeberg, *3 Enoch* (New York: Ktav, 1973, reprint). On the Hekhaloth literature, see G. Scholem, *Jewish Gnosticism* (New York: Jewish Theological Seminary, 1965) and compare the translations in *Understanding Jewish Mysticism* by D. Blumenthal (New York: Ktav, 1978). This apocalyptic theosophical development can be traced back to the Enochic material (see J. T. Milik, *The Books of Enoch,* Oxford: Clarendon, 1976).

6. Edited S. Buber, pp. 2, 3 (compare the editions of Schechter and Greenhut). Seventy represents the ultimate expression as in the seventy names of God and Metatron.

7. Chapters 86, 100, referring to King, Christ, Priest, Angel, Rod, Palm, Wisdom, Day, East, Sword, Stone, Jacob, Israel. Listing titles or names is a midrashic technique, which comes both to facilitate oral transmission and to reflect a particular theology.

8. See M. Kadushin, *Organic Thinking* (New York: Block, reprint) and *The Rabbinic Mind* (New York: Block, 3 ed., 1972).

9. See W. Brueggemann, *The Land* (Philadelphia: Fortress, 1977).

10. See G. Schaeder, *The Hebrew Humanism of Martin Buber* (Detroit: Wayne State University Press, 1973), p. 29.

11. See E. E. Urbach, *The Sages* (Heb. ed., Jerusalem, 1969), ch. 4 and refer to A. Marmorstein, *The Old Rabbinic Doctrine of God* (New York: Ktav 1968, reprint), p. 92.

12. Didache 10:6 still preserves the liturgical seal of "God of David," which was combined with "Builder of Jerusalem" in the early Palestinian recension of petition (so reflected already in Psalms of Solomon 17:21, 22).

See G. Alon, *Studies in the History of Israel* (Heb. ed., Tel Aviv, 1967), vol. I, p. 290. A shift occurs in the early Christian liturgy from temple to *Ecclesia* in the third blessing after meal. Yet it preserves the theme of ingathering in its holiness, a shift in Greek translation from the Aramaic original: "into the holy place."

13. See D. Juel, *Messiah and Temple* (Missoula, Mont: Scholars Press, 1977) and Ben F. Meyer, *The Aims of Jesus* (London: SCM Press, 1979). Both, however, depict a dichotomy between the Christian and the rabbinic views.

14. *The Land*, p. 14 and ch. XII.

15. *The Gospel and the Land: Early Christianity and Jewish Territorial Doctrine* (Berkeley: University of California Press, 1974). See the critical reviews of D. Flusser in *Jerusalem Post Weekly* (March 18, 1975) and of L. Frizzell in the *Catholic Biblical Quarterly* 37 (1975), p. 385f.

16. *The Gospel and the Land*, p. 365. A similar dichotomy is indicated in his redactional study of Matthew as polemics against Jamnian Judaism in *The Setting of the Sermon on the Mount* (Cambridge: University Press, 1966).

17. So were the works of W. Bousett (*Jesus und die Rabbiner*), of G. Kittel's *Theological Dictionary*, and P. Billerbeck's *Kommentar*. See the reputation of the latter in H. Odeberg, *Pharisaism and Christianity*, 1943, usually ignored in the discussion. One must be cautious with a scholarly or theological bias, and works should be devoted to the exploration of common religious settings and phenomena.

18. So *The Sabbath* (New York: Meridian, 1952). Later in *Israel* (New York: Noonday, 1967) he reconciles it with the emphasis on space. Compare his *God in Search of Man: A Philosophy of Judaism* (New York: Harper and Row, 1955), ch. 21.

19. *Old and New in Interpretation* (London: SCM Press, 1966), pp. 65ff.

20. On biblical theology, see James D. Smart, *The Past, Present and Future of Biblical Theology* (Philadelphia: Westminster, 1979). Refer to Brevard S. Childs, *Biblical Theology in Crisis* (Philadelphia: Westminster, 1970) and to his major evaluation of the canonical interpretation in *Introduction to the Old Testament as Scripture* (Philadelphia: Fortress, 1979). On the sociological interpretation, see Robin Scroggs, "The Sociological Interpretation of the New Testament," *New Testament Studies* 26 (1980), pp. 164–179. On the structuralist approach refer to D. Patte, *What Is Structural Exegesis?* (Philadelphia: Fortress, 1976). The approach is instructive with reference to a deep reading of the text (reflecting models, paradigms, examplars, and value systems) rather than a binary reading with its archetypal understanding, which eliminates the concrete setting and its particular faith configuration from consideration. A phenomenological approach has been indicated in the works of M. Eliade and V. Turner.

21. See D. J. McCarthy, *Old Testament Covenant* (Atlanta: John Knox, 1972) and refer to R. Bultmann, *History and Eschatology* (New York: Harper, 1957), a biblical historiography. See also O. Cullmann, *Salvation in History* (London: SCM Press, 1967).

22. The Elusive Presence, ch. 1.

23. The Elusive Presence, p. 28. The phenomenon is to be contrasted with the mythopoeic account. (See T. Mann, *Divine Presence and Guidance in Israelite Traditions*, Baltimore: Johns Hopkins, 1977.)

24. See M. Kadushin, *Worship and Ethics* (New York: Block, 1963), ch. 7.

25. See A. Neher, *The Prophetic Existence* (New York: Barnes and Co., 1969), part 3, 2. Refer also to A. Finkel, "The Jewish Liturgy of Marriage," *SIDIC* (Rome, 1981), p. 14.

26. The Tannaitic tradition and Josephus record customs and practices associated in particular with Jerusalem, as the hospitable setting for pilgrims. See J. Jeremias, *Jerusalem in the Time of Jesus* (Philadelphia: Fortress, 1962), but consult further S. Safrai's study of *Pilgrimage in Second Temple Period* (Heb. ed., Tel Aviv: Am Hassefer, 1965) and in compendium Rerum Judaicarum ad N.T. Section 1, Vol. II: *The Jewish People in the First Century* (Philadelphia: Fortress, 1976), ch. 17. On the legislation and the land, consult Brueggemann's *The Land* and Davis's *The Gospel and the Land*.

27. See Marvin H. Pope, *Song of Songs* (Anchor Bible: Doubleday, 1977), pp. 89ff.

28. *"Appiryon"* (palanquin) or the marital canopy of Cant. 3:9 is so interpreted in the Targum, Canticles Rabba and compare Pesiqtas on *"Beyom Kaloth Mosheh."* The tabernacle and the temple are both symbolic of the cosmos and God's throne in this midrashic interpretation. The wedding day of Cant. 3:11 is interpreted similarly with reference to the erection of the tabernacle and the building of the temple. See above works and Mishnah Ta'anith 4:8 (compare Midrash Canticle Zuṭa).

29. See both Pesiqtas on Hafṭarta de Neḥamtha; the references to Zion are understood as Israel.

30. See the study of V. Turner and E. Turner, *Image and Pilgrimage in Christ and Culture* (New York: Columbia University Press, 1978), consult appendix A.

31. Refer to forthcoming publication of Bernhard Anderson's presidential address on "Tradition and Scripture in the Community of Faith" at SBL Centennial, 1980 (to be published in the *Journal of Biblical Literature*, 1981).

32. See the presidential address of James A. Sanders, "Text and Canon: Concepts and Method," at the SBL annual meeting 1978 in the *Journal of Biblical Literature* 97 (1979).

33. So M. Eliade, *The Sacred and the Profane* (New York: Harper, 1957), ch. 2.

34. See S. Terrien, "The Omphalos Myth and Hebrew Religion," *Vetus Testamentum* 20 (1970), pp. 315–338.

35. See John G. Gager, *Kingdom and Community* (Englewood Cliffs, N.J.: Prentice Hall, 1975) on the sociological meaning of the kingdom of God. As for the Old Testament time of the Israelite amphictyony see the recent study of Norman K. Gottwald, *The Tribes of Yahweh* (Maryknoll: Orbis, 1979).

36. "Six things precede the creation of the world: Torah, Heavenly Throne, Temple (see Targum to Jer. 17:12), Patriarchs, Israel and the Messiah." Genesis Rabba 1:1, ed. Theodor-Albeck, p. 6 and notes.

37. Refer to A. Finkel, *Responses to God's Presence and Withdrawal.*

38. So. J. D. Crossan, "Empty Tomb and Absent Lord" in *The Passion in Mark,* ed. W. H. Kelber (Philadelphia: Fortress, 1976).

39. Genesis Rabba 68, 9 and Midrash Hagadol to Gen. 28:11, ed. Margolioth, p. 498 notes.

40. On the heavenly model and its cosmic significance see L. Ginzberg, *Legends of the Jews* (Philadelphia: Jewish Publication Society, 1954), vol. III, pp. 151, 153; vol. IV, p. 67. Note that the tabernacle is constructed according to the divine plan (Exod. 36–38, in accordance with 25–27). So Solomon's temple is constructed in accordance with the divine plan (I Kings 6, 7 in accordance with I Chron. 28:11–19). See further in A. Aptowitzer, Bet Hamiqdas sel ma'alah in Tarbig 2, pp. 137–153, 257–287.

41. See G. Klinzing, *Die Umdeutung des Kultus in der Qumrangemeinde und im Neuen Testament* (Göttingen: Vandenhoeck und Ruprecht, 1971) and refer to L. Frizzell's dissertation, *The People of God: A Study of the Relevant Concepts in the Qumran Scrolls* (Oxford, 1974).

42. *The Temple and the Community in Qumran and the New Testament* (Cambridge: University Press, 1965).

43. "Judaism in a Time of Crisis" in *Judaism* 21 (1972), p. 318. See Y. Yadin's criticism in *Temple Scroll* (Jerusalem, 1977), vol. I, p. 144 notes.

44. Consult A. Finkel, "God's Presence and the Temple Scroll" in *God and His Temple,* ed. L. Frizzell (So. Orange, N.J.: Institute of Judaeo-Christian Studies, 1981).

45. The ingathering of the elect (the *ecclesia*) in Mark 13:27, Matthew 24:31 (at the blast of the Shofar), and Didache 10:5. The seats of judgment in Matthew 19:28 and Luke 22:30 (at the messianic banquet). Both are associated with the appearance of the Son of man in his kingdom (Luke) or on his glorious throne (Matthew), which relate symbolically to the heavenly temple and Jerusalem.

46. *New Testament Theology* (New York: Scribner's, 1971), ch. 21, p. 3 and compare his *Jesus' Promise to the Nations* (*Studies in Biblical Theology* 24, London: SCM Press, 1967).

47. The purpose of pilgrimage is "to be seen and to see" God's presence. So is the dual reading of Yir'eh-Yera'eh in Exodus 23:17 (Mekhilta Simeon ad loc. and Sifre Deut., 143). Moriah (place of oracle) is called by Abraham "Adonai Yir'eh-Yera'eh" (Gen. 22:14). On pilgrimage refer to n. 26 and include M. Haran. *Temples and Temple Service in Ancient Israel* (Oxford: Clarendon Press, 1978), ch. 16.

48. Refer to Babylonian Talmud Baba Bathra 93b; Sanhedrin 23a, 30a; and Semahoth 12. See A. Guttmann, *Jerusalem in Tannaitic Law* (HUCA, 40–41, 1969–70) and G. Cohen, *Zion in Rabbinic Literature* in *Zion in Jewish Literature,* ed. A. S. Halkin (New York: Herzl Press, 1961).

49. Babylonian Talmud Pesaḥim 8b.

50. See Midrash Ps. 48:1 and Numbers Rabba 21, 19.

51. The reign of God is established on God's holy mountain, so Zech. 14. The ultimate hope expression in Jewish daily prayer is the return of God's presence to Zion; see the formulation by the early Hasideans, Midrash Samuel 31, Midrash Psalm 17, and the Palestinian recension of Amidah.

52. See the review of J. J. M. Roberts, "Zion" in *Interpreter's Dictionary of the Bible,* Supplementary Volume (Nashville: Abingdon, 1976).

53. *Scripture and Tradition* (Leiden: Brill, 1973). See also S. Spiegel, *The Last Trial* (New York: Beheman, 1979).

54. Genesis Rabba 49, 19 (ed. Theodor-Albeck, p. 502 notes). See also Midrash Hagadol to Gen. 18:19.

55. Such is the view of the Deuteronomist (2 Kings 21:16) and the later rabbinic explanation of fraternal animosity (Babylonian Talmud Yoma 9b). Shedding blood in Jerusalem causes the disruption of temple rituals (Tosefta Soṭah 14:1).

56. The theme *"homonia"* (*Agudah*) is developed in Midrash Samuel 5:15 (Simeon ben Yohai as condition for the kingdom). Compare Sifre Deuteronomy 33:5 (on *Yaḥad*) and Leviticus Rabba 30, 12. See also Lamentation Rabbati procms 20, 29. The theme of "surety" (*'Arebhim*) is indicated in Babylonian Talmud Shebhuot 39a, and see Palestinian Talmud Hagigah 3, 6 (*ḥabherim*).

57. See W. D. Davies, *Gospel and the Land,* pp. 67ff. and M. S. Chertoff, "Jerusalem in Jewish Consciousness" in *Jerusalem,* ed. Oesterrecher-Sinai.

58. Refer to V. Turner, *Image and Pilgrimage.*

59. See P. Hanson, "Apocalypticism" in *Interpreter's Dictionary of the Bible,* Supplementary Volume.

60. Edited J. A. Sanders (Ithaca, N.Y.: Cornell University, 1967), pp. 123–127.

61. See Babylonian Talmud Baba Bathra 60b, Ta'anit 30b, and Derekh Ereṣ Rabba 2.

62. Midrash Psalms ed. S. Buber, p. 267. (Compare W. Braude's translation of Midrash Psalms, Psalm 43.)

Part Four

Atonement and Redemption

8

Sin, Atonement, and Redemption

Donald G. Bloesch

Interreligious Dialogue

Does a catholic evangelicalism committed to the universal outreach of the gospel make a place for interreligious dialogue? In my judgment, such dialogue belongs to the wider mission of the church, but we must beware of the pitfalls as well as the dividends in this kind of enterprise. The temptation is to subordinate those things that make Christianity unique and distinctive to a more inclusive religious vision that views all the world religions as legitimate roads to salvation. The reward is that such dialogue leads us to appreciate the partial truths in all religious traditions. It may also open the door to renewed dedication and even genuine conversion to Jesus Christ.

We can enter interreligious dialogue, as evangelical Christians, because we believe that the truth that comes from God stands in judgment over the beliefs and practices of all religions, which are invariably mixed with egocentric motivations. As evangelicals our hope is that in dialogue *both* parties will be converted to Jesus Christ, who by his Spirit makes dialogue possible. Even the sanctified Christian stands in need of further conversion and illumination, since he is only on the way and has not yet arrived.

We hold that non-Christian religions are not wholly devoid of truth because of common grace, the universal grace given by the Holy Spirit for the purpose of preservation against evil.

163

Moreover, our position is that all people were created in the image of God and that this image is still reflected even in those whose thought and life have become darkened by sin. In addition, it is possible to contend that the Holy Spirit may well be working redemptively among non-Christian peoples because they may have access to the Holy Scriptures which are part of the spiritual heritage of some of the world religions (such as Judaism and Islam). Moreover, in countries like Japan the Bible is a best seller; this means that even in Buddhist and Shintoist households the Bible may be available; and where the Word is present, the Spirit is present, too. Because of the widespread accessibility of the Scriptures and because the gospel message is often included even in secular literature throughout the world, albeit in rudimentary form, conversions to the true God may occur even in religious environments that are predominantly non-Christian.

It is simplistic to hold that there are only two categories of human beings—born-again Christians and those who are dead in sin. There is also the pre-Christian, one who has been prompted to seek for the mercy and favor of God as a result of being exposed to the message of salvation, either through the reading of Scripture or through hearing the Christian proclamation. This person is genuinely seeking but has not yet made a commitment to Christ. Again, there is the non-Christian who has not yet heard the Good News of salvation through Christ who has been exposed to only a confused or distorted presentation of the message of faith. This person is closed to the gospel out of ignorance or fear more than idolatrous pride. Crippled by sin, the non-Christian is spiritually lost, and yet has an inner being which cries out for the God whom he/she does not yet know or only dimly knows. Then there is the anti-Christian who has heard the truth that comes from God but who has rejected this truth in preference for his/her own. This person is actively opposed to the gospel and seeks to extinguish that light. The anti-Christian is committed to a false gospel that contradicts the claims of the Christian faith. The pre-Christian, the non-Christian, and the anti-Christian are not yet regenerate, but the first is on the way to regeneration and the second and third are claimed by the grace of divine election for regeneration. The last two are still dead in sin, whereas the pre-Christian has been aroused to flee from sin and the wrath of God, has been awakened to misery but is not yet in communion with God in Christ.

All of these types of people may be found in Christian churches, and all of them may be present in non-Christian religions as well, despite the proneness to sin and error endemic to human religion. No person can claim to possess the whole truth, but all are pursued by the truth. The Christian can assuredly claim to know the truth through the revelation that has been given in Christ, but this truth exists not for one person exclusively but for the whole human race. Moreover, this truth stands in judgment over the thoughts and deeds of the Christian as well as the non-Christian. Even the Christian who has been born again and sanctified needs to be justified by the grace of God revealed in Christ. In one sense, that Christian's condition is more perilous than that of the non-Christian, the person who does not know or who has not yet heard. The Christian has heard and has responded and is therefore accountable to God for the kind of life he/she lives and for the kind of witness he/she makes. Judgment will be all the more severe because, although the Christian knows the Lord, he/she may not follow the Lord (cf. Luke 12:47–48). The Bible makes it clear that judgment begins in the household of God (I Peter 4:17).

Regarding Jewish-Christian dialogue, there is hope of making some progress because both religions emphasize the historical particularity of divine revelation as opposed to the inclusiveness of universal mystical experience. Moreover, both religions have a common Scripture, the Old Testament. As evangelical Christians, we can assume that our Jewish brothers and sisters who truly search the Scriptures are somehow in contact with the grace that we know to be the grace of reconciliation and redemption. The difference is that the gospel we proclaim does not merely fulfill the Old Testament law, but it radically calls into question the whole idea of salvation through the law. Furthermore, the Messiah who came to his own people, the

Jews, and whom we accept as the Savior of the world, was not
the Messiah who was expected. The transition from Judaism to
evangelical Christianity can only be one of conversion, though
it is a conversion to that which is integral, not alien to the
tradition of Israel. Lest this sound arrogant, I insist that the
transition from Christianity as an empirical religion to the
gospel as a divine revelation is also one of conversion. It is
conversion to the truth that we have heard but may not have
really understood, a conversion to the truth that we may be
seeking for but have not yet found.

A perennial temptation in Christian theology has been Mar-
cionism in which the church has been led to devalue the Old
Testament and thereby to sever itself from its Jewish roots. A
kind of neo-Marcionism can be detected in both Harnack and
Bultmann who saw the religion of the Old Testament as wholly
superseded by the message of the gospel. We agree with Calvin
that the church of God began with Abraham and that the
history of ancient Israel is an integral part of the sacred history
of divine revelation culminating in Jesus Christ. The self-
revelation of God in Jesus Christ was testified to by the Old
Testament prophets, though they did not understand its full
implications for their own people or for the world. There is
both discontinuity and continuity between the claims of the
New Testament and the religion of the Old Testament, and a
bona fide Christian theology dare not ignore either of these
realities.

The Meaning of Sin

Sin in the total biblical perspective signifies much more than
an act of wrongdoing: it connotes a state of ongoing enmity
with God. It is not simply the violation of a moral taboo (as in
legalistic religion) but wounding the very heart of God. Sin
involves, to be sure, a transgression of the moral law, but it is
much more than this: it is basically an inclination to lawlessness
that resides within the inner recesses of man's being (cf. Gen.
6:5; Ps. 51:5). Sin includes moral failure, missing the mark; but
its essence is a lust for power, seeking to be God (Gen. 3:5).

Biblical religion tells us that all people have fallen prey to sin (Rom. 3:23; 7:14; Gal. 3:22; I John 1:8); and, therefore, the whole human race stands in need of deliverance.

The Bible is clear that the inclination to sin, which is also sin, precedes the act of sin (cf. Rom. 7:5; James 1:14–15; 4:1). This is what led the church to speak of "original sin," the innate desire to make self rather than God the center of the universe. It is not a biological weakness so much as a spiritual infection that is passed on through human generation. As the psalmist says: "The wicked go astray from the womb, they err from their birth, speaking lies" (Ps. 58:3, RSV; cf. Ps. 51:5). Sin resides in the intentions and desires (Gen. 6:5; 8:21; Exod. 20:17). This is why the person in sin needs a new heart, new motivations, a purification or cleansing of the inward being.

The human being in its essential nature is good, for it was created in the image of divine being. Sin defaces but does not destroy this image. We were created for fellowship with God and with our neighbor. We were made a little lower than the angels and were given dominion over the world of nature (Ps. 8:5–6). The tragedy is that we have forfeited the destiny that might have been ours by seeking to usurp the role of God. The Bible affirms both the grandeur and misery of humankind. We are not zeros but glorious creatures who have gone wrong. Whereas we were intended to be in fellowship with God, we now exist in estrangement from our creator. Whereas we were intended to live in harmony with our fellow human beings and with nature, we now exist in a state of alienation with other people and with the created order.

The core of sin is unbelief, as Calvin saw so well. The prime manifestations of sin are pride, sensuality, and fear. The practical consequences of sin include discord in our relations with others, self-absorption, increasing isolation from God and from our fellow human beings, guilt, death, and hell. Sin has a collective as well as a personal dimension, for the poison in the heart of man can infect and enslave a whole people. According to Isaiah, it was not just a few wicked individuals but the whole nation that was infected by sin (Isa. 1:4). Sin in the human heart is the ultimate source of racism, nationalism, sexism, and imperialism.

Behind sin are the devil and his hosts, the fallen angels who bring temptation to men and women (cf. Matt. 4:1–11; Eph. 6:12; Jude 5–7). The devil is not the cause of sin, for otherwise human beings could not be held accountable for their sin. Yet it is the devil who provides the occasion for sin. In succumbing to temptation man falls into bondage to the devil and his hosts, described in the Bible as the powers of darkness. It is scriptural teaching that one is either in the kingdom of God or in the kingdom of the devil (though the former is more inclusive than the visible church). One cannot serve two masters, and by spurning the mastery of God one falls under the sway of the anti-god powers, the powers of darkness.

Through our sinful striving to gain power and security for ourselves, we lose our freedom. We are still free in the things below, in purely mundane relationships, as Luther perceived; but we are not free in the things above—in our relationship to God and the moral ideal. In exalting ourselves rather than God, we become helpless to help ourselves. We can no longer will the good, though we yearn for the good. We still retain our free will, but we no longer have the power to do the right. As Jeremiah put it so forcefully: "Can the Ethiopian change his skin or the leopard its spots? Neither can you do good who are accustomed to doing evil" (Jer. 13:23, NIV). Luther described fallen humanity as in bondage to sin, death, and the devil, the tyrants that account for all human misery and whom Christ came to overthrow.

Augustine gave the illustration of the man who by abstaining from the food that he needed for health so weakened himself that he was no longer able to take food. He remained a human being, created to maintain his health by eating, and yet he was no longer able to eat. Similarly, all human beings by the historical event of the fall have become incapable of that movement toward God which is the very life for which they were created. Yet they remain human beings caught in an intolerable dilemma.

Because of sin, man has become guilty before God, that is, subject to the penalty that accompanies the violation of God's law. Guilt is not simply a sense of having offended the majesty of God, but it signifies an objective state of existence in enmity with God. One can extinguish the feeling of guilt by denying the fact of sin, but the reality of sin and guilt nevertheless remains. This means that mankind is subject to the penalty that God's law demands, namely, physical and spiritual death.

There are, of course, degrees of guilt: some actions have more deleterious consequences than others. Some acts of wrongdoing cause greater injury to the self and to one's neighbor than other such acts. At the same time, even the smallest sin creates a breach in our relationship with God (James 2:10). Because God's law demands absolute perfection, even one transgression incurs the penalty of judgment and hell. Even though the sins of some persons are not as heinous as the sins of others, before God (*coram Deo*) all of our righteousness is as "filthy rags" (Isa. 64:6, NIV).

This does not mean that every act that a person commits is evil. It does mean that every act bears the stain of sin. Moreover, the direction of the sinner's action tends deeper and deeper into sin and further and further from God. Sin begets greater sin, and the final end is self-destruction. If sin were allowed to run its course, we would all be without hope.

All people have a consciousness of guilt, but only the believer can be convicted of sin. Indeed, we only begin to know the depth of our sin when we are confronted by the holiness of God (Isa. 6:1–5; I Kings 17:18; Ps. 32:4–5; 51:4; Luke 5:8). We do not know our sin fully until we are exposed to the love of God revealed in Jesus Christ. When we are awakened to the full implications of his sacrifice, then we come to realize the depths of our iniquity.

The biblical understanding of sin is often associated with the Hellenic conception of hubris, particularly as this is found among the Greek tragedians, but this is a profound mistake. Hubris signifies heroic self-affirmation in which one transgresses the limits assigned by the gods or by fate. It springs from finitude, not from a perverse will. It is a kind of moral insolence which challenges or defies the gods. But sin signifies an idolatrous pride which seeks to dethrone the gods. The tragic hero is not responsible for his plight because of ignorance of the realities of the situation in which he finds himself. The sinner is responsible because he knowingly and willingly rebels against his creator. Hubris is self-elevation which offends the gods, whereas sin is rebellion against the rule of God. Hubris is immoderation; sin, on the other hand, is hardness of heart.

Neither should sin be confounded with the modern understanding of sickness. Sin is not emotional unbalance but misplaced allegiance. It signifies not instability but wickedness. It is not a pathological state so much as a state of guilt. Sickness, both physical and mental, may well flow from sin, because as human beings we are a unity; and if we are morally off center, this is bound to affect every part of our being. Sin may be conceived of as a spiritual sickness, however, since it signifies a corruption of our inner being, the area of our relationship to the transcendent. At the same time, this is not to infer that we are no longer culpable. Once we sin, we become subject to sin, and yet because we sin deliberately or willfully we must suffer the moral consequences of our wrongdoing.

Finally, sin should not be equated with ignorance. This was a temptation in the tradition of Christian mysticism, which drew heavily upon Platonism and Neoplatonism. It was said that humans sin because of a deficiency in understanding or knowledge. Once we know the right, then we will do it. But this makes education or enlightenment a false panacea for human ills. It also overlooks the fact that sin is not merely an absence of the good nor a lack of the knowledge of the good but an assault upon the good. It certainly entails privation, but even more it signifies "man in revolt" (Emil Brunner).

Sin may well involve ignorance, but this is a guilty ignorance. We hide ourselves from the truth, because we are afraid to face up to the truth. We prefer to be ignorant of the evil that surrounds us or that resides within us, because then we think that we need not assume responsibility for combating evil. Ironically, by choosing the path of ignorance, we become all the more culpable, for we then become unwitting accomplices in evil.

Sin in the biblical view is not just missing the mark or failing to do the right. It connotes a state of being mesmerized or paralyzed by an evil spell or force. In Paul's theology, sin is almost a personal, malevolent power that holds humanity in its grasp. The answer to sin lies not in a new determination to improve ourselves but in a power superior to that of sin and the devil, namely, the living God himself. The solution to sin lies not in increased moral effort but in the grace of God (cf. Luke 12:27–28; Rom. 7:14ff.; 9:16; 11:6; II Tim. 1:9).

The Substitutionary Atonement

Evangelical theology holds that the threat and power of sin are overcome by the vicarious, atoning sacrifice of Jesus Christ, the Son of God. The word *atonement* is related to many other biblical words, including expiation, propitiation, ransom, reconciliation, and sacrifice. It is also associated with "satisfaction," a nonbiblical word which came to be used in the theology of the church to elucidate and explicate the meaning of the sacrifice of Christ on the cross. The English word *atone* is derived from the phrase *at one,* and therefore atonement basically indicates a harmonious personal relationship with God. In its modern English usage, it refers to the process by which the hindrances to reconciliation with God are removed.

Biblical scholars have been divided concerning whether the Hebrew *kaphar* and its cognates and the Greek *hilastērion* indicate expiation, the blotting out of sin, or propitiation, the turning away of the wrath of God. There has also been dispute concerning the meaning of reconciliation (*katallagē*)—whether its reference is to mollifying the offended holiness of God or to bringing an estranged humanity into harmonious relationship with a God who already forgives and who does not need to be reconciled.

It is my position that all these meanings can be discerned in Scripture, in both the Old and New Testaments. Atonement is in the final analysis a mystery, the mystery of how the divine love and the divine holiness are reconciled within the godhead. It is clear that because God is holy and because his law is inviolable, sin against his law has to be paid for or atoned.

God's holiness needs to be assuaged and man's alienation against God needs to be overcome. Reconciliation involves a mutual concord between both parties in the broken relationship.

Yet the Bible insists that God's favor cannot be bought or earned by prayers or animal sacrifices, nor can it be earned by meritorious conduct. This is because human sin makes all of our sacrifices unworthy in the sight of God. If atonement is to be made, it has to be planned and carried out by God himself. In the Old Testament, it is God who takes the initiative in arranging the sacrificial system by which ritual and moral uncleanness are purged by the shedding of blood. In certain passages of what critical scholars call "Second Isaiah," the atonement is seen as provided by a divinely sent servant of the Lord who was "wounded for our transgressions" and who "bore the sin of many" (Isa. 53:5, 12, RSV).

In the New Testament, atonement is related specifically and exclusively to the sacrificial life and death of Jesus Christ. It is made clear that God did not just conceive and initiate the plan of salvation, but God was in Christ carrying it forward to completion (II Cor. 5:18–19). What Christ did for humankind, God himself was doing in Christ. While the incarnation itself may be seen as a first step in the accomplishment of atonement, since it indicates that God identified himself with human misery, the atoning work of Christ is especially associated with his death on the cross: He came "to give his life as a ransom for many" (Mark 10:45); "We were reconciled to God by the death of his Son" (Rom. 5:10); We "have been brought near in the blood of Christ" (Eph. 2:13); "He himself bore our sins in his body on the tree" (I Peter 2:24); Christ was "offered once to bear the sins of many" (Heb. 9:28). (All RSV.)

Man needs atonement because man is accountable for sin to God. The law of God demands that the penalty for sin be paid. Sin against an infinite God demands an infinite penalty. Because as a sinner man cannot provide the perfect sacrifice, God himself takes human form and as the God-man presents the sacrifice for the remission of sins by which man is delivered from the penalty of the law—the wrath and judgment of God. This means that the cross of Christ is a sin-offering or guilt-offering, and Jesus is therefore a sin-bearer and mediator. In Hebrews 10:12 Christ's death is called a "sacrifice for sins," and in Ephesians 5:2 it is referred to as a "sacrifice to God" (RSV). The redemptive self-oblation of the suffering servant of the Lord in Isaiah is designated as a "guilt offering" (Isa. 53:10, NIV).

Yet to see the sacrifice on the cross as simply the satisfaction of the legal requirements of the law would be to miss the full depth and scope of this sacrifice. Scripture tells us that there was a cross in the heart of God before the cross in history (cf. I Peter 1:20; Rev. 13:8). Through his infinite love, God willed the deliverance of the sinner even before the sacrifice for sin offered by Christ. The cross of Christ was provided so that God's love might find a way to us. The gospel is that God decided to identify himself with the travails of a fallen humanity. In the person of Christ he took upon himself the guilt and pain of sin so that an accursed race might go free, so that his inviolable law might be satisfied. The key to the atonement lies not in the sacrifice of human innocence but in God's self-sacrifice.

The incursion of God's love into human history does not set aside the law but brings about its vindication. The cross signifies not a relaxation of the law of God but its execution. At the same time, God's forgiveness goes beyond the law, since the merits of Christ are superabundant (Thomas Aquinas). God's love fulfills the law but also transcends it, providing not only pardon for sin but also eternal fellowship with himself and with all the saints. The glory that he is preparing for us is beyond what we could ever deserve or imagine (cf. I Cor. 2:9).

The atonement also carries with it the note of triumph over the powers that hold humankind in enslavement (Col. 2:15). It signifies victory not only over sin and death but also over the demonic hosts of wickedness who keep the world in subjection by their subterfuges. The church fathers in particular emphasized this aspect of the atonement. The cross is the pivotal center of the atoning action of God in Christ, but the resurrection is the glorious culmination of this action. Through his resurrection, Christ dethrones the principalities and powers and sets the sinner free. This means that Jesus is not only sin-bearer and God revealer but also conquering king.

Scripture also tells us that the atonement of Christ was un repeatable and once for all time (Heb. 9:25–26, 28; 10:12, 14). It does not have to be completed in heaven in an investigative judgment (as Seventh-Day Adventists contend), nor does it have to be repeated on the altar in the form of the sacrifice of the mass (an idea found in traditional Roman Catholicism). Christ is now at the right hand of God the Father making intercession for us. He continues to identify with our afflictions, but his atoning work is finished. His prayer is that we acknowledge his work of salvation and that we begin to live as delivered and pardoned human beings.

Even while Scripture makes clear that Christ effects our salvation through his death on the cross and his resurrection from the grave and does not just make salvation possible, it is also insistent that the atonement is ineffectual for salvation apart from personal faith. This access to God's grace is ours only "through our faith in him" (Eph. 3:12 rsv). Paul says that God put Christ forward "as an expiation by his blood, to be received by faith" (Rom. 3:25, rsv). Faith is the subjective pole of the atonement, just as the cross of Christ is the objective pole. But this does not mean that in and of ourselves we con tribute to the atonement. Faith is made possible because Christ reaches out to us from the cross by his Spirit in order to seal the remission of sins in our hearts. When we say that Christ alone effects our salvation (*solus Christus*), we mean not only Christ dying for us on the cross but Christ living within us by his Spirit. We are awakened to faith under the impact of the objective atoning work of Christ on the cross. The atonement reaches its goal when we are united with Christ through faith. We in no way share in his atoning work, but we receive the benefits of his atoning work when we believe and obey.

The Drama of Redemption

In the context of this study, the word *redemption* is being used to refer to the whole process of salvation, though in the narrow sense it means buying back from slavery. In the Old Testament, redemption or salvation pertains mainly to concrete and material deliverance. It also carries the connotation of corporate deliverance, as when the people of Israel were set free from their bondage in Egypt and brought to the Promised Land. In some cases, redemption also has reference to interior personal salvation in the sense of a deliverance from sin and the joy of forgiveness (cf. Ps. 26:11; 49:15; 51:14; 69:18; Job 19:25).

In the New Testament, redemption is given a more definitely spiritual meaning: deliverance from the guilt and penalty of sin. It also connotes salvation from the demonic powers of darkness, which are only hinted at in the Old Testament. Basically salvation or redemption is conceived holistically, that is, it refers to the restoration and healing of the whole person. This is why redemption is associated with the resurrection of the body rather than with the immortality of the soul.

The drama of redemption begins even before the creation when God chose to identify himself with his children even in their affliction and anguish. The apostle declares that Jesus "was chosen before the creation of the world, but was revealed in these last times for your sake" (I Peter 1:20, NIV). Redemption begins in the divine election of humankind to salvation in Jesus Christ. Before the decision of faith, even before creation, there is the mystery of predestination (cf. Rom. 8:28–30). But the Bible nowhere speaks of a decree of reprobation, i.e., that some people are predestined to damnation even before their birth. Predestination is essentially good news, for it means that the whole human race is under the sign of election, the sign of the cross. Just as we assert a universal atonement, so we must also affirm a universal election to salvation. This does not mean that people are automatically saved, since they have to respond to God's gracious offer of election and redemption. It does mean that they are intended by their creator for a glorious destiny, if they will only repent of their sins and hear the Good News and be forgiven.

In the older liberal theology, redemption was held to be simply the fulfillment of creation, creation raised to its maximum heights. In this view Christology was reinterpreted as well: Jesus now became the exemplar of perfected human nature rather than the divine Savior from sin. In the biblical view, on the contrary, redemption is prior to creation, and the role of creation is to serve redemption. We are told that even at the creation, the powers of darkness were defeated and that humankind was created as a delivered people (see Ps. 74:13–14). Karl Barth has developed this theme in his *Church Dogmatics,* Volume III, Part 3.

If creation is the first stage of redemption, the second is reconciliation, where God acts to remove the discord that separates fallen humanity from his presence and favor. Among the integral elements of reconciliation are regeneration, justification, sanctification, and vocation or calling.

Justification (*dikaiosunē*) is often equated with redemption and reconciliation, but in its basic meaning it is a declaration of acquittal given by the holy God to the condemned sinner. Justification as it is used in the New Testament is essentially a forensic or legal term, though it also has a mystical and an eschatological dimension. God's forgiveness is not cheap and is conditional on his law being kept inviolable. When God justifies the sinner, the law is not abolished and the righteousness of God is not violated. This is because Jesus Christ stands in our place as our Advocate and Mediator. His perfect righteousness covers our sinfulness and imperfect righteousness, and therefore we are accounted worthy in the sight of God. The basis of our justification is the vicarious, perfect righteousness of Christ, not an indwelling, personal righteousness.

The righteousness of God is not only imputed to the sinner, but it is imparted to the sinner as well, and this is why in addition to justification we must speak of regeneration and sanctification. Justification is God's decision on man, and regeneration is God's work within man. Our justification is not conditional on our personal righteousness, however; the latter is the result and evidence of our justification. Paul referred to the justification of the ungodly (Rom. 4:5; 5:6), and Luther continued this theme with even greater emphasis. Whereas justification is perfect, because the righteousness of Christ is perfect, our regeneration and sanctification are imperfect because the Holy Spirit does not complete his work in our lives until the time of death. Some theologians have speculated that we are left in a condition of vulnerability to sin so that we might be kept humble, so that we might flee ever again to the righteousness of Christ that alone can save us from sin, death, and hell. At the same time, because we have Christ dwelling in our hearts through faith, we have the confidence of overcoming every sin, of mastering every temptation. The Christian life is a life of victory as well as of struggle. It is characterized by assurance as well as hope, but the assurance is based not on our own strength or virtue but on the promise of Christ to deliver all who come to him in repentance and faith.

Regeneration, which is the new birth into the kingdom of God, and sanctification, which is growth in holiness, are both dependent on justification, which is God's decision to accept us into his favor in the light of the sacrifice of Christ on the cross. Justification is not an event limited to the past but an ever present offer that we need to respond to again and again if we are to make progress in the Christian life. It has a definite beginning, but its impact continues throughout the whole of Christian life. Regeneration might be likened to the fertile soil; sanctification is the beautiful flower that springs from this fertile soil; justification is the rain that keeps the soil fertile.

Evangelical Christianity affirms that we are justified by faith alone. This is to say, our responsibility in salvation is simply to acknowledge and receive the perfect righteousness of Christ which covers our sins like a white robe (cf. Isa. 61:10; Zech. 3:3–5; Rev. 7:9). Faith is not a human virtue but a work of God within us impelling us to believe and respond. It is an inward awakening to the significance of the cross and resurrection of Christ, an awakening brought about by the Spirit of God. Justification by faith is not a matter of the righteousness of human striving but a full confidence in the atonement of Christ for our sins.

The obedience of faith or works of love must follow the gift of faith. Whereas we are passive when the rain of grace falls upon us, we become active as we seek to demonstrate our gratefulness for what God has done for us in Christ. Our obedience is the sign but not the price of God's favor. We cannot

merit either the grace of justification or the grace of sanctification. We can, however, cooperate with God in working out the
sanctification that he has planned for us. We are justified by
faith alone, but we are not sanctified apart from works of love.

The final stage of the drama of redemption is glorification,
when we are perfected in the image of Christ. Glorification
means a restored and transfigured humanity. It entails the
resurrection of the body and eternal life in fellowship with God
and all the saints. It involves a new heaven and a new earth
(Isa. 66:22; Rev. 21:1), not the negation but the transformation
of creation. It signifies a cataclysmic intervention of God into
human history to consummate the kingdom that has already
been inaugurated by the coming of Christ.

Evangelical Christianity does not hesitate to speak of a millennial hope before the final consummation when some of
God's promises will be realized on earth. This is why we can
face the immediate future as well as the absolute future with
optimism because we know that God is in control. Jesus Christ
is even now Lord of the world, and the principalities and powers
are made to serve his will and purpose even in their destructive
work. God does not cause evil, but be brings good out of evil.
Even in the most horrendous calamities, the Spirit of God is at
work confirming the divine promise that all things work together for good for those who know God (Rom. 8:28).

The Christian is summoned not only to faith but also to
vocation, which comprises a fourth aspect of reconciliation. Not
only Christians but all people are called to be ambassadors and
witnesses of the grace of Christ which has been poured out for
all and which is intended for all. Even though we will find
ourselves in many different occupations, our vocation is to be a
sign and witness of the redemption that God has procured for
us in Christ. We will all realize this holy vocation in different
ways, but if our motivations are pure, we will endeavor to give
all the glory to God alone and not to ourselves, not even to the
church.

The life of discipleship is a demonstration of costly grace,
the grace that cost God the life of his own Son and the grace
that may cost us our reputations, our health, the love of family

and friends, and even our lives. To take up the cross and follow
Christ entails suffering, but this suffering does not make repa-
ration for sin, as did the suffering of Christ. Our suffering is a
sign and witness to his suffering that alone atones for the sins
of the world. Our suffering does not procure salvation as did
the cross of Christ; instead, it reveals and upholds his salvation
before the world. In our discipleship, we work out the implications of a salvation already given (cf. Phil. 2:12–13), but we do
not lay hold of a salvation that is not yet ours. We prepare
ourselves to enjoy the glory which is the crown and goal of
salvation, but our suffering does not merit this glory, for this
glory is already assured to us through justification. Indeed, if we
would die before undergoing the purifying process of sanctification in this life, we would still be assured of heaven, for the
title to heaven is already ours through faith alone (cf. Luke
23:39–43).

Discipleship entails striving to keep the commandments, not
to gain salvation but to show our gratefulness and loving
appreciation for all that God has done for us in Christ. We
cannot fulfill all that the law demands, but we can keep the law,
because we have the Holy Spirit living and working within us.
Yet because impure motivations continue to reside within us,
even when we are being sanctified through obedience to the
law, we must confess that we are still only sinners saved by
grace. After having done all, we are still unworthy servants
(Luke 17:10), and therefore we can claim our heavenly inheritance only on the basis of the alien righteousness of Christ.

Salvation by Grace

With the leading spokesmen of evangelical Christianity—
Augustine, Luther, Calvin, and Barth—we affirm that we are
justified and redeemed by grace alone (*sola gratia*). Our works
are the fruits and evidences of a grace already assured to us
through the sacrifice of Christ on Calvary and sealed within us
by the outpouring of the Holy Spirit. Our salvation is assured
"not because of deeds done by us in righteousness, but in
virtue of his own mercy, by the washing of regeneration and

renewal in the Holy Spirit" (Titus 3:5, RSV). Because grace is invincible and effectual, theologians in our tradition have been led to speak of "sovereign grace," the grace that accomplishes what it sets out to do.

We can be heralds of grace and servants of grace, but we cannot be winners of grace, since grace is always given to the undeserving. Likewise, we cannot be dispensers of grace, for grace is not within our power or under our control. We can be co-workers with God in making known the victory of grace, but we can never be co-mediators or co-redeemers with Christ. We are the objects of grace, not the source or cause of grace.

Even sanctified Christians continue to be sinners and, therefore, stand in need of the grace of God. We now have power over sin through grace, but we cannot escape the presence of sin either within or around us. We are still vulnerable to sin, and this is why we must cling to grace all the more. To deny that Christians have sin is to deny the gospel and to render the work of Jesus Christ of no account (cf. I John 2:12; 4:10; Rev. 1:5).

The Reformed and evangelical doctrine of *sola gratia* does not imply a divine determinism that overrules the will and personality of human beings. Grace does not annul human freedom but restores it to its true purpose—communion with God and fellowship with the people of God. True freedom is not the anarchic freedom to will error as well as truth but the freedom given to us at creation that results in life and happiness. True freedom is to live according to the law of our being, namely in communion with our Creator and Redeemer. A railway engine is meant to run on tracks, and if it remains on the tracks it finds freedom. But if in order to gain freedom, it jumps the tracks the result is not freedom but ruin.

Through sin we have lost the capacity to be free in the way God intended. We still possess a free will, but we lack the power to use this will to do the good or to come to God. Our free will is enslaved by the passions of the flesh, which signify not simply physical lusts but unlawful spiritual cravings. When grace comes upon us, we receive new life—creative moral power. Our freedom is restored; we can now begin to live in obedience even

though imperfectly. Because free will in and of itself is incapable
of setting us on the road to life, evangelical Christians prefer to
speak of Christian liberty, the liberated will which is enabled to
obey through grace.

The reconciling act of God in Jesus Christ has for its purpose
the new life in Christ. Christ "died . . . that . . . we might live with
him" (I Thess. 5:10, RSV). Through this restored relationship to
God, our consciences are cleansed; we are now equipped with
new moral power (II Peter 1:3–7). We are delivered from the
tyranny of sin and enabled to live for Christ with Christ reigning
as Lord in our lives (II Cor. 5:14–15; Rom. 14:8–9).

Grace does not exclude resistance but overcomes it. Grace
prevails even when men and women persist in living by their
own power. The prophet Isaiah declared: "I will strengthen
you, though you have not acknowledged me" (Isa. 45:5, NIV; cf.
Jer. 20:7). God's loving mercy is experienced as wrath when we
deny and reject it, but it nevertheless gains mastery over our
lives. His grace appears in the form of judgment when we live
as though grace had not been given, but it is never permanently
withdrawn from us. Because we can thwart the intention of
grace and thereby arouse the wrath of God, we must not be
complacent in our state of grace. Paul declared: "You have
received the grace of God; do not let it go for nothing" (II Cor.
6:1, NEB; cf. Heb. 12:15).

To affirm salvation by grace alone is not to deny the call to
sainthood that is given to all Christians, and indeed to all of
God's people. Grace is given not that we might continue to live
in sin but that we might begin to obey and conform our wills to
the will of the Father in heaven (cf. Rom. 6:15–19). The purpose
of grace is obedience under the cross, a life of holiness that will
be well-pleasing to God. It can be pleasing to God, however, not
because of its intrinsic merits but because it is grounded in and
directed by grace.

The church fathers often said that God became man so that
man might become as God. They did not mean that humanity
would be raised to the level of deity but that humanity might be
raised to fellowship with deity. They also believed that people
might come to reflect in their own lives the goodness of divinity.

The man-god, the Christian goal according to Athanasius, can never be the equivalent of the God-man, who is Jesus Christ. Between the two, there is an infinite qualitative difference. At the same time, the saint, who never ceases to be a sinner, can mirror and attest the reality of divine grace that was fully embodied in Jesus Christ alone. He can come to be a veritable sign of the passion and victory of Jesus Christ. His holiness is derivative, not inherent; it always points beyond itself to the perfect holiness that is in Christ. The drama of redemption is fulfilled when God's people become a holy people, a people who live by divine forgiveness but who are at the same time concerned to demonstrate the righteousness of God in their lives. This was the vision of the Hebrew prophets as well as of the apostles and the church fathers. The cross and resurrection of Jesus Christ and the subsequent outpouring of the Holy Spirit make it possible for this vision to be at least partially realized in earthly history. The consummation of the kingdom lies beyond history, but the upbuilding and advancement of the kingdom take place now as the sons and daughters of the new age proclaim the Good News of the coming of God's all-conquering grace into the world of sin and death.

9

Sin and Atonement

Seymour Siegel

"Whatever became of sin?" asks Karl Menninger in a well-known book. People, it seems, have stopped talking about sin. This does not mean, of course, that they have stopped sinning. Quite the contrary seems to be the case. One of the wily tricks of the *yetser hara,* the evil inclination, is to attempt to convince people that it does not exist. Sin is present in our lives today as it always has been. What is different is that it has been given new names—sickness, ignorance, weakness—and the seductive label—liberation.

What do we mean when we speak of sin?

In order to answer this question we must describe our notion of what makes up a human being. Anthropology is an indispensable twin of theology.

In this discussion two aspects of human nature are immensely important. First, human beings are theological. They cannot live without some commitment to some structure of meaning and value in their lives. This structure may be conscious or unconscious, known or unknown. It is revealed most frequently in a period of crisis. When we are faced with difficult decisions or moments of shattering impact we begin to realize what the structure of our values is. To use Paul Tillich's most meaningful formulation: we all have some ultimate concern. There is something, someone, or some cause which is the highest rung of our hierarachy of values for which we are willing to sacrifice everything. Many things have served as ultimate concerns: the ego, the state, the party, the pursuit of truth, even the trappings of religion. We are commanded in the Bible: "Thou shalt love the Lord thy God with all thy heart, with all thy soul and with all thy might" (Deut. 6:5). That which we love with all our heart, with all our soul and with all our might is our "god." The main choice of life is whether we should serve God or a "god."

The second important aspect of human nature is the assertion that the human is defined by freedom. Freedom is the possibility inherent in the human being of acting one way or another way. The rabbinic psychology posits two *yetsers*, two inclinations present within the consciousness of the human being. One of these is called the *yetser hatov*, which is the tendency within us to turn ourselves to the good, to conquer self-interest and self-centeredness. The *yetser hatov* makes it possible for us to be obedient to God, to serve others even to the point of self-sacrifice. It is the good *yetser* that makes it possible for us to practice the good.

The other tendency within us—far more powerful, it seems— is the *yetser hara*, the evil inclination. This is the tendency within us that propels us away from the good and toward the evil. The *yetser hara* has its roots in pride and idolatry. In pride we put ourselves in the center of things. Our aggrandizement, our pleasure, our reputations form the core of all our values. This expansion of the ego is at the expense of our true commitment, which is to God. The rabbis assert that God says he cannot abide in the same place with the prideful person. There just isn't enough room for both. The other ally of the *yetser hara* is idolatry. Idolatry consists of substituting something finite, passing, and mortal as our ultimate concern rather than that which ought to be our source of allegiance and total commitment. These two tendencies—idolatry and pride—turn us away from God, involving us in deeds, thoughts, and commitments which are sinful. They turn us away from the good and make us cling to the evil.

Both of the *yetsers*—the good one and the evil one—are rooted in our freedom. If we had no freedom it would be nonsensical to speak of turning one way or the other way. We would not turn, we would be pushed. If, as human beings, we were completely determined, we might do wrong things—but this would not be sin. The ability to sin is a great tribute, for it asserts that we are free. Modern "liberationists" or determinists (they are not the same) do not aggrandize the human spirit by denying the reality of sin. They diminish the human spirit.

The *yetser hara,* which turns us toward evil, can be identified with sensuality, as hedonism; but it is not, in normative Judaism, identified with the body. The body is not evil. It is, after all, a creation of God. The *yetser hara* uses the body and its desires to entice men away from the good. The body itself can also be moved by the *yetser hatov,* the good inclination. This is evident when sexuality or eating is done according to the directives of God. The notion that the body is the source of evil is of Hellenistic origin and is not part of normative Judaism. When the *yetser hara* is overcome, it is a result of the study and practice of Torah and God's grace.

The *yetser hara* expresses itself also through pride. Whereas in sensuality human beings descend to the level of an animal who is at the mercy of instinct, in pride human beings pretend that they are more than human, in other words . . . God. When the serpent tempted Eve in the Garden of Eden to disobey the command not to eat from the Tree of Knowledge, he promised that if she did succumb she and her husband would be "like God." This is the eternal temptation of sin. We wish to be like God in making our own law and providing our own salvation and eventually our own immortality. The truth, of course, is that we are amphibious creatures—partly animal and partly spirit. In sensuality we try to forget our spiritual nature and act like animals. In sin as pride we forget our animal dimension and pretend that we are entirely spirit.

The evil *yetser,* which is the cause of sin, is combated, as we said above, by the study of the Torah and works of lovingkindness. "Blessed are Israel," the rabbis say. "As long as they are devoted to the study of Torah and works of lovingkindness the Evil Yetser is delivered into their hands" (Eccles. Rabba: 9, 7). In the rabbinic viewpoint, the Torah by itself is not sufficient to defeat the *yetser hara.* "The conquest in the end comes from God" (Schechter, *Some Aspects of Rabbinic Theology,* p. 278). Thus the words of the Daily Prayerbook: "Make us cleave to the Good Yetser and to good deeds; subjugate our Evil Yetser so that it may submit itself to Thee." The underlying idea is "man's consciousness of his helplessness against the powers of temptation, which can only be overcome by the grace of God" (Schechter, p. 280).

Even the *yetser hara* is not completely evil. It also has its place in the creation. Otherwise God would not have created it. Thus Scripture says: "And God saw everything that he had made and, behold, it was very good" (Genesis 1:31). This refers, say the rabbis, to the evil *yetser.* The question is put, "Indeed can the evil *yetser* be considered as very good?" The answer is that if not for the evil *yetser* a man would neither build a house, nor marry a wife, nor beget children, nor engage in commerce. The point seems to be that one of the strategies to be used against the evil inclination is to turn it to good purposes. Thus, the desire for acquisition of goods which does reflect self-aggrandizement is also the motive power for the economic and commercial progress that characterizes society. Thus life is a continuous battle within the human soul for domination. All too frequently, it is the evil *yetser* which triumphs.

If the foregoing is true, then the conclusion is that all men sin. Sin may not be "original" in the sense that the term is interpreted by some Christians. Sin is ubiquitous. There is no person so righteous that he/she always does good and does not sin. There is a bit of self-aggrandizement even in the highest reaches of the spirit. Humans do good not only for the sake of the good but also to be admired, to be justified, and to be rewarded. The rabbis say that the only commandment which is fulfilled purely is that of circumcision. The subject is too young to "sin." However, there is nothing so base that some element of the *yetser hatov* is not present therein. This is the reason that evil almost always justifies itself in terms of some good. Even our bodily functions have some "spiritual" dimension attached to them. Animals eat when they are hungry. Only human beings are gluttons. Animals have sex only at stated times. Men are lechers. Animals defecate without concern about privacy. Men cover themselves or hide themselves. Even Adolph Hitler, the greatest of all sinners, justified his actions in terms of some higher good: He was, after all, doing the world a great service in ridding it of "vermin." It is this mixture of motives that makes human life so ambiguous, so puzzling, so dangerous, and so interesting.

If the above analysis is correct, then individuals can "sin" even when they are not formally religious. If it is true that all men have some "ultimate concern" which functions in life as "god," then all are committed to something. It is also true that they do not fully obey their "god." The loyal party member permits a bit of self-indulgence; the seeker after power relaxes; the Jew does not fulfill the Torah; the Christian does not fully follow Christ. Though these "sins" differ in content, they do not differ in form. There is a feeling of alienation, guilt, and remorse. This is part of the human condition. In this sense we all carry the burden of sin.

Let us delve a bit deeper into the motivation for sin. After all, how does the *yetser hara* succeed so often and so universally? If we acknowledge and commit ourselves to our "ultimate concern," why do we fail so often?

The Hebrew language has three main words to describe sin. These three words are used in the confession of the High Priest during the service of the Day of Atonement. They, therefore, represent the normative statement about the typology of sin. The three words are: *chet, avon,* and *pesha.*

Each one of these terms points to a special quality of sin.

Chet is related to a term taken from archery. It refers to missing the mark, just as an arrow misses the bull's-eye. The term refers to the phenomenon of sinning through ignorance, misunderstanding, lack of skill. Frequently, people sin because they have convinced themselves that they are doing the right thing even while they are doing the wrong thing. It also points to the tragic phenomenon of human life that frequently people's good intentions result in the opposite of what they had hoped. They are not aware that their aim is bad, that their calculations are awry, or that their predictions are all wrong. "The ultimate treason," points out T. S. Eliot, "is to do the wrong thing for the right reason." More harm is done in the name of goodness, love, religion, and justice than in the name of the devil himself. Parents frequently think that they are doing the best for their children by being indulgent; teachers feel that they are helping their students by not insisting on high standards; governments institute programs to help the downtrodden which increase the misery of those who are the object of concern. This is one of the really tragic aspects of human existence. It is an expression of sin reflecting *chet*. A *chet* is partially forgivable—after all, the intention was good. It is also partially blameworthy. As human beings we should inform ourselves of the probable consequences of our actions. We should attempt to grow in awareness and wisdom so that we have a better chance to fulfill our intentions. In the ancient days, when the sacrificial system was functioning, it was the duty of the doer of a *chet* to offer a sacrifice called *chatat*.

Avon is related to a root which means crooked. It refers to the type of sin which is not a defect of the intelligence but a defect of the will. The individual's response is: I know I am doing wrong. I really want to do the right, but I cannot help myself. The individual is overcome with desire, weakness, lack of will, knowing what is good, but not having the power to do it. The analogy which I find meaningful is that of a dieter who knows that eating ice cream is not good. However, the dieter yields to temptation and exhibits weakness—thus sinning. The doer of the *avon* is culpable and should not have submitted to temptation. Most of the sins we commit stem from our weakness, our petty desires, and our inability to do the right, even when we know that we are doing the wrong.

The most serious sins are the result of *pesha*, rebellion. Sin is rebellion. We know what is wrong. We have the power to resist the wrong. We, however, will to do the wrong because we wish to assert our own ego, to affirm our own identity. In doing the wrong, in defying God, we affirm our own independence, our own self-confidence. The sin is not merely to gain pleasure or even power over others. It is to defy God in the name of our own autonomy. This is basically the sin of Adam who had everything in the Garden of Eden except the fruit of one tree. He saw this as a challenge to his own selfhood. He wanted to be like God. I sin—therefore I am.

The *pesha* sin is the most blameworthy. It is born of rebelliousness and inauthentic self-assertion. It is also the most significant. There is a poignancy, even some nobility (misplaced, it is true) in attempting to stand on our own two feet without dependence on anything or anyone. The Rabbi of Kotzk, who was one of the great teachers of the *chasidim,* is quoted as saying that he greatly admired Pharaoh, the king of Egypt. He had the stubbornness to stick to his guns even in the face of dire calamities, plagues, and misfortunes. "That was a man," he is reported to have said. This is one of the reasons that great sinners are sometimes converted into great saints. They have directed their remarkable energies, enthusiasms, and courage to the wrong end. They are, therefore, outrageous sinners. They have but to turn this energy to the good and they will be saints. The Talmud says that on a place where a repentant sinner stands, a perfect righteous man cannot stand. Part of this is admiration for those who have tasted the forbidden fruits of the world and yet abandoned them for the righteous path. However, there is also a recognition that some sinners possess a large measure of spiritual energy. During their sinful days they dedicated these efforts in promoting the evil. In their repentance they have redirected the same energies toward pious ends. Perpetrators of *pesha* have spirit; they are rebellious, not passive and pathetic in their sinfulness. They can become saints.

The inner outcomes of sin are alienation and disorder. Our faith in our ultimate concern makes our humanness possible. Without this faith men are either the slaves of their impulses or driftless; they are in a state of *anomie.* Since sin is an offense against the God we worship, its inevitable outcome is alienation from the very source of our being. We can no longer relate wholeheartedly to the source of meaning. We have offended him. We are ashamed and embarrassed. Instead of the encounter, there is concealment. Like Adam in the garden after he had sinned, the sinner tries to escape God, to flee from him. Luckily,

God continues to pursue us even in our sinfulness. This pursuit is a further cause for the state of alienation. Many would like to be rid of God altogether since his presence does annoy and upset.

An analogy which is frequently used comes from interpersonal relations. When we have sinned against someone we love—a spouse, a friend—we feel alienated from the person we love and respect. We cannot look the other in the face. We avoid his/her company. We cross the street to prevent an encounter. Another strategy is to act inauthentically, without enthusiasm or wholeheartedness. The pangs of guilt are a wall which separates us from these whom we have offended. The sense of shame comes from the feeling that we have betrayed that which we, literally, hold to be most sacred. There is also a longing to return to authentic relationship. This shame and longing form the motivation for healing and reconciliation.

Sin also brings with it disorder. The emotional and spiritual life of the individual is affected by wrongdoing. This may lead to actual illness. Psychiatrists such as Frankl, Menninger, and Binswanger have stressed that existential anxiety, flowing from a lack of meaning and harmony, *shalom,* with the source of life is a basic cause of mental and even physical disorder.

The psalmist has described the relationship between sin and sickness: "Happy is the man whose transgression is forgiven, whose sin is pardoned. When I kept silent concerning my guilt, my bones wore away (Ps. 32:1, 3). (Keeping silent about transgression—either denying or forgetting that it has taken place— does not lead to happiness but pain and sleeplessness.)

This phenomenon leads to the conclusion that our essential nature, that is, the state of our being that reflects the divine intention, called for fellowship with God in faith and trust. When this fellowship is disrupted as it is in our existential nature (that is, humans as they really are), disruption, disharmony, and illness result. Rabbi Joseph H. Soloveitchik points out that the experience of sin can have, as we have said, psychological and physical correlates: "anguish, fear, despondency, depression, anxiety, even rashes, dizziness, etc." Rabbi Soloveitchik compares the experience and symptoms of sin and guilt with grief and bereavement, the symptoms of loss. "Both can be seen as the suffering of an intolerable sense of loss, both involve withdrawal, masochism, self-hate and in extreme cases a full array of somatic symptoms."

Loneliness and shame, anguish and guilt, alienation and despair are the fruits of sin. These feelings are frequently distorted, denied, and covered up. But there breaks through a disgust and revulsion at being in such a state. This is the drive toward repentance.

The Hebrew term for repentance is *teshuva*. The root means turning, returning, and renouncing. Repentance involves turning, the redirection of life's energies from the bad to the good. It also involves returning to the basic nature of our existence, which is to be in fellowship with that which we worship as our ultimate concern. As sinners, we have strayed far away from our true essence. We are alienated from the source. We must return.

The process of *teshuva* is intricate and subtle. It involves becoming a new person: "Since you have done teshuva it is like you have become a new creature, as it is written, 'and the recreated nation will praise the Lord'" (Midrash Tehilim). (*Teshuva* equals being born again.)

Two authors have written very profoundly about *teshuva* in our times. One is the German philosopher Max Scheler. His book, *On the Eternal in Man* (Harper & Row) contains a chapter titled "On Repentance and Rebirth." The other writer is Rabbi J. B. Soloveitchik of Yeshiva University, whose lectures on repentance delivered during the Ten Days of Teshuva are an annual event in the religious circles of New York. The lectures have recently been published in Hebrew and English by the Israeli author, Pinchas Peli. Rabbi Soloveitchik acknowledges his debt to Scheler, contributing many insights from the Judaic point of view.

Scheler disagrees with those thinkers who see the notion of repentance as unproductive. These thinkers argue that since repentance deals with past actions, it is self-flagellation to dwell on that which has already happened. Even God cannot change the past. Since we cannot recover the past, there is no sense in dealing with it. Scheler argues that though we cannot change the past, we can change the meaning of the past for us. This change of meaning is part of repentance, the "self-healing of the soul."

The meaning of the past is never wholly complete. It is always redeemable through repentance. If guilt brought about by past actions remains unrepented, it has a debilitating effect on the personality. When guilt is acknowledged and repented for, then the effect of the past is radically changed. "Repenting is equivalent to re-appraising part of one's life and shaping it with a mint-new worth and significance." In repentance the situation which resulted in sin is recreated, cleansed, and totally reshaped. The meaning of the past is totally different. Think of a reformed alcoholic. That first shot of whiskey has a totally different meaning now in a reformed situation than it had when the person was still an alcoholic. Then it was the first of a series of deeds leading to enslavement. Now it is the first of a series of deeds leading to liberation. Repentance, therefore, is a process of facing up to past deeds; acknowledging their former sinful significance; expressing disgust and regret at having committed them; and resolving to be a new person, with a new past, a new present, and a new future. The turning removes the guilt and liberates the person.

Soloveitchik explicates the meaning of *teshuva* as it is expressed in the work of the greatest of Jewish philosophers, Moses Maimonides, who included a section on the Law of Teshuva in his masterwork, the *Strong Hand* or the *Mishne Torah*. Maimonides says that the first step in *teshuva* is confession. As individuals we must acknowledge our own guilt. We have to tell the truth to ourselves about ourselves. This is extraordinarily difficult some times, for we are, as T. S. Eliot expressed it, creatures who cannot bear too much reality. In Judaic tradition, this confession does not have to be made to a priest—but to God alone. The confessions of the synagogue especially during the Day of Atonement are in the plural so that there can be an inclusion of the individual in the group confession.

The next step is called *charata,* which means regret. We must not only acknowledge our past sins, we must regret them, be sorry they were ever committed. The third step in the process of *teshuva* is a strong resolve not to repeat the sin. This resolve is tested when the occasion arises again to do the wrong thing, and the penitent resists the temptation.

The final process is reconciliation with God and the rebirth of a new man. This person is a different one than the person who had sinned. The past and its significance has altered. Alienation has been overcome. Estrangement has been bridged. Loneliness for God has been overcome, and humanness has been restored.

All of this comes through an act of will on the part of the sinner. Of course, as we said previously, the sinner is helped by God's grace. But this grace is extended only if the movement toward God has already begun. "He who comes to cleanse himself," say the rabbis, "he is helped from above."

This whole process is one of enormous depth. It is not self-evident nor easy. Solomon Schechter, in his classic work *Aspects of Rabbinic Theology,* begins his chapter on "Forgiveness and Reconciliation with God" with these words: The various aspects of the doctrine of atonement and forgiveness as conceived by the Rabbis may best be grouped round the following Rabbinic passage: "They asked Wisdom (Hagiographa), 'What is the punishment of the sinner?' Wisdom answered, 'Evil pursues sinners' (Prov. 13:21). They asked Prophecy, 'What is the punishment of the sinner?' Prophecy answered, 'The soul that sinneth, it shall die' (Ezek. 18:4). They asked the Torah, 'What is the punishment of the sinner?' Torah answered, 'Let him bring a guilt-offering and it shall be forgiven unto him, as it is said, "And it shall be accepted for him to make atonement for him."' (Lev. 1:4). They asked the Holy One, blessed be he, 'What is the punishment of the sinner?' The Holy One, blessed be he, answered, 'Let him do repentance and it shall be forgiven unto him, as it is said, "Good and upright is the Lord: there will he teach sinners in the way"'" (Ps. 25:8).

It is God himself who wants the sinners to repent and to return to him.

Scripture and the rabbinic literature never tire of assuring sinful man of the availability of *teshuva* and atonement. No life is so derelict, so sin-hardened that it is beyond redemption.

Teshuva creates within us a new heart. The self, freed from sin, is open to other people and to a closer relationship with God. Organized around an authentic center, life regains its freedom and wholeness. The great Day of Atonement is the time for repentance and atonement. Note the verse: "For on this day atonement be made for you, to cleanse you; from all your sins before the Lord shall you be clean."

Rabbi Soloveitchik points out that there are two aspects to the process we have been discussing: atonement (*kappara*) and purity (*tahara*). In the first the stain of sin is removed. The soul is freed from the burden of sin. But this is not sufficient. There must also be purity. The soul must be restored to its original quality as the bridge between the human being and God. Repentance yields *kappara*, the sin is forgiven and the stain is removed. Yet we do need God's grace to bring us to purity to reestablish our relationship with him. That is why the verse concludes, "Before the Lord shall you be clean." In Judaism it is the grace of God given freely to him who comes that cleanses and restores. "Fortunate are you, O Israel," say the rabbis. "Who purifies you and before whom are you purified? Your father who is in Heaven." Through him in direct relationship we remove the sin and reestablish the relationship.

Jewish mystics (see Sefer Hatanya, Iggeret Hateshuva) point to two kinds of *teshuva:* the lower and the higher (*teshuva tataa* and *teshuva illah*). In the first, the mercy of God forgives the sins of those who transgressed. The higher *teshuva,* "the superior form of *teshuva,* the cleaving of spirit to spirit," requires great effort. It is not enough to remove the barrier. The soul must make an effort to reunite with God, achieving the unity which is so necessary for the realization of God's purpose on earth. "We are accustomed to thinking of the work of *teshuva* as beginning after sin, but that until man sins there is no context for repentance. However, this is not so. All our work is after the sin of Adam. It is thus that all our work has as its purpose to restore the world to that original order and wondrous state. Thus all our work is the work of *teshuva,* and if one goes astray and sins, this sin is an additional diminution in the work of *teshuva.*" This statement, made by a contemporary Jewish thinker, summarizes the whole matter. The work of the human being on earth is to return creation back to its Creator; to restore the original rightness with which creation began. At first, of course, we have to restore our own souls. By doing that we are bringing about the unity of God and his creation.

Every year we have Yom Kippur, the Day of Atonement. The work of repentance is never completed. As long as we live we are prey to pride, sensuality, rebellion, self-aggrandizement, separation, and alienation. We fall and stumble—but the opportunity of *teshuva* remains until the end of days when we will have a new heart and a new spirit. That day has not as yet come. We dare not desist from the task of bringing it closer.

Part Five

Mission and Proselytism

10

The Problem of Proselytization
An Evangelical Perspective

Vernon C. Grounds

For all the radical differences between Judaism and Christianity, these two monotheistic religions share striking similarities. They share a kind of mother-daughter relationship; or, as the apostle Paul puts it in his letter to the Romans, Christianity is a branch grafted into the olive tree of Israel. Family commonalities ought, therefore, to elicit little surprise. Both faiths venerate the Old Testament as Holy Scripture. Both worship the God of Abraham, Isaac, and Jacob. Both believe in a promised Messiah, whether as in the case of Judaism it is still a prospective belief or as with Christianity retrospective. Both subscribe to the same moral principles epitomized in the Ten Commandments; hence both highlight love, justice, and personal responsibility. In addition, while once again stressing their vast differences, both religions recognize the duty of bearing witness and making converts.

I, as an evangelical, must speak about Judaism from the perspective of a relatively uninformed outsider, yet there seems little doubt that Jews have traditionally regarded witness as a sacred obligation. In the words of Daniel Polish, the term *witness*

> . . . has no cachet in the religious language of the Jews. Its appearance in our conversation is an importation from neighboring territory. In its most elemental sense, redolent, as it is in

English, with overtones of legal process, it is, of course, familiar. The Hebrew equivalent of "witness" *ed*, carries a network of associations in its wake. Isaiah 43:10—"'you are my witnesses' says the Lord," sounds a central chord of the Jewish experience. . . .

The witness, in the strictest sense of the term is not simply one who speaks for another. Rather he is one who takes formal oath and gives testimony to some fact concerning the other. Such oath in biblical theology is serious business indeed, with immediate implications for the witness and consequences for future generations. Biblical oaths have a physical component: the witness places his hand under the thigh of the one to whom he is swearing. This is what Eliezer does to Abraham in Genesis 24 as he is about to embark on the mission that will assure his master of the descendants whom he had been promised. This graphic act has its counterpart in the Roman practice that provided the etymological root of the English word testify: the witness takes the preliminary oath with his hands clutching his own testes. The implication of these acts underscores the dreadful seriousness of witnessing. To witness is to declare that upon which one would stake, not his good name alone, but something far more serious—the existence of his progeny and their descendants.[1]

Ben Zion Bokser, discussing "Witness and Mission in Judaism," refers to the "profound awareness" in Talmudic literature "that the Jewish people were under a commitment to share the teachings of their faith with the peoples of the outside world." The rabbis, for example, interpreted the whole career of Abraham as that of a missionary actively "disseminating his faith." Typically they regarded Genesis 12:5, "And Abram took Sarai his wife . . . and the persons which they had acquired in Haran" (NASB), as an allusion to the converts won to their God by that faithful patriarch and his wife.[2]

Bokser also writes that during the Graeco-Roman era, Judaism was vigorously evangelistic, waging "an active missionary campaign to win converts and Godfearers to its banner. In many cases, the missionaries were Jewish traveling merchants who propagated their beliefs among the people with whom they came in contact. We have the evidence of contemporary documents that these efforts were far-reaching."[3]

As evidence of the far-reaching missionary activity of Jews in these centuries, Bokser cites the "gibe at the Pharisees" in Matthew 23:15. "Woe unto you, scribes and Pharisees, hypocrites! for ye compass sea and land to make one proselyte, and when he is made, ye make him two-fold more the child of hell than yourselves."

Sometimes in their zealous concern Jewish proselytizers would even resort to the strong-arm techniques which equally zealous Christians were later to employ so shamelessly. At least Josephus records that in the age of the Maccabees, Judaism used force in attempting to convert the Idumeans and Ituraeans.[4]

In the light of this concern with witness and conversion, one can understand why Samuel Sandmel thinks the Christian church spread so rapidly in the Roman world because—among other reasons, to be sure—"its way had been prepared by a Jewish missionary impulse."[5] That impulse was squelched, however, when Constantine in the fourth century forbade Jews to make converts, as Muslim rulers likewise did in the seventh century. But surreptitiously Jewish missionary activity continued.

In medieval Spain, though, a church council decreed death for any Jew who so much as attempted to win over a Christian, and by 1492 Spanish Jews faced one of three dire choices: flee the country, be killed, or profess conversion. No wonder that Judaism lost its missionary spirit. No wonder, either, given persecutions and pogroms, that Jews throughout most of the Christian epoch have been reluctant to obey Jehovah's directive, "Ye are my witnesses." And yet a modern Jewish philosopher, Hermann Cohen, could remind his suffering people that their very suffering was the concomitant of a divine task, that of bearing witness to the world. "This historical suffering of Israel gives it its historical dignity, its tragic mission, which represents its share in the divine education of mankind. What other solution is there for the discrepancy between Israel's historical mission and its historical fate? There is no other solution but the one which the following consideration offers: to suffer for the dissemination of monotheism, as the Jews do, is not a sorrowful fate; the suffering is, rather, its tragic calling, for it proves the heartfelt desire for the conversion of the other peoples, which the faithful people feels."[6]

Recently, moreover, American Jews under the leadership of Rabbi Alexander Schindler and Rabbi Sanford Seltzer—no doubt there are other leaders as well—have been urging that Judaism revert to its ancient practice and seek to bring converts into its fold from among the religiously unaffiliated. Thus, in his presidential address to the Board of Trustees of the Union of American Hebrew Congregations on December 2, 1978, Schindler said: "I believe that it is time for our movement to launch a carefully conceived Outreach Program aimed at all Americans who are unchurched and who are seeking roots in religion. . . . My friends, we Jews possess the water that can slake the thirst, the bread that can sate the great hunger. Let us offer it freely, proudly—for *our* well-being and for the sake of those who earnestly seek what it is ours to give."[7]

This program, I understand, is low-key but multifaceted, utilizing newspaper ads and articles, books, tracts, filmstrips, and instruction classes. It is, please note, aimed only at the unchurched and religiously unaligned segment of our population. Yet it is a program, according to Rabbi Alan Flan, which is developing "sensible, responsible, intelligent ways to give people an idea of what the options for Jewish life entails." Flan has therefore exhorted his coreligionists, "We should open our arms to the person who is seeking to become a Jew."[8] And perhaps, one surmises, even stimulate that desire.

As for Christianity, its very genius is evangelism. Emil Brunner's aphorism, "The church exists by mission as a fire exists by burning," expresses the drive and dynamic of the New Testament. Let me give a rapid review of some relevant texts. During his ministry, Jesus, as reported by the fourth Gospel, utters this astonishing claim, "I am the way, the truth, and the life: no man cometh unto the Father, but by me" (John 14:6). Then after the resurrection he lays a mandate of universal sweep on his disciples: "Go ye therefore, and teach all nations, baptizing them in the name of the Father, and of the Son, and of the Holy Ghost, teaching them to observe all things whatsoever I have commanded you: and, lo, I am with you alway, even unto the end of the world" (Matt. 28:19–20).

This mandate is repeated at the ascension when Jesus delineates the global dimensions of the church's ministry: "But ye shall receive power, after that the Holy Ghost is come upon you: and ye shall be witnesses unto me both in Jerusalem, and in all Judea, and in Samaria, and unto the uttermost part of the earth" (Acts 1:8).

In obedience to the Lord's solemn commission, Peter, preaching in Jerusalem on the day of Pentecost, summons his polyglot audience to conversion: "Repent, and be baptized every one of you in the name of Jesus Christ for the remission of sins, and ye shall receive the gift of the Holy Ghost. For the promise is unto you, and to your children, and to all that are afar off, even as many as the Lord our God shall call" (Acts 2:38–39). A little later he delivers a second sermon and renews his summons, "Repent . . . and be converted, that your sins may be blotted out" (Acts 3:19).

Like Peter, only even more powerfully, Paul after his own dramatic conversion pleads with Jews and Gentiles for a simultaneous renunciation and commitment—a renunciation of whatever religion they formerly professed and a commitment to the new and solely salvific faith in Jesus Christ. So, explaining his motive and mission to the church at Rome, he declares: "I am debtor both to the Greeks, and to the Barbarians; both to the wise, and to the unwise. So, as much as in me is, I am ready to preach the gospel to you that are at Rome also. For I am not ashamed of the gospel of Christ: for it is the power of God unto salvation to every one that believeth; to the Jew first, and also to the Greek" (Rom. 1:14–16).

In that same letter he exclaims with intense emotion: "Brethren, my heart's desire and prayer to God for Israel is, that they might be saved. For I bear them record that they have a zeal of God, but not according to knowledge. For they being ignorant of God's righteousness, and going about to establish their own righteousness, have not submitted themselves unto the righteousness of God" (Rom. 10:1–3).

Writing to a group of Christians in Corinth, Paul defends himself against the allegation of inconsistency: "For though I be free from all men, yet have I made myself servant unto all, that I might gain the more. And unto the Jews I became as a Jew, that I might gain the Jews; to them that are under the law, as under the law, that I might gain them that are under the law; To them that are without law, as without law, (being not without law to God, but under the law to Christ,) that I might gain them that are without law. To the weak became I as weak; that I might gain the weak: I am made all things to all men, that I might by all means save some" (I Cor. 9:19–22).

And it is Paul who affirms in his Letter to the Galatians: "But though we, or an angel from heaven, preach any other gospel unto you than that which we have preached unto you, let him be accursed. As we said before, so say I now again, If any man preach any other gospel unto you than that ye have received, let him be accursed" (Gal. 1:8–9).

Texts like these—and in the New Testament there are many more—have inspired Christians to become tireless evangelists and missionaries carrying their message literally to the ends of the earth and indiscriminately viewing every nonconverted human being, pagan, Jew, Hindu, Muslim, animist, and atheist alike, as a soul for whom the Savior died and with whom the Good News must be shared. Taken at face value, these texts challenge Rabbi Schindler's opinion that "there is no clear New Testament basis or mandate to justify the efforts to convert Jews." They challenge, too, his assertion that Jews are "outside the need for a Christian form of redemption."[9]

Granted that from the Jewish perspective the issue is by no means as simplistic as I have stated it, what I have stated is incontestably the understanding of the New Testament missionary imperative which has traditionally been held by Christians. Consider, for example, the Bethel Confession, formulated by German Christians during the early stages of Naziism with none other than Dietrich Bonhoeffer as one of its primary authors:

The Church has received from its Lord the commission to call the Jews to repentance and to baptize those who believe on

Jesus Christ to the forgiveness of sins (Matthew 10:5ff.; Acts 2:38ff; 3:19–26). A mission to the Jews which for cultural reasons refuses to baptize any more Jews at all is refusing to be obedient to its Lord. The crucified Christ is to the Jews a stumbling block and to the Greeks folly (I Corinthians 1:22ff.). "The Crucified One" as little accords with the religious ideal of the Jewish soul as it does with the religious ideal of the soul of any other nation. Faith in him cannot be given by flesh and blood even to a Jew, but only by the Father in heaven through his Spirit (Matthew 16:17).[10]

The language is unambiguous. Jews, no less than Aryans, having come to repentance and faith, must be baptized into the Christian church.

Hence, to sum up the historic belief and practice of Christianity regarding this matter—and American evangelism still adheres to this position—obedience to the crucified and risen Lord demands witness to and, God so disposing, conversion of Jews.

With all of its theological presuppositions and outworkings, this position inevitably lays evangelicalism open to the charge of being intolerably proud and arrogant. Among the accusations leveled against it is that of an insufferable dogmatism. Not content with a humble and genteel relativism, Christianity in its evangelical branch claims to possess almighty God's fixed and final truth. So Harriet Van Horne, *New York Post* columnist, praised presidential candidate Jimmy Carter for having "risen above the narrow tenets of his church," but at the same time suggested that "it might be more tactful for Governor Carter to cite the Judeo-Christian ethic rather than attributing all his talk of love and humility to the teachings of Jesus."[11] Indeed, she inquired, "Why should any religious sect consider its view of God the only one?" Or, we might well add, its view of salvation?

And precisely its view of salvation exposes evangelicalism to the charge not only of dogmatism but of exclusivism as well. The sole repository of redemptive truth, it alone—so runs the evangelical claim—holds the key which unlocks the door into a blessed eternity. Its interpretation of who Jesus was and what He did is the one guaranteed way of redemption. Peter asserts this flatly, and evangelicals hold that Peter's words are God's Word. "Neither is there salvation in any other: for there is none other name under heaven given among men, whereby we must be saved" (Acts 4:12). And the entail of this exclusivism is according to its critics a shockingly obtuse eletism, voiced ironically in some lines by a bard whom I have been unable to identify:

> We are the Lord's elected few.
> Let all the rest be damned.
> There'll be no room above for you:
> We don't want heaven crammed.

That, I must emphatically protest, is not the spirit of authentic evangelicalism; but it is, I confess, an attitude occasionally displayed by some Christians.

Still further, evangelicalism is accused of narcissism, a "vulgar group narcissism," to purloin a phrase from John Murray Cuddihy. It is accused, too, of what in Roman Catholic circles was once designated triumphalism or what an early twentieth-century fundamentalist, Ford Ottman, called the imperialism of Jesus, a crusading mentality that engenders fanaticism and motivates an aggressive, coercing, high pressure proselytism . . . and might, consequently, in the name of God, be sowing the poisonous seeds of anti-Semitism. Evangelicals like myself are aware of these charges and, while conscientiously thinking through and living out our faith, struggle unremittingly to prevent deep conviction from developing into the kind of deadly animosity which stoked the furnaces of Auschwitz.

Not only that. We are compelled to deal with the question which Rabbi Schindler raises. Why do we contend (Can we possibly do it without being acrimoniously contentious?) that Jews are not, definitely not, "outside the need for a Christian form of redemption"? Why do we teach and preach that Judaism as a religion fails to qualify Jews as non-candidates for evangelism? That question is being answered in depth and at length as we carry on our dialogue in this conference. We evangelicals are candidly setting forth the answers which we find convincing though they may not prove at all persuasive to our Jewish friends. I assume, then, that it falls within my province as a participant to give a brief answer which I take to be the New Testament answer.

Alienated from God by sinful disobedience, Jews, together with all members of the human family, are lost. But in his unchanging faithfulness and fathomless grace God has been redemptively at work in history reconciling the self-estranged race of Adam to himself. In doing that he long millennia ago challenged Abraham to enter into a unique relationship with himself and thereby embark on a unique mission. In faith Abraham responded. The subsequent history of Israel issues from the covenant thus established. The Jews, God's chosen people, became the recipients of supernatural truth and an efficacious system of atoning sacrifice. The Israelitish theocracy, however, was simply a framework within which God was providing the possibility of a faith-full and faithful relationship with himself duplicating the Abrahamic pattern. From among these people who were Jews ethnically, he was drawing into redemptive fellowship with himself a people who were Israelites spiritually. Yet he intended that Judaism *qua* religion be temporary and preparatory, the foundation on which a new faith, a new covenant, and a new relationship would in the fullness of time be established.

Following the New Testament argument, therefore, as elaborated especially in the anonymous letter to the Hebrews, we evangelicals maintain that by the whole Christ-event Judaism *qua* religion has been superseded, its propaedeutic purpose accomplished. Since Messiah has come and offered his culminating sacrifice, there is, as we see it, no temple, no priesthood, no altar, no atonement, no forgiveness, no salvation, and no eternal hope in Judaism as a religion. Harsh and grating expressions as to its salvific discontinuity are called for— abrogation, displacement, and negation. And those expressions are set down here, I assure you, with some realization of how harsh and grating they must indeed sound to Jewish ears.

Admittedly, Christian theologians have disagreed sharply among themselves concerning God's present relationship to his chosen people; and those disagreements persist within the Protestant wing of Christendom Gerald Anderson, for one, strongly avers that "the covenant in Christ does not displace, cancel, repudiate or annul the covenant with Israel." He avers, rather, that "Christ *fulfills* and *completes* the covenant," and in support of his argument he appeals to both a Protestant and a Catholic theologian. "Emil Brunner emphasizes that the New Testament 'radical understanding of doctrine of justification by faith implies . . . not merely continuity with the Old Testament conception of faith as faithful obedience, but at the same time constitutes its completion. . . .' Rosemary R. Reuther rightly recognizes that 'the most fundamental affirmation of Christian faith is the belief that Jesus was Christ; he was that Messiah whom the prophets "foretold" and the Jewish world "awaited." On this affirmation everything else in Christian theology is built.'"[12]

Gerald Sloyan sides with Anderson as to the continuity of the unique bond between God and Israel. He concludes his book-length investigation of Paul's text, "Christ is the end of the law for righteousness" (Rom. 10:4), by declaring: "To claim that Christianity derives from the Hebrew revelation is to see the election, covenant, promises, and Law of the Jews as permanently valid. No service can be done to God by declaring his work completed by the Christian revelation which has as its result the destruction or negation of the Hebrew revelation. Christ is the end of the Law as its completion, but not as its abrogation."[13]

The contrary thesis of discontinuity goes back, however, to the earliest centuries of the church. Tertullian, rebutting Marcion's polemic against Christianity as a religion which worships a God who changes his mind, sees in the very abolition of the Old Testament system a confirmation of Jehovah's faithfulness.

> We too claim that the primary epistle against Judaism is that addressed to the Galatians. For we receive with open arms all that abolition of the ancient law. The abolition itself derives from the Creator's ordinance. . . . But if the Creator promised that the old things would pass away, because, he said, new

things were to arise, and Christ has marked the date of that
passing, . . . the apostle . . . invalidates the old things while
validating the new, and thus has for his concern the faith of no
other God than that Creator under whose authority it was even
prophesied that the old things were to pass away. Consequently
both the dismantling (*destructio*) of the law and the establishment
of the gospel are on my side of the argument. . . . Therefore the
whole intent of this epistle is to teach that departure from the
law results from the Creator's ordinance (V, 2).[14]

And previously in Book IV of that same work, *Adversus Mar-
cionen,* Tertullian refuses to concede that the new covenant
contradicts the old. It is "different" but not "contradictory." "I
do admit that there was a different course followed in the old
dispensation under the Creator, from that in the new dispensation under Christ. I do not deny a difference in records of
things spoken, in precepts for good behavior, and in rules of
law, *provided* that all these differences have reference to one
and the same God, that God by whom it is acknowledged that
they were *ordained* and also *foretold*" (IV, 1).[15]

Tertullian can serve as a spokesman for those evangelicals
who interpret the new covenant as different from the old covenant yet not a renunciation of its promises—a fulfillment, instead. By faith in the culminating and final sacrifice, adumbrated and typified by the Hebrew sacrificial system, a believer,
whether Jew or Gentile, becomes with Abraham a true Israelite,
included within God's redeemed people.

It should be added that evangelicals who embrace a premil-
lenarian eschatology foresee a prophetic future for the Jews as
an ethnic entity, with Palestine as the center of Christ's planetary
kingdom. But this restoration nationally does not affect the
destiny of Jews individually. God's prophetic promises will
assuredly be kept; but if a Jew is to experience the Abrahamic
relationship to his creator, it must be through faith; yes, faith in
the Messiah who has already come, Jesus Christ. In short, as
James Parkes, the distinguished Anglican scholar who was an
authority on Jewish-Christian beliefs and a devoted friend of
the old covenant people, summarized the relationship between
these two biblical faiths, Judaism is "not an alternative scheme

of salvation to Christianity, but a different kind of religion."[16] And that is why from the evangelical perspective Jews fail to qualify as non-candidates for evangelism. There is no "alternative scheme of salvation to Christianity."

But the traditional position is so offensive that many Christians have been joining with Jews in a determined battle to bring about its modification or, preferably, its abandonment. This battle is going on along three fronts—civility, history, and theology. First, an appeal is made to *civility:* evangelicalism ought to consider far more seriously the virtue of a kind of henotheistic tolerance. Second, an appeal is made to *history:* evangelicalism ought to ponder far more deeply the horror of anti-Semitism. Third, an appeal is made to *theology:* evangelicalism ought to evaluate far more open-mindedly the option of doctrinal reconstruction.

Take, to start with, the appeal to civility. This subject has been brilliantly explored and expounded by John Murray Cuddihy in his sociological study, *No Offense: Civil Religion and Protestant Taste.* One of the major figures on whom he focuses is Reinhold Niebuhr, the world-renowned Protestant ethicist, long a luminary at Union Theological Seminary in New York City. In an address on "The Relations of Christians and Jews in Western Civilization" which he delivered in 1958 before a joint meeting of his own faculty and that of the Jewish Theological Seminary, Niebuhr opted outright for a permanent moratorium on the evangelization of Jews. He endorsed the view proposed by philosopher Franz Rosensweig that Christianity and Judaism are "two religions with one center, worshipping the same God, but with Christianity serving the purpose of carrying the prophetic message to the Gentile world." This, Niebuhr avowed, is a far better view than those conceptions of the two faiths (even, Cuddihy asks, that of the apostle Paul?) "which prompt Christian missionary activity among the Jews." Granted that there are some differences between the two religions. Yet those are really minor, and a Jew can find God "more easily in terms of his own religious heritage than by subjecting himself to the hazards of guilt feelings." Moreover, Christianity is "a faith which, whatever its excellencies, must appear to (the Jew) as a symbol of an oppressive majority culture." Because of ineffaceable anti-Semitic stains, "Practically nothing can purify the symbol of Christ as the image of God in the imagination of the Jew." Such was the essence of Niebuhr's address.

I can do no better service at this point than simply set before you Cuddihy's devastating critique of this blockbusting proposal.

Note, first, how the *Children of Light* distinction between faith and its "expression" reappears; expression has now become— perhaps under the influence of Tillich—"symbol." Note also that Christian faith seems to exist only in its symbols, viz., "as it appears" to the Jew—"conditioned" (tainted)—or as it appears to the believer, i.e., as bearer of the "unconditioned." The "truth-value" of Christianity "in itself" seems to play no role. Note, further, that Christianity appears, to the Jew, as "culture" (an "oppressive majority" culture); and, further, that—given history—it "*must*" so appear to him; Jews are not free vis-á-vis Christianity to see it for what-in-itself it really is.

In this attitude of Niebuhr, it may be asked, is there not a stubborn residue of the same condescension to Jews that he is in the very act of disavowing? For Christians, like Niebuhr, are apparently able to understand not only their own Christianity and its true attitude to Jews, but also how Christianity must "look" to Jews. Christians, in other words, are able to take the role of Jews to Christianity, whereas Jews, for their part, are, by implication, deemed incapable of reciprocating by taking the role of Christians to themselves. Furthermore, Christians are the only ones who understand this whole process inasmuch as they alone understand that the Jewish *lack* of understanding is itself "understandable." Further, Jews are *expected* by Christians to be incapable of finding the Christian position on Jewish conversion "understandable." And, finally, only Christians, it would seem, and not Jews, find this Jewish inability to understand in turn understandable. Note, finally, a curious further implication of Niebuhr's proposal: namely, that even in the (one would have supposed) "privileged" matter of defining one's own religion's relation to another religion, Niebuhr is proposing that that other's "outsider" view of one's own religion—even if

erroneous, nay, *because* it is erroneous—become normative for
one's own definition of one's own religion.
    The mind boggles!

Little wonder, consequently, that Cuddihy thinks Niebuhr's
address might be adjudged "an exercise in expiatory masochism" and even a "sell-out."
    Yet the famous ethicist does have reasons, to be sure, for
advocating this radical break with Christian tradition. After all,
doubt, humility, and toleration on his reckoning are the ear-
marks of a truly religious person. Certitude, pride, and intoler-
ance are, on the contrary, incompatible with a recognition of
the "historical contingency and relativity" which inevitably
accompany human finitude, to say nothing about the logic-
twisting effects of human sin. In Niebuhr's judgment, "our toleration of truths opposed to those which we confess is an
expression of the spirit of forgiveness in the realm of culture. . . .
Like all forgiveness, it is possible only if we are not too sure of
our own virtue. . . . toleration of others requires broken confidence in the finality of our own truth." And tolerance is the
offspring not of indifferentism but rather of that intellectual
modesty exhibited by high-minded individuals "with a sufficient
degree of humility to live amicably with those who have contradictory opinions."[17]
    But these reasons strike Cuddihy as specious. He wonders
whether the root motive for Niebuhr's proposal is civility, a
desire to avoid being a Pauline scandal and stumbling block to
his numerous intercredal friends. Never once apparently does
Niebuhr raise the issue of truth. How tactless to do that! For, as
Rabbi Arthur Hertzberg has remarked, "The survival of Judaism
in America is endangered by many things; but I believe that it's
single greatest enemy is vulgarity."[18]
    With all this as background, listen now to Cuddihy's answer
to his self-propounded question, "Why, then, was the Christian
mission to the Jews abandoned by the Protestants?"—as it has
been by sizeable segments of non-Roman Catholic Christianity
and by a number of influential Roman Catholic theologians:
"Not because Christ and Paul had not commanded it (they

had); not because it was false to Christianity (it was of its essence); but because of appearances; *it was in bad taste*. As Marshall Sklare notes, by 1970 the Jewish Community was publicly opposing the Christian mission to the Jews 'on the grounds that Reinhold Niebuhr had elaborated a decade before,' namely—in Sklare's words—because of 'the unseemliness' of such evangelization."[19]

Impressed though I am by Cuddihy's probing study, I incline nevertheless to place more weight than he does on Niebuhr's epistemological skepticism. The inability to apprehend truth with certainty and finality means we can repose only a "broken confidence" in our faith-formulations. Civility and relativism, in other words, are Siamese twins. And why risk social ostracism by insisting that one's friends embrace one's dubious surmizes about reality and destiny?

In the second place, the modification (preferably the abandonment) of the traditional Christian assumption that Jews, like the adherents of all other religions, need to accept the gospel is being urged as an antidote against the recurrent malady of anti-Semitism. Thus an appeal is made to history. Ponder, evangelicals are rightly exhorted, the heart-breaking pages of Israel's tragic saga. Realize that it is Christianity which at bottom has been either primarily, or at any rate largely, responsible for the centuries-long persecution that reached its nadir in the Nazis' ghastly "final solution of the Jewish problem." Trace the connection between New Testament anti-Judaism and the anti-Jewish pogroms in Christian (I choose to let the adjective stand without enclosing it in exculpating quotation marks) Europe and America. Do that and you may decide a moratorium on the evangelism of your Jewish friends and neighbors is in order.

Here, frankly, evangelicals are hard put to gain clear perspective. Not regarding the incredible, emotion-numbing insanity of an Auschwitz. Not that by any means! Instead, we are hard put to evaluate objectively the allegation that the preaching of the gospel has inspired anti-Semitism and may—God forbid!—do so again in the future. How just, we must interrogate our souls, is that allegation?

The core of the gospel, we are reminded, is the cross, the

story of a judicial murder. Perpetrated by the Romans, it was brought about by the hateful connivance of those enemies whom Jesus had stirred up within his own nation. Can this story be told, we are asked, without eliciting the vindictive taunt (or thought), "Jewish Christ-killers! Jewish Christ-killers!"? Can it be told, as traditionally it has been, and not breed animosity against, say, members of a Brooklyn synagogue who have never heard the names of Annas and Caiaphas? Can it be told and not serve to exonerate the infliction of suffering on the Jews as a penalty merited by their guilt? Recall that at the close of the third century Chrysostom condemned the "odious assassination" of Christ by the Jews, for whom there is, he declaimed, "no expiation possible, no indulgence, no pardon." Recall, too, that in the twentieth century so noble a Christian as Dietrich Bonhoeffer, challenging the Aryan clauses which Hitler had adopted, wrote this sentence: "The church of Christ has never lost sight of the thought that the 'chosen people,' who nailed the redeemer of the world to a cross, must bear the curse for its action through a long history of suffering."[20] With amplest good reason, therefore, Jules Isaac asserts in his *Teaching of Contempt,* "No idea has been more destructive and has had more deadly effect in the scattered Jewish minorities living in Christian countries than the pernicious view of them as the 'deicide people.'"[21]

Besides believing that Israel as a nation was guilty of murdering its incarnate God, Christians also believe, we are further reminded, that Jewish guilt grows higher and higher as Jesus' own people stubbornly persist in their refusal to accept him as Messiah. And this is the belief of not merely benighted fundamentalists. No, it is a common Christian belief. Even a theologian of Karl Barth's stature and sensitivity entertained it. In 1957, a long time after Auschwitz, he authorized without change what he had written in 1942: "There is no doubt that Israel hears; *now less than ever* can it shelter behind the pretext of ignorance and inability to understand. But Israel hears—and does not believe!"[22] And in not penitently acknowledging its Messiah Israel goes on obdurately heaping up its guilt.

Not surprisingly, therefore, history reveals that a dark and destructive attitude toward Jewish people develops as a concomitant of gospel proclamation. In the story of Jesus the sinister villain is Israel: it is the lightning rod that draws to itself the sizzling electricity of Christian wrath.

As evangelicals, what ought to be our response to this indictment? We have, I reply, an inescapable obligation to do whatever we can in order to clear away the misunderstandings and misinterpretations which have dyed the pages of history with Jewish blood. We must point out, for one thing, that the nation Israel as an entity was no more guilty of crucifying Jesus than we were; maybe, in fact, we were more so. Suffice it to say here that a careful examination of the Gospels puts the burden of responsibility for the crucifixion of Jesus on the shoulders of the imperial government in Palestine. So Jules Isaac inquires whether the Roman soldiers and their commanding officer were acting on orders from Judas or Caiaphas. "They were acting," he comments, "on orders from Pilate who had sent them." Then Isaac comments again, "Common sense tells us that in such cases the greater responsibility lies with those who command the greater power—in other words with Pilate."[23] Hence in refuting the charge that the Jewish people were Christ-killers, we evangelicals must attest with Roy Eckardt that "'Roman responsibility' is a purely historical, superseded matter, while 'Jewish responsibility' is hardly at all a historical matter; it is an existential one."[24] For what Christian today, he asks, would ever shout at a citizen of Rome the taunt, "You killed Christ!"? That would be the nonsensical equivalent of indiscriminately charging a crowd of contemporary Americans, "You killed Abraham Lincoln!"

We evangelicals must likewise attest that any Jewish responsibility was limited to a handful of corrupt leaders and their hangers-on. Eugene Fisher argues that in a way those leaders were not really leaders: "Cut off from the people and living by collaboration with Rome, the temple priesthood must have developed a quite natural 'seige mentality.' Eager to please their Roman superiors, they would zealously seek to bring to the attention of Pilate even the slightest hint of rebellion. . . . They were not the truly religious leaders of the day, the Pharisees.

Rather the individuals involved were only the 'chief priests and the scribes,' the Sadducean party of the aristocracy who had sold out to Rome in the view of the people and represented no more than their own selfish interests."[25]

We evangelicals must attest, once more, that since Jesus died for the sin of the world, every human being bears the responsibility for the cross, Christians no less than Jews (and Christians, I repeat, more than Jews). Lest this attestation stir within our deceitful hearts even a flicker of self-righteousness, we evangelicals need to remember that it is actually a belated echo of Article IV of the Catechism of the Council of Trent promulgated in the sixteenth century: "In this guilt are involved all those who fall frequently into sin; for, as our sins consigned Christ the Lord to the death of the cross, most certainly those who wallow in sin and iniquity *crucify to themselves again the Son of God, as far as in them lies, and make a mockery of him.* This guilt seems more enormous in us than in the Jews, since according to the testimony of the same apostle: *If they had known it, they would not have crucified the Lord of glory;* while we, on the contrary, professing to know him, yet denying him by our actions, seem in some sort to lay violent hands on him" (Hebrews 6:6; I Corinthians 2:8).[26] The recognition of our personal responsibility for the Savior's death is, as James Daane suggests, "the spiritual solvent that ought to dissolve anti-Semitism in the Christian community."

> Penitent for his own role in crucifying the Son of God, cognizant of his infinite guilt for such an act, the Gentile Christian can, within the spirit of true repentance, condemn only himself. When he thinks of the sins of other sinners—which he naturally does and must do—if he is truly sorry for his own sins, he can only compare other sinners *favorably* with himself. With Paul, he can only say about sinners: "of whom I am chief." Confession of one's own responsibility for the death of Christ involves the recognition that one's guilt is infinite. Where this is recognized and acknowledged, how can the sin of another be regarded as *greater*? How can the Jew be regarded as "most" responsible?[27]

So, we evangelicals must attest that the Gentile refusal of God's Messiah is equally as reprehensible as the rejection of Jesus by a twentieth-century Jew, except that, as God knows the conflicting emotions within the labyrinth of every psyche, He is aware, as we cannot be, of the next-to-invincible difficulty a Jew may experience in opening his heart to the claims of a Christ whose followers have caricatured him as a cruel sadist rather than a compassionate Savior.

Consider, in the third place, the appeal to theology as a ground for imposing a moratorium on the evangelization of Jews. For latterly, in the aftermath of Vatican II and with the increase of Jewish-Christian dialogue, not forgetting the continuing effect in the United States of a civil religion that labors to avoid sectarian offense, Catholic and Protestant scholars have pushed for a drastic revision of traditional Christology and *pari passu* the revision of traditional soteriology. Chief among these has been Rosemary Reuther whose controversial book, *Faith and Fratricide,* boldly raises this explosive issue: "Is it possible to say 'Jesus is Messiah' without, implicitly or explicitly, saying at the same time 'and the Jews be damned'?"[28] Here it is out of the question—neither is it my specific assignment—to examine her argument that the New Testament is anti-Judaic and thus latently anti-Semitic. Reuther's purpose, as stated by Thomas Indinopulos and Roy Bowen Ward, is to demonstrate that "the anti-Judaic root of Christianity cannot be torn out until the church's Christology is rid of its negation of the ongoing validity of the Jewish faith."[29]

Ignoring her provisional and, even an evangelical may quite dispassionately report, unsuccessful venture at an acceptable non-Judaic reformulation of Christology, let us shift our attention to another Roman Catholic theologian, Gregory Baum, and notice how he has sought to accomplish the same objective. Himself of Jewish background, he too calls for a reconstruction of Christology that will eliminate its pathological anti-Semitism. He is confident that by "ideology critique" the revision can be accomplished. Bravely he blazes the trail which must be hewn out: "From the beginning, the Church preached the Christian message with an anti-Jewish ideology. When in later centuries, the Church gained political influence and social power, the anti-Jewish ideology translated itself into legal structures that excluded the Jews, with the result that the Christian gospel in fact came to promote the oppression of a living people. Because the enslavement of human beings goes against the spirit and substance of the Gospel, it is possible, I hold to remove these ideological deformations from Christian teaching, however ancient and venerable they may be."[30]

In the soul-scorching blaze of Auschwitz, which serves as "an altogether special sign of the times," Christianity, Baum contends, has no other option than penitent theological reconstructionism. "The Church is now summoned to a radical reformulation of its faith, free of ideological deformation, making God's act in Christ fully and without reserve a message for life rather than death." Speaking his mind more fully and specifically on this score, Baum declares: "There seems to be no reason why the Christian church, on the basis of the believing response to the Holocaust and a new Christian piety, should not be able to re-think and re-formulate the Christ-event in a way that retains Jesus unalterable as the source of God's judgment and new life for the believing community, but specifies that this dispensation of grace is only a prelude to the complete fulfillment of the messianic promises when God's will be done on earth in the new age."[31]

This, then, in one short sentence is how Baum hopes to engineer the recasting of traditional Christology: "Jesus is the Christ in an anticipatory way." The Baumian version of Christology "does not make Jesus the messiah of Israel who fulfills *all* the divine promises, who completes and closes the order of redemption and who is identified with God in such a way that there is no access to divinity through other dispensations. At the same time, such a christology, to remain in continuity with the Christian past, must clarify the pivotal place which Jesus holds in the history of salvation and the manner in which the absolute manifests itself in Jesus—that is to say, how it remains correct for Christians to say that God is substantially present in Jesus Christ."[32]

This carries a corollary, as Baum unflinchingly admits: Jesus is no longer *the* way to God, the only Savior apart from whom a redemptive relationship with the creator is impossible. Such exclusivism must be abandoned.

Reuther and Baum have an ally in Father John T. Pawlikowski, O.S.M., professor at the Catholic Theological Union in Chicago and chairman of the NCC Faith and Order Study Group on Israel. He finds fault with Paul's vision of the Jewish future sketched in Romans 9–11 because it "ultimately ends on a conversationist [*sic:* conversionist?] note that I find unacceptable." So, for him, "more radical surgery is imperative." In his judgment "parts of our traditional Christology [are] severely inadequate and should in fact be discarded. . . . as Christians we should come to view the Jewish 'no' to Jesus as a positive contribution to the ultimate salvation of mankind, not as an act of unfaithfulness or haughty blindness."

Pawlikowski is keenly conscious that his reformulated Christology "will profoundly alter Christianity's self-definition," but he is persuaded that it will "make possible a more realistic relationship to Judaism and to all other non-Christian religions."[33]

"A profound alteration of Christianity's self-definition. . . ." Profound indeed, so profound that an evangelical must apply to Pawlikowski's proposed reconstruction the strictures Indinopulos and Ward level against Reuther and, inferentially, Baum. This reformulation has so distanced itself from historic Christian belief that what is presented as "christological" will not "prove intelligible, much less acceptable to any of the recognizable branches of Christianity. . . . The implication of our author's Christological 'reinterpretation' is that in order for Christology to cease being anti-Semitic, it must cease being recognizable as Christology, that is, 'salvific.' To us, this appears as self-defeating—a case of stopping the disease by shooting the patient."[34]

Which is why, Indinopulos and Ward warn the ecumenical advocates of reconstructionism, the "inherent contradiction" between the two divergent religions, Christianity and Judaism, cannot be overcome "without either the Christian quitting his faith or the Jew converting to Christianity."

We come back then, more or less full circle, to the problem
of witness and conversion. Since Christianity, as evangelically
construed, is of necessity evangelistic, can Christians earnestly
share their faith with Jews and not come under censure for
proselytizing? I think they can. As an evangelical, I draw a
sharp distinction between proselytizing and witnessing, rejecting
proselytism as a perversion of witness. As an evangelical, I am
glad to have the Second Vatican Council voice not my mere
sentiment but my strong conviction: "In spreading religious
faith . . . everyone ought at all times to refrain from any manner
of action which might seem to carry a kind of coercion or a
kind of persuasion that would be dishonorable or unworthy,
especially when dealing with poor or uneducated people. Such
a manner of action would have to be considered an abuse of
one's own right and a violation of the right of others."[35]

As an evangelical, I also gladly endorse the editorial note
appended to that Vatican II statement: "It is customary to distinguish between 'Christian witness' and proselytism and to
condemn the latter. This distinction is made in the text here.
Proselytism is a corruption of Christian witness by appealing to
hidden forms of coercion or by a style of propaganda unworthy
of the gospel. It is not the use but the abuse of religious freedom."[36] Moreover, as an evangelical, I gladly subscribe to the
affirmation made by Tommaso Federici in his study outline for
the Roman Catholic Commission for Religious Relations with
the Jews.

> The Church thus rejects in a clear way every form of proselytism.
> This means the exclusion of any sort of witness and preaching
> which in any way constitutes a physical, moral, psychological or
> cultural constraint on the Jews, both individuals and communi-
> ties, such as might in any way destroy or even simply reduce
> their personal judgment, free will and full autonomy of deci-
> sion. . . . Also excluded is every sort of judgment expressive of
> discrimination, contempt or restriction against the Jewish people
> as such . . . or against their faith, their worship, their general
> and in particular their religious culture, their past and present
> history, their existence and its meaning.[37]

In addition, as an evangelical, I gladly countersign the emphatic repudiation of proselytism issued by the World Council of Churches: "Proselytism embraces whatever violates the right of the human person, Christian or non-Christian, to be free from external coercion in religious matters, or whatever, in the proclamation of the Gospel, does not conform to the ways God draws free men to himself in response to his calls to serve in spirit and in truth."[38]

Still further, I, as an evangelical and as a human being who knows his own motives are never unmixed, appreciate James Megivern's helpful analysis in his article, "A Phenomenology of Proselytism." I realize, as he indicates, that three major dynamics seem to underlie the proselytizer's activity: first, the "necessary-for-salvation" motive; second, the "one-and-only-truth" motive; and third, the "obedience-to-a-divine-command" motive.[39]

I realize likewise that operating dynamically in the proselytizer may be latent and "less exalted motives, with consequences that no respectable religion could ever want to justify"—a "domination-motive," an "insecurity-motive," and an "egocentric-motive."[40] But while keenly appreciative of the subtlety and strength of these perhaps unconscious dynamics, I do not draw from them or Megivern's other arguments a warrant for declaring "a moratorium on Christian missions as we have known them."[41] Instead, I am constrained to view positively the three major motives which he mentions. Like my fellow-evangelicals I share the conviction that Christianity, as the flower and fulfillment of its Old Testament root, is the one-and-only truth, the solely salvific religion. Certainly we are not obtusely insensitive to the enormous problems inherent in that conviction. Neither are we obtusely insensitive to the difficulties which our truth-claim creates in intercreedal dialogue. Joseph A. Bracken rightly points out that, if a dialogue-partner holds such a conviction, he is not engaging in a mutual search for truth; he is covertly using dialogue "as an instrument to convert the others to one's own antecedent confessional viewpoint." "If one believes that one already has the truth and that truth of its very nature is incapable of change or development, then clearly one will engage in dialogue only up to a point, the point, mainly, when

one's antecedent beliefs would be called into question. . . .
Ultimately, one's antecedent views on the nature of truth will
dictate the manner of one's participation in a dialogue-situation,
and the only honest thing to do in advance of actual participation is to decide where one stands on this prior issue."[42]

Peter Berger is of the same opinion: "Dialogue between Jews
and Christians (again, for perfectly understandable reasons)
rarely deals with the truth claims of the two communities."[43] So
interreligious discussion at this deep epistemological and philosophical level are mandatory to prevent dialogue from being a
polite shadowboxing. But as long as we evangelicals remain
convinced that by God's grace alone, not by virtue of our superior intellectual power, we do in fact possess the truth and thus
know the solely salvific gospel, we are under obligation to share
it. And now Megivern's other motive, obedience to a divine
command, comes into play—in our case, obedience to our
Lord's mandate, "Preach the gospel to every creature" (Mark
16:15). Only his mandate and our obedience may have as their
motive a dynamic which Megivern does not mention though it
is the master-motive in Christian theology, ethic, and mission—
love.

"God is love," the New Testament proclaims, and motivated
by love and nothing but love he has undertaken the whole
process of creation and redemption in order to share the beati-
tude of his love with finite experients. We hear the message of
that love which at an incalculable cost to himself God freely
offers to all of us. (I read Abraham Heschel's moving exposition
of Jehovah's pathos, his empathic identification with humanity
and with Israel in particular; and in my heart the Johannine
affirmation reverberates, "God is love.") Illuminated by God's
Spirit, we respond in faith. And having experienced personally
the wonder of his love, we are motivated to love him and,
loving God, obey him. "If ye love me," Jesus said, "keep my
commandments" (John 14:15). And one of his commandments
is universal evangelism.

More than that, love for the God sacrificially self-revealed in
Jesus Christ motivates love for all whom he loves. The inseparable linkage of love-for-God and love-for-neighbor is indicated

in these deceptively simple New Testament words: "We love him, because he first loved us. If a man say, I love God, and hateth his brother, he is a liar: for he that loveth not his brother whom he hath seen, how can he love God whom he hath not seen? And this commandment have we from him, that he who loveth God love his brother also" (I John 4:19–21).

And if love motivates us (though its motivating power is confessedly often weak, ineffectual, and short-circuited), we rejoice to share with our neighbors the best we have to give, and that best is the gospel of Jesus Christ. George A. F. Knight therefore speaks on behalf of all evangelicals when he, a sympathetic friend of Israel, writes: "There is one thing, and only one thing that we must communicate to all men, and that is Christ. To refrain from doing so . . . is a form of religious anti-Semitism which is as basically evil as the philosophy of the Nazis."[44]

Thus in the end the problem is not *why* but *how:* as undeserving recipients of redemptive love how can we lovingly share the gospel with Jewish non-Christians? If we share it prayerfully, graciously, tactfully, honestly, sensitively, and non-coercively, we will not be guilty of the proselytizing that understandably disturbs Rabbi Balfour Brickner: "It is not the Gospel that is a threat to the Jews. The threat is from those who use the Gospel as a club to beat others into a brand of belief and submission with which they may disagree or find no need."[45]

Our evangelism, if love-motivated and love-implemented, will fall within the category of witnessing approved by Rabbi Bernard Bamberger: "I see no reason why Christians should not try to convince us of their viewpoint, if they do so decently and courteously; and I believe that we Jews have the same right."[46]

One might devoutly wish that he were a theological genius and a sociological wizard capable of undoing the Gordian knot of Jewish-Christian relations. But that tangle, I fear, will stay tied until, an evangelist might exclaim, the millennium has dawned. Meanwhile Reuther charts the path which we must follow with a measure of resignation and a capitulation to realism: "Possibly anti-Judaism is too deeply embedded in the foundations of Christianity to be rooted out entirely without destroying the whole structure. We may have to settle for the sort of ecumenical goodwill that lives with theoretical inconsistency and opts for a modus operandi that assures practical cooperation between Christianity and Judaism."[47]

Is that too modest an agreement? Or can an evangelicalism that intolerantly opposes any least anti-Semitic innuendo, carry on its evangelistic mission while cooperating ecumenically with its Jewish friends and neighbors? My hope, my prayer, is that it can.

Notes

All Scripture references are taken from the King James Version, unless otherwise noted.

1. Daniel Polish, "Witnessing God After Auschwitz," eds. Helga Croner and Leon Klenichi, *Issues in the Jewish-Christian Dialogue: Jewish Perspectives on Covenant, Mission, and Witness,* (New York: Paulist Press, 1979), p. 134.

2. Ben Zion Bokser, "Witness and Mission in Judaism," Croner and Klenchi, op. cit., p. 93.

3. Ibid., p. 95.

4. Cf. W. Cruickshank, *Encyclopedia of Religion and Ethics,* vol. 10, p. 402.

5. Quoted by Marvin R. Wilson, "Christians and Jews: Competing for Converts?" *Christianity Today* (March 21, 1980), p. 29.

6. Quoted by Elliott Dorff, "The Meaning of Covenant," Croner and Klenchi, op. cit., p. 48.

7. Quoted by Peter L. Berger, "Converting the Gentiles," *Commentary* (May 1979), p. 35.

8. From a not yet identified newspaper article.

9. Readers Response, *Worldview* (July-August 1978), p. 45.

10. Dietrich Bonhoeffer, *No Rusty Swords,* John Bowden trans., Edwin Robertson, ed. (New York: Harper and Row, 1965), p. 241.

11. Quoted by John Murray Cuddihy, *No Offense: Civil Religion and Protestant Taste* (New York: Seabury Press, 1978), p. 3.

12. Gerald Anderson, "The Church and the Jewish People: Some Theological Issues and Missiological Concerns," *Missiology: An International Review,* vol. II, no. 3 (1974), p. 287.

13. Gerald S. Sloyan, *Is Christ the End of the Law?* (Philadelphia: Westminster Press, 1978), p. 181.

14. Quoted by David P. Efroymson, "The Patristic Connection," *Antisemitism and the Foundations of Christianity,* Alan T. Davies, ed. (New York: Paulist Press, 1979), p. 104.

15. Ibid., p. 103.

16. Quoted by Thomas A. Indinopulos and Roy Bowen Ward, "Is Christianity Inherently Anti-Semitic?" A Critical Review of Rosemary Reuther's *Faith and Fratricide, Journal of the American Academy of Religion,* vol. 45 (1977).

17. For the quotations and comments cf. John Murray Cuddihy, op. cit., pp. 38–45.

18. Quoted by ibid., p. 115.

19. Ibid., p. 43.

20. Dietrich Bonhoeffer, op. cit., p. 212.

21. Quoted by James Daane, *The Anatomy of Anti-Semitism* (Grand Rapids: Wm. B. Eerdmans Publishing Company, 1965), p. 18.

22. Quoted by Indinopulos and Ward, op. cit., p. 211, n. 1.

23. Quoted by Paul R. Carlson, *O Christian! O Jew!* (Elgin, Ill.: David C. Cook Publishing Co., 1974), p. 123.

24. Ibid., p. 123.

25. Eugene Fisher, *Faith Without Prejudice* (New York: Paulist Press, 1977), pp. 80–82.

26. Quoted by ibid., p. 76.

27. James Daane, op. cit., p. 26.

28. Quoted by Indinopulos and Ward, op. cit., p. 195.

29. Ibid., p. 203.

30. Gregory Baum, "Catholic Dogma After Auschwitz," Alan Davies, op. cit., p. 141.

31. Ibid., p. 146.

32. Ibid., p. 147.

33. Quoted by Gerald Anderson, op. cit., pp. 284–85.

34. Indinopulos and Ward, op. cit., p. 205.

35. Ben Zion Bokser, op. cit., p. 102.

36. Loc. cit.

37. Loc. cit.

38. Cf. *Ecumenical Review,* 1 (1971), p. 11.

39. James J. Megivern, "A Phenomenology of Proselytism," *The Ecumenist,* vol. 14, no. 5, p. 66.

40. Ibid., p. 68.

41. Ibid., p. 69.

42. Joseph A. Bracken, "Truth and Ecumenical Dialogue," *The Ecumenist,* vol. 18, no. 5, p. 70.

43. Peter Berger, op. cit., p. 39.

44. Quoted by Martin A. Cohen, "The Mission of Israel After Auschwitz," Croner and Klenchi, op. cit., p. 178.

45. Readers Response, *Worldview* (July-August 1978), p. 46.

46. Quoted by Marvin Wilson, op. cit., p. 30.

47. Quoted by Indinopulos and Ward, op. cit., p. 210.

11

Mission, Witness, and Proselytism

Blu Greenberg

The conference organizers allowed us great leeway in addressing this sensitive topic. Fully aware that any one of a number of alternative topics under this rubric would have been "safer," more academically respectable, and certainly more discreet, I have nevertheless chosen to go directly to the heart of the matter—to the most vexsome center—how a Jew, or Jews, feel about the Christian mission. Having freely made that choice, I stand before you today with great ambivalence.

In good Jewish fashion, I argue with myself:

On the one hand, the Christian mission to the Jews is the cutting edge of evangelical-Jewish relations today. There is much ado in the Jewish community today over mission, much alarm over the attempts of Christians to recruit converts at our most vulnerable points—marginal individuals, brand new Soviet Jewish immigrants, teen-agers in search of adult identities, and the like.[1] Moreover, the evangelical mission groups are now more sophisticated, better supported, growing stronger and faster.[2] Not only are more people listening, but evangelical Christianity is, so to speak, becoming mainstream. It seems likely, then, what with the current "evangelical renaissance,"[3] all of this activity—"to go and preach Christ"—will increase. In defense, the Jewish community is assuming its most aggressive proselytic stance, that is, to win back those who have been wooed away.

226

On the other hand, I tell myself, there is the other reality—
the new posture of many evangelicals. When I read "Jews and
Evangelicals in Conversation" I was not only informed, I was
very moved.[4] To me it seemed as if there was a kind of *teshuvah*
on the part of evangelicals—not simply repentance but *teshuvah*
in the sense of "turning toward"—evangelicals open to Jews as
Jews, finding a place for Jews and Judaism in the eternal scheme
of things. My grandparents walked four extra blocks so as not
to have to pass in front of a church in Eastern Europe. Yet here
am I, an Orthodox Jew, standing before you in the Mission
House of Trinity Evangelical Divinity School, not the least bit
defensive about my Jewishness, even taking quite for granted
your graciousness and openness to me. And must I not also
bear in mind the incredible alliance and support—for whatever
reasons—that evangelicals have given to the Jewish State of
Israel, to Jews restored to their Holy Land? The reasons do not
matter. How can I speak, even whisper, the slightest criticism
before such people?

On the other hand, there is Christian Scripture on the Jews.
There is much in the New Testament that I can connect to and
even appreciate as a Jew, but each time I read it, I come away
with new fears for me and my line. I have to ask myself uneasily:
what guarantees do I have that my Jewish grandchildren will
not suffer anti-Semitism as a result of Christian theology on the
Jews?[5] What will be the impact, say five generations from now,
of the sign on the bulletin board down the hall that reads . . .
"Wednesday: Pray for the Jewish World."

On the other hand, here am I, entering into the realm of
someone else's theology. Who am I, an outsider, to tell anyone
else how to interpret their sacred Scriptures? What chutzpah!
But then, will what I say or what any Jew says, make any difference in the matter? Hardly likely . . . .

Therewith, the ambivalence. Nevertheless, or rather despite
it, I shall proceed, for I know that real dialogue takes place
when we talk not only of the pleasing but of the painful. I also
understand that all things in life are interconnected—that there
is a link between responsible scholars and leaders and the rest

of the community, that the inner and outer sancta have con-
necting passageways. Therefore, I shall first share with you my
view of Christian mission, a view which I think is widely held by
Jews; and then, bearing evangelical claims in mind, try to offer
a different model of Christian mission, one which might be
structurally and theologically acceptable to evangelicals, yet
which I as a committed Jew could also live with. Regarding the
latter, i.e. the model, I speak only for myself, knowing that there
are many Jews who would consider me as having "sold out."

Mission, witness, proselytization—code words that have sent
shudders up and down the spines of caring Jews in every
generation. Yet what does it really mean? It is to preach that
redemption and salvation come only through Jesus Christ, that
Christ died for human sin, that Christianity superseded Judaism.

Setting aside revelation in Christ and Jewish rejection of
Jesus for a moment, supercessionism (and mission theology as
its logical conclusion) would be quite understandable simply at
the level of psycho-social dynamics: the need of early Christianity to define itself as "apart from" first-century Judaism, out
of which it was irreversibly born. Add the other two factors—
revelation and internecine strife—and supercessionism, proselytism, and a sense of mission become natural parts of a healthy,
vibrant, growing, rich-blooded Christianity. It is a sign of faithfulness, not a heretical stance.

Now that's one part of me—the part that sees mission as a
detached observer might see it, coolly, objectively; it is thoroughly valid. You have the truth and you want to share it out of
love or commandment or any number of legitimate motives.
"Christian witness, whether to Jews or to anyone else, is God's
mission, not our own," says a recent Christian pronouncement.[6]

But now there's the other part of me, the real me, in fact, the
Jew who knows where she's come from and who tests Christian
mission against another whole set of criteria:

First, I react to Christian mission as a Jew who believes that
election counts for something. To be born a Jew, to live out my
life as a Jew, to marry another Jew, to bear Jewish children—
these are very special gifts. Divine election as a Jew is to me a
special calling. I often feel overcome with emotion when I

attend a *bris*, the circumcision ceremony, or one of the ritual ceremonies we are now developing for the birth of infant girls. These events bring out the deepest feelings in me, feelings of continuity, of connection, of community, and the binding ties of the Jewish family. The new infant is more than the child of its parents. He/she is also the latest link in the long chain of tradition. This notion of election is quite different from racism— for it does not deny that one can move in or out, nor that one can be reborn to another faith. It simply means that my cool detached thoughts about Christian mission are scrambled by another code—the miracle of being born, not only to biological parents, but to a whole community and to Torah.

Second, I reflect on Christian mission to the Jews from the perspective of Jewish history. I know this general truth: whenever the Good News was combined with power, it became the bad news for Jews. In every era in Christian Europe, the closer Christians got to their sacred texts, the more painful things became for Jews. The more strongly Jesus was believed to have atoned for human sin, the more sins were committed against the Jews.

And third, I see mission through the unique and historically discontinuous event of the Holocaust.[7] I see it through the eyes of a community of survivors—biological survivors, the holy ones, and psychological survivors like myself, whose souls were seared although their bodies were untouched. Irving Greenberg has written: "After the Holocaust, no statement, theological or otherwise, should be made that would not be credible in the presence of burning children."[8] A most powerful theological criterion, and one that applies to Christian mission to the Jews as well.

The question here is not one of silence of the established church, nor acknowledgment of Christian acts of mercy and lovingkindness. It is neither complicity and bystandership nor incredible, individual Christian selflessness and sacrifice. Nor is it the relative response of fundamentalists or reformers. These are profound issues and scholars everywhere have begun to deal with them quite thoroughly. The issue here is much more simple. From the standpoint of evangelical theory on mission to the Jews, the Holocaust offers an opportunity for reality testing. Would those who preach conversion for all Jews really want a world *Judenrein,* a world free of Jews? Having come so close, we are all forced to ask ourselves that terrible question: what would a world with no Jews really feel like? After the Holocaust, can any well-meaning Christian look into my eyes and make that claim, the call for a kind of "spiritual final solution"?[9]

And more: can Jews really be saved through Jesus? Jesus himself, his original apostles, and any of his followers who might have had one Jewish grandparent somewhere would have all been prime targets for the gas chambers. Or conversely, would any decent Christian have felt a theological victory, had Hitler given the Jews a chance to save themselves by affirming Christ?

Regarding proselytism, the Holocaust offers another area for reality testing, albeit from a somewhat different perspective. The test of functionalism may not be theologically legitimate or persuasive, but nevertheless it should be considered insofar as it sheds light on the theology of "the other." If the Jews did not accept Christianity after the *Hurban,* the destruction of the second temple in 70 A.D., and if they are still not prepared to embrace it after the Holocaust, does it not seem highly unlikely that they will ever be converted away from Judaism? In Jewish law you need two witnesses to establish a fact.[10] Perhaps events can also witness.[11] Two cataclysmic events have witnessed and established forever the stiffneckedness of this people, clinging passionately to their ancient faith, rebuilding after destruction with even greater intensity and devotion.

In light of the three criteria then—election, historical anti-Semitism, and the normative event of the Holocaust—the idea that only through Christ will Jews be saved is out of order. Let me say it in undialogic fashion. It is obscene! We Jews think of the saving remnant in terms of one and one and one more. To lose one teen-ager or one Russian Jewish immigrant family, after what it has taken for one Jew to make it to the last third of the twentieth century, is sad enough. To have them pried away through mission/proselytism is an act of spiritual rape.

Now I know the dilemma that evangelical Christians face, and I am not trying for the jugular. I know, too, that most contemporary evangelicals who are in no way responsible for past acts of anti-Semitism or for the horrors of the Holocaust, still do feel a tremendous remorse, even a shared grief with Jews. Yet, one is still rooted in faith and Scripture. Scripture says, go convert the Jews. What is a decent Christian to do?

I know how it feels. As an orthodox Jew, as one who believes in revelation, who loves Torah, and who tries to live her life according to *Halakah,* yet also as a woman of the twentieth century who is committed to the new values for women, I have experienced the dilemma in my own life many, many times: the tension one feels between faithfulness to Scriptures and the need to respond to unfolding religious realities, the conflict one feels about Biblical authority and infallibility when it clashes with historical and social necessity, the tension between absolute and pluralist models, the anxious feeling one has at times that by chipping away a tiny piece one begins to weaken the whole structure. Yes, I understand the dilemma a well-meaning evangelical faces.

Nevertheless, I would maintain that for Christians to claim a concern and community with Jews, and yet keep the status quo regarding mission to the Jews is no longer a credible posture. To paraphrase Kenneth Kantzer's question to evangelicals vis-á-vis Israel: "How can you be different from someone, critical of them and still say you are for them?" How can an evangelical of good faith claim to love the Jews, have a commonality with them, yet all the while want them to be something which they are not and can never be—true Christians?

And yet. How can a committed Christian, one who takes Scripture and dogma seriously, not respond to the call to mission?

I believe there are several ways out of the dilemma. None of them are easy: in fact, they are surely quite painful to any Christian who believes in Jesus Christ and who loves and abides by his word. At the risk of offending even more than I might have already offended, I would like to suggest one possible area to explore, one model of Christian mission to the Jews. It requires splitting mission into two parts: mission-proselytism and mission-witness.

Mission proselytism: Only by joining us or only through Christ will Jews be redeemed. To act on this aggressively, as proselytism implies, is unconscionable in light of the past, eternally untenable as far as Jews are concerned, and probably falls short of the above-mentioned reality tests that Christians must apply to their own theology. This is the sacrifice Christians will have to make to coexist with Jews, now until the end of days.

Mission witness: Fulfilling the Word of God in the call to mission, but interpreting it in an old/new way, similar to the way Jews have classically understood mission and witness. It is mission in the broadest sense of the term: to bring the message of a redemptive God to all the world. "You are my witnesses," says God to the prophet Isaiah (Isa. 43:10).[12] The Midrash comments on the passage, "If you are my witnesses, then I am the Lord. If you are not, then, as it were, I am not God."[13] The people are witnesses to God's being. The existence of the Jewish people, that they have survived, is a testimony to the existence of God, to his being the Redeemer and the Lord of history.

But there is more to it than that. God is known through his believers; his message and his teachings are understood through the lives of his people. Their mission to the world, to serve as a light to the nations, is achieved by giving witness to his ways through believers' daily actions. In Judaism, we have the concept of *kiddush hashem* and its counterpart, *hillul hashem:* by living in a certain way we sanctify the name of God; or conversely, by living ignobly we desecrate the name of God. The ultimate test of *kiddush hashem* for a Jew (and the ultimate testimony any human being can give), is the willingness to die, as a Jew, for the sanctity of God's name. Interestingly, *kiddush hashem* is also the phrase we use for the martyrs who chose to die as Jews rather than convert.

Christians can do the same thing regarding mission and witness. Christians can and should and do give witness to the same God. They do this, however, through the life of Jesus, his teachings, his death and resurrection, his atonement for human sins, as well as the promise of redemption, of salvation through

Jesus for all those who have been born or reborn or wish to enter into Christ.[14]

The distinction lies, however, in one important point, a limitation or sacrifice Christians must make: that your salvation or your witness does not deny my validity or my salvation. The difference then, between proselytism and witness is that Christ is not the only means of salvation open to human beings. God—Christ's father or Jesus' God, depending on which tradition you come through—is the only means of salvation. What this implies about the Jews who rejected Jesus is that they were not blind to God, but rather continued to be faithful to the original covenant which was never abrogated.

This is a major and minor change at one and the same moment. Major because it challenges the absolutist model of Christian mission; major because it allows Christians no blurring of the lines between God and Son of God; major because even if goodwill theologians agree, it will take a massive effort to permeate this message through the life of the Christian community and through the Christian seminaries. (That is another whole problem in itself.)

More important, however, it is a minor change, because all the rest of Christian theology—Jesus' teachings, his life, his resurrection—can stand. The whole of Christianity will not topple. Its tenets will barely be altered. Its faithful will hardly be shattered. What assurances can we offer? We can point to other traditions that gave up the conversionary ghost and survived. One example is Roman Catholicism, for which ecumenism renewed rather than diminished its strength. Our second proof comes from rabbinic Judaism, which virtually eliminated the proselytic stance of the First Jewish Commonwealth, and yet continued to thrive. It did not make the truth of Judaism dependent on converting the whole world.

Furthermore, this non-conversionary model allows mission to the Jews as witness to Christ to also stand. This means that mission-witness will have some effect in terms of conversion, just as Jewish testimony to a Jewish way of life and Jewish values has. But this is fair game in a system that neither locks in nor locks out adherents, in contrast to the aggressive proselytism based on and motivated by false choices of salvation.

Effectively, it reverses the supercessionist trends of Christianity on which proselytism, teachings of contempt, and the seeds of violence were sown. In its place, it acknowledges that God has enough love to hold the two faith groups in chosenness simultaneously, much like a father or mother who loves each child in the most special way.

Moreover, it will free up Jews from a defense posture so that they can understand and affirm their indebtedness to Christianity for witnessing monotheism to the larger, Gentile world. Without this Christian emphasis on exclusivity, Jesus (and Paul, too, for that matter) becomes a link or bridge between Jews and Christians and not the breaking point that he has always been.

This model implies major rethinking on the part of traditional Jews, those most closely parallel to evangelicals in terms of commitment to Scriptures. In the past, traditional Jews have almost universally dismissed any possibility of serious theological validity to various Christian claims. Needless to say, it does not mean that Jews must now affirm Jesus as Christ or Jesus' resurrection. It does mean, however, that Jews must assume a less patronizing and more seriously pluralist acceptance of Christians' faith claims. This would represent a kind of ecumenical golden rule: Do unto others as you would have others do unto you.

Having arrived at the theological model, how do we validate it and link it to Scriptures? I would suggest three ways:

First, consider the hermeneutic of revelatory events, the belief that revelation of Scriptures is further illuminated and reinterpreted by later revelatory events. In this case, the Holocaust and the rebirth of the State of Israel are those revelatory events. Just as the life and death of Jesus changed history and theology, so now the Holocaust and the rebirth of Israel—the death and the resurrection—shed light on the next period. How? After the Holocaust, and the choices it forces on Christians, and after the living, thriving Jew has re-entered his Holy Land, Jews and Christians alike must appropriate these events as metahistorical symbols of God's power to sustain his people. Christians who refuse to see this are guilty of the very same thing which they accused Jews of long ago—blindness to the new revelation.

Carrying this one step further, Paul Van Buren has suggested that after the Holocaust, mission be interpreted as the obligation for Christians to keep the Jews alive, to protect them, and to come to their aid.[15] Whether Christianity takes this ultimate step remains to be seen. To a partial observer, this would be a logical consequence of using the Holocaust and Israel as revelatory events.

A second possibility does exist and that is to say the gospel stands, but that the human conscience, informed by the *whole* of tradition, may apply a kind of civil disobedience to a part of the sources. With all respect to the divinity and sanctity of the New Testament, one refuses to obey statements which deny the validity and sanctity of a Jew or of any other person. This, in fact, is what many evangelicals have already done in their own quiet way. Unlike modernist rejections, illicit in the sense that they are based on sufficiency of human reason, this rejection is based on the reality of sacred history—the unconditional command of love, an unbounded love that overrides any tensions or hatred of the other. In effect, this is what Pope John XXIII did in redefining the relationship between Jews and Catholics.

The third possibility is to play out the areas of tension—supercessionism, proselytism, etc., on the eschatalogical stage. Let God, so to speak, decide at the end of days. Jews, I believe, would be perfectly happy with this trade-off. If Christians could do this elsewhere—transmute the failures of a political and social Messiah salvation into eschatological hopes and not diminish themselves in the process—it could work once again where Jews are concerned.

I am not so naive as to think that the elimination of supercessionist and exclusive salvation themes in Christianity will end all areas of friction between Jews and Christians, nor even so naive as to think that any of this will be achieved by sleight-of-hand or possibly even in our lifetimes. There still is deicide; there still is the false law-love dichotomy; there is still the matter of the first or second coming. But if we attempt to share in honest conversation what offends as well as what uplifts, perhaps we can overcome one by one those things that divide and hurt and thereby make ourselves freer to share those things that divide and uplift.

All I have tried to do is offer one possible model for resolution of one particular problem, and I have tried to do it in a manner that does least damage in terms of the sacredness of Scriptures to evangelicals. This latter characteristic is important to me, for it represents the integrity of Christians as well as a strong bond that Jews and evangelicals share. Moreover, it opens the avenue to another kind of witness, the kind in which each testifies to the other of our particular strengths and our unique qualities as well as the shared values we try to preserve in the face of increasingly secularized society.

What kinds of things can we witness to each other? Christians have something to learn from Jews about the special cohesion of the Jewish family and its relationship to community. To a great extent, I think this grows out of the Jewish commitment to law and ritual, which binds and strengthens the family. Christians ought to reconsider the law-love dichotomy, including the fact that "to do" or "to act" is as much a matter of love as it is to say, "I believe."

Jews have much to learn from evangelicals about the experience of rebirth as a man or woman of faith within one's faith community. The truth is that we do have many rebirth rituals in Judaism: Passover reenacts the birth of the people Israel; *mikvah,* the ritual of immersion, precedes marriage and renews the procreative cycle; *Shavu'ot* demonstrates that we reaccept and reaffirm the covenant; *Yom Kippur,* symbolizes the death and rebirth of an individual each year. Yet the notion and sensation of being reborn as a person of faith has largely been obscured in our celebration. To see how Christians refresh themselves in this manner is a lesson that Jews can learn.

Having said what I said earlier about mission-proselytism, let me make one final comment. Although I've called it obscene and have described it as spiritual rape, somehow I don't feel personally threatened. I think that is because I feel very strong as a Jew, not in the sense of power but in terms of commitment to my tradition and my people. I so love being Jewish—the Jewish Sabbath, the traditions, the Torah, the liturgy, the history—that nothing could entice me away, even, I believe, on pain of death. What's more, through the miracle of election, through diligence and good fortune, my husband and I have been able to generally pass these feelings on to our five children. So while I am intellectually and theologically critical of mission-proselytism, the issue does not have as much emotional impact on me as, say, the tensions in the Middle East or the Soviet treatment of Jewish refuseniks.

Thus, as a Jew secure in her tradition, I am in a sense both free enough and distanced enough to learn something else from Christian mission: that if you love something so deeply you do not keep it only to yourself or your family or your immediate community. You reach out to share it with others, including those who are on the fringes, who are the misfits, the marginals, those who do not have the support systems of loving family and friends. When Christianity speaks of God's strength being revealed in weakness, I understand it best through the deeds of evangelicals who do not overlook those who are weak and apparently powerless. Christian mission moves to marginal people. This is a lesson for me; I believe it is a lesson for the Jewish community at large, not simply to win back those of our own who have been wooed away, but to move to the edges of our faith community, to bring back the assimilated, the disconsolate, the insecure, and to strengthen them with the beauty and comfort and meaning of the Jewish tradition.

Notes

1. For example, the American Board of Missions to the Jews last year opened a center in Brighton Beach in New York City, a neighborhood heavily populated by newly arrived Russian Jewish immigrants who are easy prey for the aggressive outreach program of the mission center. They are approached from their first days in this country, are offered incentives, free camps, day care, etc. For a survey and analysis of the extent of missionary activity in New York City, see the report of David Mann for the New York City Jewish Community Relations Council, 1979.

2. See Proposal of the Task Force on Missionary Activity, internal memo, Jewish Community Relations Council (1000), pp. 2 5.

3. This term was coined by Donald Bloesch, who has written several works on evangelicalism, including *The Evangelical Renaissance* (Grand Rapids: Eerdmans, 1973). Arnold Markowitz, director of the Hotline Service on Mission and Cults, has pointed to several instances of Baptist churches allowing the use of their space for missionary activity. In some cases, the minister was unaware of the mission work, but in most instances there was tacit awareness and covert support.

4. Marc H. Tanenbaum, Marvin R. Wilson, and A. James Rudin, eds. *Evangelicals and Jews in Conversation on Scripture, Theology, and History.* (Grand Rapids, Michigan: Baker Book House, 1978). See particularly Chapter 1 by Marvin R. Wilson.

5. Many books have been written on the linkage between Christian theology and anti-Semitic acts. See particularly the work of Jules Isaac, *The Teaching of Contempt: Christian Roots of Anti-Semitism* (New York: Holt, Rinehart and Winston, 1974); James Parkes, *The Conflict of the Church and the Synagogue* (New York: Atheneum, 1974); A. Roy Eckardt, *Elder and Younger Brothers* (New York: Schocken, 1973); Rosemary Reuther, *Faith and Fratricide: The Theological Roots of Anti-Semitism* (New York: Seabury Press, 1974), chapter 4; Raul Hilberg, *The Destruction of the European Jews* (Chicago: Quadrangle Books, Inc., 1961), chapters 1 and 2; Franklin Littell, *The Crucifixion of the Jews* (New York: Harper & Row, 1975).

6. From the report of an international consultation held in Oslo under the auspices of the Department of Studies, Lutheran World Federation, as cited in Eckardt's paper, p. 9. See below, footnote 7.

7. There is considerable debate in both Jewish and Christian scholarly communities on the uniqueness of the Holocaust. See Irving Greenberg, "Cloud of Smoke, Pillar of Fire" in Eva Fleischner, ed., *Auschwitz: Beginning of a New Era?* pp. 7–55; Emil Fackenheim, *God's Presence in History* (London: University Press, 1970); A. Roy Eckardt, "Thinking About the Holocaust," Paper prepared for the Indiana University Scholars Conference on the Holocaust (November, 1980), pp. 10–16; and A. Roy Eckardt, *Long Night's Journey Into Day* (Wayne University Press: forthcoming). See also two articles on this topic by Steven Katz and Henry L. Feingold, in *Shoah* (New York: National Jewish Resource Center), (March 1981), vol. 2, no. 2.

8. Greenberg, "Cloud of Smoke, Pillar of Fire."

9. Rudolf Pfisterer, the German theologian, has called Christian mission to the Jews a spiritual final solution. See Eckardt, "Thinking About the Holocaust," pp. 12–19.

10. Deut. 17:6.

11. This is not as unlikely a metaphor as one might think. Inanimate objects can be invoked as witness (Gen. 31:48—stones; Ps. 89:37—the moon); so, too, historic events of great magnitude.

12. One might easily ask: Why not call for the elimination of the concept of mission altogether? From a practical perspective, I think the chance of success of any particular scheme lies in the most moderate rather than in the most sweeping of proposals. We must bear in mind that the willingness of Christians to listen when the argument is predicated on mutual respect and a sense of justice (as opposed to power or leverage) is nonetheless counterbalanced by their desire to protect and remain faithful to dogma and history.

13. *Midrash Yalkut Shimoni*, Isaiah Chap. 43, Note 455 (New York: Title Publishing Co., 1944).

14. Here I would disagree with Eckardt's thesis that post-Holocaust Christian theology must call resurrection—and for that matter all of Christian theology and history—into question. I disagree, not for theoretical reasons—for I believe his conclusions are logically correct—but for practical reasons. I know that human beings can and often do hold a world view or a faith commitment where not everything is perfectly logical, internally consistent, or entirely made up of compatible parts. Thus, resurrection can be affirmed independent of supercessionism; and preaching Christ can be done without trying to convert the Jews, especially since Jews already share the same God; and salvation through Jesus need not ipso facto rule out religious pluralism.

15. Paul Van Buren, *Discerning the Way* (New York: Seabury Press, 1980), pp. 180ff.

12

Mission, Witness, and Proselytization
A Jewish View

Sanford Seltzer

In an era characterized by efforts at interconfessional rapprochement and the development of transdenominational movements within Christianity, the role of Judaism and the Jewish people in the unfolding of the divine plan remains unresolved. Israel continues to be a theological problem. The future of ecumenism is clouded by the growing division between evangelical interpretations of mission and witness and those Protestants and Catholics committed to a theology of mutual recognition between Judaism and Christianity.[1]

J. Coert Rylaarsdam laments the "disease in Christian mission to Jews" and holds out the promise of Jews and Christians as "brothers in hope, members of separated communities of faith, but servants of the same God in a single ongoing drama of redemption."[2] Krister Stendahl understands Paul's reference to God's mysterious plan for Israel in Romans 11 as "an affirmation of God-willed coexistence between Judaism and Christianity in which the missionary urge to convert Israel is held in check."[3] Eva Fleishner emphasizes that not only has the Catholic church officially repudiated any and all forms of proselytizing of Jews, but as a consequence "Christianity's mission to the Jews is reversed or transformed into the effort to live in greater fidelity to the faith it has received from Judaism in the specific way of the Jew called Jesus whom Christians acclaim as Christ."[4]

Conservative evangelicals speak out with equal fervor and conviction. Arthur Glasser writes: "We feel it incumbent upon Christians to reinstate the work of Jewish evangelism in their missionary obedience."[5] Gerald Anderson adds: "Christians have much to regret and repent for in the history of their relations with the Jewish people, but while there is no special mission to the Jews, neither is there any special exemption of the Jews from the universal Christian mission."[6] He reminds his readers that Reinhold Niebuhr's near successful quest to put an end to Christian efforts to evangelize Jews was "motivated more by sociological than theological considerations."[7]

Two citations from the proceedings of the first Evangelical-Jewish conference sponsored under these auspices also merit mention in this context. Marvin Wilson presents a concise definition of evangelical as "a Christian who believes, lives, and desires to share the gospel."[8] Carl Edwin Armerding, in an essay titled, "The Meaning of Israel in Evangelical Thought," writes: "I would like to think that evangelical Christianity, admittedly and unabashedly committed to Jesus Christ and the scriptural message, is the kind of concerned, loving, caring, and thinking community to which, like the house of Mary, Martha, and Lazarus, our Jewish friends would seek to repair."[9]

Against this backdrop of increasing Christian disagreement over the meaning and future of Jewish existence, the various branches of contemporary Judaism, whatever their differences, and these are not insubstantial, have been united, or so it appeared by their distress over the resurgence of Christian missions to the Jews, however subtle or well-intentioned these overtures were. They joined as well in their emphatic rejection of Judaism as a proselytizing faith stressing instead the rabbinic injunction that the righteous of all peoples have a share in the world to come. "It is as arrogant," wrote the late Abraham Joshua Heschel, "to maintain that the Jewish refusal to accept Jesus as the Messiah is due to their stubbornness or blindness as it would be presumptuous for the Jews not to acknowledge his glory and holiness in the lives of countless Christians."[10]

That Jews had once actively missionized and that Judaism had left an indelible impact on the ancient world is undeniable.

George Foot Moore's observation: "The conviction that Judaism as the one true religion was destined to become the universal religion was a singularity of the Jews,"[11] is consistent with the accounts of Jewish missionary successes rendered by Josephus, Greek and Roman historians, rabbinic sources, and, of course, in Matthew 23:15.

But this was part of the dead and buried past, a segment of the record of the historic Jewish experience reserved for the researcher and scholarly discussion. Scholars might differ as to the precise chronology and circumstances governing the cessation of Jewish missionizing endeavors, but that and that alone was the extent of the debate. To be sure, Judaism was open to men and women who voluntarily opted to become Jews; and the tradition was quite clear that the *ger tzedek*, the proselyte, was as beloved of God as the born Jew, perhaps even more.[12] But no proselyte was to be accepted without the proper orientation and prior and ample warning regarding the frequent plight of the Jewish people. The rabbis were unequivocally disapproving of conversions performed solely for the sake of matrimony as well.

The same commonality of theme was generally evident in Jewish thought in dealing with the scope and thrust of Deutero-Isaiah. Israel's mission was to teach God's Word by example. She was to so conduct herself among the nations in which she dwelt, that through her dedication to Torah the world would be inspired and humanity perfected under the kingdom of the Almighty. That the duties and responsibilities of a holy people might result in pain and suffering and even tragedy as they often did were unavoidable burdens of that legacy. "The Jews," writes Henry Slonimsky, "become protagonists in the most august drama, the making of man. They are the people whose actual course of life furnishes the material for the apotheosis in Isaiah 53 and the image there conceived is so supreme that it was borrowed and used to invest the central figure of the Christian religion."[13]

There were those, particularly among the founders of Reform Judaism, who saw the divine vocation of the Jew in the more literal context of Isaiah 49:6. Isaac Mayer Wise wrote that "the mission of Israel was and still is to promulgate the sacred truth to all nations on earth."[14] He claimed to discern among "advanced Gentiles" a gradual approach to the content of what he termed "Israelism."[15] For Kaufman Kohler, "the idea of Israel's mission formed the very soul and life force of the Jewish people in its history and literature."[16]

Others swept up in the fervor of an imminent messianism preached a universalism achievable only "when the Jew shall have completely cast away his obstructive exclusiveness and ceremonialism and the Christian his Christology."[17] In 1910, Isadore Singer pleaded with world Jewry to reclaim the New Testament as an integral part of historic Judaism and to remove the blank page between Malachi and Matthew. "Has modern Judaism," he asked, "after an interval of 1,839 years, the will and the force to resume the great monotheistic world propaganda which our ancestors limited by national passions abandoned shortly before their war with Rome?"[18]

In the opening years of this century, countless Reform rabbis preached and taught the Jewishness of Jesus and called for his reclamation as a Jew and his return to a rightful place in the synagogue where he was nurtured and in the gallery of immortal leaders of the Jewish people. On Sunday morning, December 20, 1925, Stephen Wise preached perhaps the most controversial sermon of his distinguished career, "The Jewish Attitude Toward Jesus of Nazareth." "Shall we not say that this Jew is soul of our soul and the soul of his teaching is Jewish and nothing but Jewish?"[19]

But the pronouncements of Wise and Kohler and the others fell upon deaf and often hostile ears. The occasional voice lifted in behalf of the resumption of mission was greeted by a formidable silence. Jewish energies were directed toward the cessation of the Christian evangelical enterprise. It was only in the Reform prayer book that the idea persisted and even here in liturgical themes so intentionally phrased as to transform them into vague, innocuous, and poetic ideals. Thus, in the waning moments of the Day of Atonement, the congregation reads the following: "Grant that the children of Israel may recognize the goal of their changeful career so that they may exemplify by their zeal and love for mankind the truth of Israel's message, one humanity on earth even as there is but one God in heaven."[20] A similar sentiment is found in the ritual for Sabbath Eve. "Almighty and merciful God thou hast called Israel to thy service and found him worthy to bear witness unto thy truth unto the peoples of the earth. Give us grace to fulfill this mission with zeal tempered by wisdom and guided by regard for other men's faith."[21]

As of December 1978, it was no longer possible to speak quite as definitively of a Jewish view of mission, witness, and proselytization. "Jewish views" was now a more legitimate description. It was then that Rabbi Alexander Schindler, president of the parent body of Reform Judaism, the Union of American Hebrew Congregations, called on its Board of Trustees to authorize the creation of a Task Force on Reform Jewish Outreach among whose goals was to be the launching of "a carefully conceived program aimed at all Americans who are unchurched and who are seeking roots in religion."[22] Schindler was explicit in his insistence that his message was not intended to paint Judaism as the one and only true faith or to impugn the allegiances of those who had selected other equally exalted paths to God. But he was equally candid when he said: "Let me not obfuscate my intent through the use of cosmetic language. Unabashedly and urgently I call on our members to resume their time honored vocation and to become champions for Judaism. . . . these words imply not just passive acceptance but affirmative action."[23]

The Board of Trustees of the Union approved the establishment of the Task Force which is currently at work, its structure slightly modified by its emergence as a joint venture of both the Union of American Hebrew Congregations, essentially a congregational body, and the Central Conference of American Rabbis, the rabbinic arm of Reform Judaism. It abides by the conditions of its mandate which are to undertake a thorough and comprehensive study of Rabbi Schindler's recommendations so as to ascertain their validity and their implementability. The results of that study were delivered to the Biennial convention of the Union in Boston, Massachusetts, in December, 1981.

Even now, outreach to the religiously unchurched remains a matter for investigation and not for action.

Yet that caveat in no wise diminishes the significance of the Schindler proposal for the future of Christian-Jewish relationships. His promise that whatever programs may ultimately be instituted will not be directed toward practicing Christians or members of any other faith community does not lessen its impact any more than the reassurance that whatever is done will be done with dignity and forebearance. The perspectives from which both evangelicals and non-evangelicals confront the Jewish people have been altered. A new dimension has been introduced into the dialogue.

Jews also have been challenged. The assumptions underlying post-Holocaust Jewish survival have been tested. The call to mission requires that Jews focus once more on that dichotomy of role which has always been so taxing for Jews and which Arthur Cohen characterized as the tension between the "natural and the super-natural Jew." "Christianity shares with us the mystery of our presence. Though it compromises its own history when it destroys us, it treasures the mystery of our presence and marvels at the constancy of our disbelief. This is only to say that the non-Jew conserves the dogma of our supernatural vocation while we, its legatees and bearers, would sacrifice dogma for fact, vocation for our natural condition."[24]

Cohen's formulation of the problem nearly twenty years ago struck a discordant note in a Jewish community convinced that after Auschwitz only a demythologized Jew could ever survive. His bitterest critic, Richard Rubenstein, summarized what many others undoubtedly felt: "Why must he complain that Jews want primarily to be normal or even just a bit vulgar and bourgeois? Why does he agonize over the fact that Jews have wisely elected to reject saintliness as a profession?"[25] A generation later the issue again has surfaced.

Shortly after the creation of the Task Force On Reform Jewish Outreach, Rabbi Balfour Brickner, then Director of the Union of American Hebrew Congregations Commission on Inter-religious Affairs, wrote to a select number of Catholic and Protestant leaders eliciting their comments. Thirty-one persons were contacted. Eighteen replied. The responses were generally favorable viewing the renewed possibility of Jewish mission as a demonstration of the vitality of Judaism and the Jewish people. "Whether the engagement with the outsider actually leads to conversion or changes of religious affiliation is not important," said Peter Berger. "Rather what is essential is that very committed individuals and every community of such individuals engage with all the significant alternatives."[26]

The respondents praised Schindler for not implying that Judaism was superior to other faiths and indicated that the move would not damage interfaith relationships. On the contrary, it was felt that the level of the discussion would be enhanced now that issues heretofore ignored or avoided had been opened. Krister Stendahl wondered whether it was possible to distinguish between outreach to the unchurched and nonproselytizing. He asked: "If your mission is non-proselytizing is there also a way in which a Christian mission to Jews can be seen as non-proselytizing?"[27] Harvey Cox and Eugene Fisher in a similar vein saw the proposal raising more questions than it answered in dealing with who truly was a Jew. "I am opposed to Christians trying to convert Jews," said Cox. "I do not extend my opposition to the case of secular Jews for whom Judaism has ceased to have any personal meaning. . . ."[28]

"What does non-religious mean," asked Fisher, "in the context of a tradition which does not make the same distinction in the same way between saved and secular, religious and profane, as that which prevails in Christianity and which even in Christianity is a matter of considerable internal debate?"[29] Fisher desired more clarification as to whether the definition of the unchurched included the millions of lapsed Catholics in the world. "Does not," he added, "the church have a prior claim to work among this group?"[30]

Whatever their reservations, these essentially positive statements of nonevangelical Christians were consistent with a commitment to the theological parity of two faith communities joined in the struggle against secularism. Thus in a letter to Rabbi Schindler, Leonard Swidler congratulated him on the reclamation of Judaism's atrophied universalistic strain. "I am sure," he wrote, "this will improve ecumenical relations between Jews and Christians for it will tend to foster a sense of parity rather than Christian paternalism. In the atmosphere of the former, one can have dialogue, but not in the latter. Mazel tov."[31]

The ambiguity of terms, such as religiously unchurched or even its subsequent modification to religiously nonpreferenced requires a far more scrupulous examination than had been initially contemplated. A 1978 study by the Princeton Religious Research Center and the Gallup Organization titled, "The Unchurched American," revealed rather conclusively that it was erroneous to equate lack of religious belief with the absence of formal church or synagogue affiliation. That study defined unchurched as a person who was neither a member of a church or synagogue and who had not attended either institution in the past six months apart from weddings, funerals, or special events such as Christmas, Easter, or Yom Kippur.[32] The survey disclosed that eight out of ten persons polled stated that one could be a good Christian or a good Jew without participating in formal services of worship. Sixty-eight percent of the unchurched Christians believed in the resurrection of Jesus and 64 percent that Jesus was either God or the Son of God. Fifty-seven percent affirmed a belief in the hereafter and 70 percent said that prayer was efficacious.[33] When asked to account for the apparent inconsistency between professions of religious commitment and the absence of formal institutional membership, those interviewed answered that the church had lost its spiritual emphasis and was so preoccupied with institutional politics that it was ineffective in helping people find their way in the world.

The confusion over exactly who are the unchurched is even more pronounced in defining the so-called secular Jew, a concept Dr. Fisher recognizes as beyond the Jewish vocabulary and which Eugene Borowitz, writing as a Jew, describes as the "secularization of Jewish spirituality."[34] It is here that the Christian-Jewish argument may encounter yet another of its numerous impasses. Jews have never made the distinction between religious and nonreligious as precisely as Christians nor have they compartmentalized the meaning of Jewish peoplehood.

It is true that the tripartite division of American society into
neat categories of Protestant, Catholic, and Jew has contributed
to the present state of affairs. It is only in recent years that
Christian and Jewish thinkers have given serious concern to
the shallowness of American religiousity most aptly called by
Will Herberg a "religiousness without religion, a religiousness
with almost any kind of content or none, a way of sociability or
belonging rather than a way of reorienting life to God."[35]

It may not be possible for Christians to accept the criteria of
Jewishness, as stipulated by Jews, if these run counter to a
Christian understanding of Judaism and of the prerogatives of
Christian mission. Jews in turn must be prepared to acknowl-
edge this situation and in an open society endure the possibility
of Christian outreach to so-called secular Jews.

It is somewhat paradoxical that although nonevangelicals
have generally decried the activities of Jews for Jesus and other
Hebrew Christian missionary movements, their suppositions
that secular Jews are acceptable candidates for conversion are
consistent with the attitudes of evangelicals who have long seen
no contradiction between one's ethnic identity as a Jew and
one's witness to Christ. Gerald Anderson observes: "In our own
time there is evidence that many Jews who have accepted Jesus
as the Messiah take a new pride in their Jewishness."[36] Richard
R. DeRidder adds: "The denial that one can be both a Jew and
a Christian is simply not true. Christianity in its gospel of the
Christ of universal grace does not doubt that God still moves
into Jewish lives by the pathway of faith while waiting pa-
tiently . . . for Jewish recognition of Jesus."[37]

The semantic and substantive difficulties inherent in defining the unchurched and the nonpreferenced in ways congenial
to both Jews and Christians awaits the serious attention of both
faith communities and is already the subject of evaluation by
the Task Force on Reform Jewish Outreach. While nonevangelicals have gone on record as approving of some form of Jewish
mission, the evangelical view has not as yet been documented.
Four representatives of the evangelical community were among
the recipients of Rabbi Brickner's questionnaire. None responded, a circumstance which, while hardly conclusive, may

well be a significant barometer of evangelical disapproval and perhaps dismay. A March 1977 editorial in *Christianity Today*, noting first the unwillingness of Jews to recognize Jesus as the Messiah, went on to say that it would be inconceivable for evangelicals not to share the Good News with Jews as with all others. That statement came as no surprise. What was unexpected was the subsequent paragraph of the editorial. "If evangelical relations are to prosper we must then acknowledge the right of each group to make voluntary converts from among the followers of the others."[38]

To be sure, the article was written nearly two years before the Schindler proposal, but if it be truly reflective of the evangelical position, its seeming internal contradiction notwithstanding, it would reduce the degree of Jewish apprehension. But if the editorial was not representative of evangelical thought and if mainstream evangelicals echo the sentiments of Carl Henry, "the basic issue between Christian and Jew remains: is Jesus of Nazareth the messiah of promise?"[39] then the call for active Jewish outreach is of a totally different theological complexion.

It is one thing for evangelicals to suffer the recalcitrance of a stiff-necked people. It may be another for them to concede that it is both possible and permissible for salvation to be of and by the Jews. It is one thing to explain the continued existence of Judaism and the Jewish people as a divine mystery accompanying Christ's church on its way through the world "as a mirror and guarantor of God's love which transcends our yes or no."[40] It is another to acknowledge the truth of Israel's message and the permanence of its mission.

The call for Jewish outreach was not greeted enthusiastically by other branches of Judaism, nor was there any unanimity within the ranks of Reform. Many saw it as an unfortunate, regressive decision which could only endanger the hard-won gains achieved in Jewish-Christian relationships and result in the further alienation of evangelicals. Rabbi David Polish, a distinguished past president of the Central Conference of American Rabbis, expressed the feeling of many opponents when he wrote that "there could be no more inopportune time than now to jeopardize a truce that could perhaps become a

peace. Some would seize the occasion as a pretext for lifting a
reluctant suspension of their mission, perhaps blaming Jews
for rejecting a profound Christian concession."[41] Polish's fears
are not to be dismissed idly. The memories of generations of
Jews who when offered the cross or martyrdom chose to die
with the *Shema Yisroel* upon their lips are never far from the
surface of the collective Jewish psyche and do not fade regard-
less of time and place. It may well be impossible for evangelicals
to comprehend the depth and intensity of these feelings for
Jews. There is no clearer illustration of the enormity of that
barrier than the following excerpt taken from an article titled
"The Conversion of the Jews," by William Sanford LaSor, a
professor of Old Testament at Fuller Theological Seminary.
"Until we know the Jew and love him as a person, until we
share something of his memory of the Holocaust, until we
sincerely believe that we are in his debt. . . . it seems to me that
talk about evangelizing the Jew is only empty rhetoric. . . . What
have you and I done today to help some Jew trust us?"[42]

Many Jews literally held their breath in anticipation of the
evangelical rejoinder to the call for Jewish mission. Those anxi-
eties, predicated on bitter experience, were so overwhelming
that much of what Schindler said was either ignored or not
even heard. The nature of what would be done, the methods
that would be used, the persons who would be reached were all
irrelevencies, swept asunder in the groundswell of a visceral,
almost instinctive, No! Jewish fears of evangelical retaliation,
ingrained as they are by the painful lesson of the centuries and
then restated in the death camps of Europe, make the success
of a reasoned and rational reply doubtful if not impossible.

But if the experience and precedents of the past, let alone
the present, are of any value, the tenacity of the Jews to their
faith and to their people is well-known. No more significant
index of the perseverance of Jewish identity exists than in the
data showing that despite the growing incidence of exogamous
marriages involving Jews, less than 1 percent of Jewish partners
convert to Christianity while between 30 percent and 40 percent
of non-Jewish partners become Jews. Increasingly, mixed-
married couples affiliate with synagogues and determine to

raise their children as Jews even as the non-Jewish partner has resolved to retain his or her religious identity.[43] These continuing trends would confirm Milton Himmelfarb's opinion that "if anything, the intermarriage of Jews seems less ideological today, less rebellious than it did in the 1920s."[44]

Nor is it inappropriate to quote from the comments of a Queens College sociology professor, Thomas Robbins: "Any faith or religious tradition that can only survive through . . . the requirement that other faiths renounce proselytization would appear to be desperately feeble."[45] The one proviso to be added is that the validity of such reasoning depends on the safeguards of a democratic society in which coercion and oppression for the harboring and expression of ideas contrary to the will of the majority are expressly forbidden and where people are not labeled moral or immoral solely on the basis of highly subjective interpretations of religious texts.

There were others in the Jewish community whose opposition to a program of outreach to non-Jews rested on the equally sincere belief that however worthy the project, it would detract from the more important task of putting our own religious house in order. Contemporary Jewry, they argued, had first to bear witness to itself as engaged in a sacred task before extolling the virtues of Judaism to strangers. They were correct in their recognition of the need. But what they failed to perceive was that the very possibility of mission and its restatement as an ideal compelled the Jew to do precisely that.

The rebirth of the State of Israel was of profound theological significance for Christians whose failure to come to terms with the reality of Jews as flesh and blood remains a stumbling block to interfaith understanding. Of greater moment for Jews was the physical fact of Israel as a refuge for the survivors of the Holocaust and its concrete testimony that at long last they were a people like every other people, no longer rootless and disembodied.

The fulfillment of the ancient promise stirred the Jewish spirit and revived the Jewish soul. It underlined the commentary of Hannah Arendt. "Because only savages have nothing more to fall back upon than the minimum fact of their human origin,

people cling to their nationality all the more desperately when
they have lost the rights and protection that such nationality
once gave them. Only the past with its entailed inheritance
seems to attest to the fact they still belong to the civilized
world."[46]

But this jubilation over the land of Israel was also a vivid
reminder of how traumatic the sojourn of the people of Israel
had been among the nations of the earth and of how far was
the inner journey yet to be traversed by the Jew in the restoration of the authentic Jewish self. The rehabilitation was as yet
incomplete. The paradox of Jewish survival resides not in the
manifest reality of the Jewish people despite the vicissitudes of
history, but in the deeper struggle to unhesitatingly embrace
inwardly that which is proclaimed to Judaism's friends and foes.
God's covenant with Israel is permanent and binding. Judaism
lives neither to be superseded nor rejected as the word of
God.

The capacity of Jews to speak of mission is of far greater
importance than its actualization. To couch one's destiny again
in religious language is to at long last be redeemed from the
externally imposed image of an accursed and deicidal people.
To dare raise the possibility is to witness the restitution of Jewish
self-esteem and to suggest a renewed yearning in Jewish life for
the recovery of the transcendent. Above all, one experiences a
sense of the holy as Jews again struggle with the dilemma
posed by the vision of consecration in Isaiah 6: "And I heard
the voice of the Lord saying, whom shall I send and who will
go for me? Then I said, here I am, send me."

Notes

1. See Harold H. Ditmanson, "Some Theological Perspectives, Christian
Mission and Jewish Witness," *Face to Face,* Anti-Defamation League of B'nai
B'rith, New York (Fall-Winter, 1977), p. 6.
2. J. Coert Rylaarsdam, "Mission To Christians," ibid., p. 18.
3. Krister Stendahl, "Limits of Christian Mission," ibid., p. 19.
4. Eva Fleishner, "In the Light of the Holocaust and Religious Pluralism," ibid., p. 16.

5. Arthur Glasser, "Christian Missionaries and A Jewish Response," *Worldview*, vol. 21, no. 5 (May 1978), p. 40.

6. Gerald Anderson, "Christians Challenge the Rabbi's Response," *Worldview*, vol. 21, nos. 7–8 (July/August 1978).

7. Ibid.

8. Marvin Wilson, "An Evangelical Perspective on Judaism," *Evangelicals and Jews in Conversation*, edited by Marc H. Tanenbaum, Marvin R. Wilson, and A. James Rudin (Grand Rapids: Baker Book House, 1978), p. 4.

9. Carl Edwin Armerding, "The Meaning of Israel in Evangelical Thought," ibid., p. 138.

10. Abraham Joshua Heschel, *Face to Face*, p. 21.

11. George Foot Moore, "Judaism, In the First Centuries of the Christian Era," *The Age of the Tannaim*, vol. 1 (Cambridge, Mass: Harvard University Press, 1954), p. 323.

12. "Dearer to God is the proselyte who has come of his own accord than all the crowds of Israelites who stood before Mt. Sinai. For had the Israelites not witnessed the thunders, lightenings, quaking mountains, and sounding trumpets they would not have accepted the Torah. But the proselyte who saw not one of these things came and surrendered himself to the Holy One Blessed be he and took the yoke of heaven upon himself. Can anyone be dearer to God than this man?" As found in C. G. Montefiore and H. Lowe, *A Rabbinic Anthology* (New York: Meridian Books), p. 568.

13. Henry Slonimsky, *The Philosophy Implicit in the Midrash, Essays* (Cincinnati: Hebrew Union College Press, 1967), p. 31.

14. James Heller, *Isaac M. Wise, His Life, Work and Thought* (Union of American Hebrew Congregations, 1965), p. 537.

15. Ibid., p. 538.

16. Daniel J. Silver, "A Lover's Quarrel with the Mission of Israel," *Contemporary Reform Jewish Thought*, edited by Bernard Martin (Chicago: Quadrangle Books, 1968), p. 147.

17. Joseph Krauskopf, *A Rabbi's Impressions of the Oberammergau Passion Play* (Philadelphia: Rayner Publishers, 1901), p. 12.

18. Sanford Seltzer, "Reactions to Jesus in the Reform Rabbinate," unpublished thesis, 1959, p. 9.

19. Ibid., p. 1.

20. Union Prayer Book, vol. II, Central Conference of American Rabbis (New York, 1962), p. 345.

21. Union Prayer Book, vol. I, Central Conference of American Rabbis (Cincinnati, 1951), p. 34.

22. Alexander M. Schindler, Presidential Address (December 2, 1978, Houston, Texas), p. 6.

23. Ibid.

24. Arthur A. Cohen, *The Natural and the Supernatural Jew* (New York: Pantheon Books, 1962), p. 281.

25. Richard Rubenstein, *After Auschwitz* (Indianapolis: Bobbs Merrill Co., 1966), p. 187.

26. Peter Berger, "Converting the Gentiles," *Commentary* (May 20, 1979), p. 38.

27. News Release, Union of American Hebrew Congregations (May 20, 1979), p. 3.

28. Ibid., p. 5.

29. Ibid., p. 4.

30. Ibid.

31. Leonard Swidler correspondence with Alexander M. Schindler, December 21, 1978. Unpublished.

32. "The Unchurched American" (The Princeton Religious Research Center, 1978), p. 2.

33. Ibid., pp. 11–12.

34. Eugene Borowitz, "The Changing Forms of Jewish Spirituality," *America* (April 28, 1979), vol. 140, no. 16, p. 347.

35. Will Herberg, *Protestant, Catholic, Jew* (Garden City, New York: Anchor Books, 1960), p. 260.

36. Gerald Anderson, op. cit.

37. Richard DeRidder, *Worldview* (July/August, 1978), op. cit.

38. *Face to Face*, op. cit., p. 2.

39. Ibid., p. 17.

40. H. Berkhof, "Israel as a Theological Problem in the Christian Church," *Journal of Ecumenical Studies*, vol. VI (Summer, 1969), p. 337.

41. David Polish, "Jewish Proselyting, Another Opinion," *Journal of Reform Judaism*, vol. XXVI, no. 3 (Summer, 1979), p. 7.

42. William Sanford LaSor, "The Conversion of the Jews," *The Reformed Journal* (November, 1976), p. 4.

43. Sanford Seltzer, "Membership Status of Non-Jews," *An Horizon Report*, Union of American Hebrew Congregations (August, 1980).

44. Milton Himmelfarb, "Secular Society, A Jewish Perspective," *Religion in America*, edited by William McLoughlin and Robert N. Bellah (Boston: Beacon Press, 1968), p. 282.

45. Thomas Robbins, *Worldview* (July/August, 1978).

46. Hannah Arendt, *The Origins of Totalitarianism* (New York: Meridian Books, 1958), p. 300.

Part Six

The Past and the Future

13

Six Hard Questions for Evangelicals and Jews

Kenneth S. Kantzer

In early spring of each year, Jews around the world celebrate Holocaust Remembrance Day. It is a reminder to Jews and Gentiles alike of the unspeakable tragedy of the Holocaust under Hitler and the Nazis. Jews will never forget it, and they vow it shall never happen again. *Christianity Today* joins with the Jewish people in remembering this infamous event. With them, we are determined that nothing like it shall ever happen again.

We believe it is especially appropriate on this occasion to raise six hard questions for both evangelicals and Jews:

1. Are evangelicals anti-Semitic?
2. Who killed Jesus?
3. Is the New Testament anti-Semitic?
4. Should Christians seek to evangelize Jews?
5. Should Jews fear evangelicals?
6. How can evangelicals and Jews work together?

No doubt it would be easier to avoid these sticky questions. But the occasion is far too momentous, the day too serious to allow ourselves to drift apart simply because we are unwilling to take the trouble to understand each other. We evangelicals and Jews need each other too much to gloss over our differences

257

with superficial banalities. We owe it to each other to speak with
open hearts and complete honesty.

Are Evangelicals Anti-Semitic?

Anti-Semitism is, of course, difficult to define. It includes
infinitely more than genocide: for that is only the worst form of
anti-Semitism—the final step in a long journey. On the other
hand, anti-Semitism must not be so broadly defined as to preclude criticism of particular acts or of specific groups of
Jews. "Faithful are the wounds of a friend," says Scripture. It
is possible to criticize a Jew without being anti-Semitic, just as
it is possible to criticize an evangelical without being anti-
evangelical.

On the whole, evangelicals tend to slough off suggestions
that they are anti-Semitic. They admit that nominal Christians,
particularly medieval Catholics and some members of the liberal church in modern Germany, were anti-Semitic; but evangelicals stand opposed to this. Beyond that, however, we must
confess that Luther and the Reformers and many evangelical
Protestants since then have made statements that Jews certainly
have a right to consider anti-Semitic. We regret these anti-
Semitisms of the past and present. Southern Baptist president
Bailey Smith vigorously insists that he did not intend as anti-
Semitic his recent remark that God does not hear the prayers of
Jews. He says he loves and honors the Jews and that he was
simply expounding a fine point of Baptist theology in his well-
known reference to Jewish prayers. At any rate, other evangelical leaders, including such thorough conservatives as Jerry
Falwell, have publicly dissociated themselves from Bailey Smith's
remark. Says Falwell, "God hears the cry of any sincere person
who calls on him." These leaders have vigorously rejected the
Smith statement and made clear their opposition to all anti-
Semitism. Still, we sorrowfully acknowledge anti-Semitic statements and actions. We are thankful, therefore, that we detect a
spirit of repentance among evangelicals.

But repentance without restitution, like faith without works, is useless. What must evangelicals, and especially evangelical leaders, *do* to show that their repentance is sincere?

1. It is important that, where guilty, they publicly acknowledge past anti-Semitism, and declare it to be sin. If evangelicals are unwilling to set the record straight on this matter, any mouthing of repentance is rightly suspect.

2. Evangelical leaders must avoid any direct or indirect support for anti-Semitic causes. We believe contemporary evangelicals pass this test fairly well. Anti-Semitic leaders of the past, such as Gerald L. K. Smith and Gerald Winrod, and the anti-Semitic movements of the present such as the Ku Klux Klan, have absolutely no following among even the most conservative evangelical leaders. Of course, some evangelicals have espoused political and social causes that are not generally popular among Jews (who have tended to be liberal in these matters). But so far as we can see, they do this without any anti-Semitic overtones. And many evangelicals favor middle-of-the-road or liberal policies more congenial to the Jewish mainstream. It is also striking that the most politically conservative evangelical spokesmen are frequently the most pro-Jewish and pro-Zionist in their convictions. At any rate, evangelical leaders do not now align themselves in any way with anti-Semitic causes.

3. It is not enough just to condemn anti-Semitism in the past and remain aloof from anti-Semitic causes. Evangelical leaders and pastors must also use their teaching ministries to present solid instruction as to the antibiblical and anti-Christian nature of all anti-Semitic attitudes or actions. To heighten evangelical sensitivities concerning the horrors of anti-Semitism and the need Jews have for true Christian friends, church leaders would do well to show films like *Avenue of the Just* or *Night and Fog,* and discuss them as a deterrent to future wrongs.

4. Further, evangelical leaders must ferret out, expose, and actively oppose incipient and overt anti-Semitism that creeps into a society structured for centuries along anti-Semitic lines. Hitler did not arise in a cultural vacuum. His persecution of the Jews was the end product of a long history of anti Semitism in which, alas, evangelicals too played an ignoble part. Incipient anti-Semitism leads to gross anti-Semitism, which may terminate

in genocide. So evangelicals must root out even the incipient forms we often think are harmless. Are we careful to show an appropriate respect for Jews in our casual remarks, attempts at humor, or social and business relations?

5. Evangelicals must guard against the unconscious anti-Semitism in themselves and others that lies concealed in the structures of society. Jews, naturally more sensitive to this, can help evangelicals here by forthrightly pointing out such attitudes. A public school English teacher, for example, can instill prejudices for life by his or her treatment of Shylock in Shakespeare's *Merchant of Venice*.

6. As evangelicals demonstrate in tangible ways their abhorence of anti-Semitic actions, they will declare a crucial truth to the Gentile world at large: *to attack Jews is to attack evangelicals, and such attacks will be resisted by evangelicals as attacks against themselves.* Only in this way can evangelicals make their repentance credible. Evangelicals, we grant, may well have begun to move in this direction. They may well be the Jews' best friends, but they certainly still have a long way to go.

Who Killed Jesus?

Careful students of Scripture may regard this question as irrelevant, if not ridiculous. But among untaught evangelicals and nominal Christians it is significant. The blame Gentiles heaped on Jews for the death of Christ created a profound sense of unfairness and resentment that has become a fixture of Jewish culture. Today, the repetition of this unjust charge produces an emotional, unconscious antagonism deep in the hearts of many Jews. Evangelical scholars, in writing on the New Testament, must bear this in mind and show uninformed readers the scriptural teaching. A superficial reading of the New Testament leads some to conclude that the Jews as a whole condemned Jesus to death and the Romans performed the execution. A more careful reading shows it was only *certain* Jewish leaders who brought the charge and stirred up the mob. Romans executed Jesus partly because Pilate lacked the courage to stand against those leaders and the excited mob.

But this is only part of what the New Testament says on this question. Christians also believe that the death of Jesus was part of God's overall plan. He chose the Jews to be a messianic people—a people through whom the world would be richly blessed (Gen. 12:1–3: "Thou shalt be a blessing . . . and in thee shall all families of the earth be blessed"). In his perfect life and sacrificial death, Jesus was the representative of the Jews in their messianic role to bring ultimate blessing to the whole human race (John 4:22: "Salvation is of the Jews").

But the world today does not accept Jesus and his salvation, just as earlier it rejected God and his messianic people. In this sense, the Jewish leaders (and Pilate) were more representative of the unbelieving world than of the Jews. Jesus presented himself as the true Jew doing God's messianic work as their representative. It is important that evangelical pastors, teachers, and leaders spell out clearly and specifically to their churches and constituencies that neither Jews of Jesus' day not Jews of today are corporately to be held responsible for the death of Jesus.

Is the New Testament Anti-Semitic?

Closely related to the question of who killed Jesus is the broader question of anti-Semitism in the New Testament. Paul, who is often considered to be the most anti-Semitic of all the New Testament writers, was himself a Jew, intensely proud of his Jewishness. The same is true of John, who, for all he said about Jewish leaders, left no doubt that Jews were the true people of God. All the New Testament writers except Luke were Jews. They boldly identified with the Jews, who, in contrast to Gentiles, cherished the Hebrew Scriptures and the idea of a coming Messiah.

One practical application of the alleged anti-Semitism of the New Testament requires special consideration. We must distinguish between what would not be anti-Semitic in the mouth of a first-century Jew and what those same words might convey about a Jew when spoken today. Both Christian and Jewish scholars recognize that the so-called anti-Jewish polemic in the New Testament is in reality an in house debate among Jows.

But two thousand years of anti-Semitism provide a wholly different context from that of the first century. New Testament words repeated in today's context are interpreted to mean something quite different from what these same words meant in their New Testament context. This is not so much a theological problem as a hermeneutical one, and it demands very sensitive, discerning action on the part of the church. Whenever a pastor or leader reads or refers to a passage from the New Testament relating to this topic, it is imperative that he interpret it so that he places it in its holistic Bible context, for these passages *are* misunderstood, perhaps not by the well-taught, but by the ill-taught. To avoid a misunderstanding of the New Testament message, therefore, evangelicals must provide their hearers with a careful interpretation set in its original Jewish context. Christians are not sensitive to this problem, but they would be if their grandfather, two uncles, and six cousins had died in the furnaces of Buchenwald.

Should Christians Seek to Evangelize Jews?

From its very beginning, Christianity sought to win converts to its faith. Evangelicals believe that Jesus Christ is their divine Lord and Savior and wish to share this good news with all others. Ultimately, salvation depends on faith in Christ. Any evangelical who does not believe this either is not a genuine evangelical, or is a very poorly instructed one. Jews, therefore, can expect evangelicals to seek adherents to Christian faith. They would be poor evangelicals if they did not.

But is it possible for evangelicals to obey the biblical mandate to evangelize in ways acceptable both to them and to Jews?

We begin by noting that both Jews and evangelicals today are firmly committed to religious freedom. Every religious group has the right to practice and propagate its own faith. At times Judaism has been a missionary religion. Jews have every right to seek to convert Christians to the Torah of God. They, in turn, must grant evangelicals the right to seek to win all people to the Christian message.

Of course, both Jews and Christians must repudiate certain kinds of evangelism. Some evangelistic techniques are not consistent with true respect for other people and, therefore, with the respect that every biblical Christian should have for every Jew. Evangelists ought not place unworthy pressures on Jews to induce them to become Christians. Any sort of manipulation or bribery is wholly out of order. We abhor any deception in seeking to present Christ to Jews. A small minority of Jewish Christians disguise their Christianity to attract unsuspecting Jews to accept Christianity. This is deceitful, contrary to the New Testament teaching, and unworthy of evangelical Christians. Evangelicals have more reasons to oppose this type of deception than do Jews, but we have often failed them by our silence. Evangelicals must speak out boldly and unequivocally against any deceitful practices. We must insist on ethical integrity as the first law of any Christian witness.

Should Jews Fear Evangelicals?

On what grounds, then, can we argue that Jews should *not* be afraid of evangelicals who are open and sincere in their evangelizing of Jews? We believe a number of reasons show that Jews ought to trust evangelicals as true friends.

1. Events of the last few years have shown that evangelicals have sought to identify with Jews. At times they may have embarrassed Jews by their well-meaning but not very sophisticated support, but in public and private they have made known their backing of Jewish causes; many have consistently supported the nation of Israel and Zionism; and they have defended the Jew in high and low places. G. Douglas Young, late president of the Institute of Holy Land Studies in Israel, and Arnold T. Olson of the American Bible Society and president emeritus of the Evangelical Free Church of America, are only two of many evangelical leaders who have staunchly supported Jews at home and abroad.

2. Our next point is extremely sensitive, and we do not wish to introduce a red herring. Yet we fail to see why evangelicals' support for Jews is negated by their desire to evangelize. Just the opposite is true. Their special concern for the Jew, drawn from the Bible, often translates into an even stronger motivation to share their faith with those toward whom they feel a unique relationship. Moreover, a Jew does not necessarily cease to be a Jew when he becomes a Christian any more than a Gentile ceases to be a Gentile when he becomes a Christian. Would he not technically remain a Jew—even though he might be reckoned apostate—since Judaism teaches that a Jew who sins is still a Jew?

We do object when Messianic Jews disguise their true intent and claim to be simply a Jewish party for the purpose of attracting Jews to Christianity. But if a Jew is defined as the son of a Jewish mother who voluntarily identifies himself as a Jew, one with other Jews of the past and present, brings himself under the teachings of the Hebrew Scriptures, and follows Jewish practices as a true expression of his own piety, then surely there is no reason why his acceptance of Jesus as Messiah means that he ceases to be a Jew. We do not accept the view of Chaim Potok that a Jew cannot become Christian without converting out of Judaism. Christianity, Potok argues, destroys the essence of Judaism by completing its messianic goal, so the Jew who becomes a Christian has no further purpose in existing as a Jew. As we read the Bible, however, the messianic role of the Jew is permanent, both as a burden and as a glory, and will never be accomplished until the end of history (Isa. 2:1–4 and Rom. 11:26: "And so all Israel shall be saved").

3. This leads us to a third reason why Jews can trust evangelical Christians for continued support: the role accorded to Jews by the Bible. This provides Christians, faithful to both Old and New Testaments with powerful built-in safeguards to keep them from falling into anti-Semitism. They owe a great debt of gratitude to the Jewish people. According to the Bible. God chose them to be the instruments for his redemptive purposes in the world. Through them God gave his revelation in the Hebrew

and Christian Scriptures, and, finally, the Christian Messiah and Savior.

But if gratitude has a short memory, evangelicals have an even more compelling reason for special concern over Jews: many of them believe Jews are specially protected by God. Jews also have a future role in God's plan; therefore, to fight them is to fight God (the Jews are still specially loved by God for "his gifts and call are irrevocable," Rom. 11:28–29). God has even specially commanded them, so many evangelicals believe, to treat Jews well ("I will bless those who bless you, and him who curses you I will curse," Gen. 12:3).

4. Finally, Jews can count on evangelical concern because of the general stress in both Hebrew and Christian Scriptures on the fundamental nature of the ethic of love. Evangelicals do not always act in love, but in their Bible they have an immensely powerful and continuous encouragement to love Jews. And it warns them that eventually they are accountable to God for their deeds.

How Can Evangelicals and Jews Work Together?

Jews and evangelicals must join in working for racial and human justice in our homeland and in the Middle East, and for Jews and all people everywhere. They must stand united against all kinds of man's inhumanity to man. For their part, Jews should not limit their opposition to anti-Semitism, but also stand against the hatred and super patriotism that can foster it. Christians, on the other hand, need to share equally with the Jews in the ongoing battle against anti-Semitism. They must make all legitimate Jewish concerns their own, and they must especially identify with Jews and join with them in equally vigorous opposition against even incipient forms of anti-Semitism. We evangelicals need to make our identification with Jews so plain that—let us repeat—when anyone attacks Jews as Jews, or displays any form of anti-Semitism, he must know that he is also attacking evangelicals and violating their basic convictions. And he will then need to do battle against both Jews and evangelicals.

We would do well to heed the warning of a Christian of a former day. In his later years, German pastor Martin Niemoeller lamented: "In Germany they came first for the Communists, and I didn't speak up because I wasn't a Communist. Then they came for the Jews, and I didn't speak up because I wasn't a Jew. Then they came for the trade unionists, and I didn't speak up because I wasn't a trade unionist. Then they came for the Catholics, and I didn't speak up because I was a Protestant. Then they came for me, and by that time no one was left to speak up." God forbid that American evangelicals will bring such a fate upon themselves.

But evangelicals and Jews have much more in common than a mutual desire for survival. Under God, both know themselves called by God to work for human good. Jews and evangelicals can cooperate to preserve all truly human values. We share the ethics of the Ten Commandments and the prophets. We are deeply committed to both political and religious freedom. In America, at least, we are committed to the separation of church and state. But we are also coming more and more to see that Western society, our nation, and even our public schools dare not be value free. Actually, there is no such thing as a value-free society. Our Western culture cannot hold together as a society where we should like our children to live without the Judeo-Christian heritage on which it was built. To remove these commonly held religious and moral values from Western society would be wholly undesirable and even disastrous for both Jews and Christians.

Rather, we should gratefully accept and promulgate the common values of our Judeo-Christian faith: the sanctity of human life, the stewardship of the earth's resources, the importance of the family as the basic unit of society, respect for the individual and his inalienable rights, and the moral imperative to love one's neighbor.

Of course, these are *religious* values, but they are also values to be preserved and defended by any stable government for the common good, for the personal and social welfare of the nation. We dare not permit those who reject these basic human values to prevent Christians and Jews from building them into our government, our public schools, and the basic social fabric of our society. Evangelicals and Jews must stand together to preserve our freedoms, our democratic society, and most of all, those basic values we owe ultimately to the Jews. As the messianic people of God, they have brought these infinite blessings to us Gentiles; and for this we evangelical Christians are deeply thankful.

14

The Holocaust and the Reality of Evil[1]

David Wolf Silverman

No Jew of my generation can forget or dismiss the Holocaust. The pall of its occurrence hangs over our lives and periodically dims our hopes. No Jew of my generation can read the special memorial prayers on the Day of Atonement without a shudder when the precentor recalls those whose deaths were "cruel and abnormal." The psychic shock waves suffered by every affirming Jew and by many indifferent Jews are still felt. How deeply or widely Jews were affected is not yet completely understood or comprehended today. It is a defensible assumption, however, that the echoes, reverberations, and repercussions of the Holocaust are constitutive of the background and are operative in almost everything that happens in Jewish life.

On the historical human plane, the Holocaust is, therefore, a *living force*—one which is unfortunately confined to Jewish recollection. The *frisson* of dread which took hold of Jewish consciousness during the incident at Entebbe when Jews were *separated* from non-Jews by the terrorists is a direct consequence of the lived presence of the Holocaust. The three decades which separated the Auschwitz platform (where Dr. Mengele, the Angel of Death, selected Jews for the gas chambers) from the Entebbe Air Terminal were spanned in an instant. To my mind, it was this act of "selection" which finally firmed the determination of the leaders of the State of Israel to undertake their daring operation of rescue. The possibility of the recurrence of the Holocaust even in miniscule form could neither be tolerated nor suffered.

The Holocaust, therefore, is not a datum—inert, lifeless, and past. Its impact is immediately recognizable in the one land where a majority of the survivors of the death camps live—the State of Israel. And it is concerning this State and the condition of the Jewish people prior to its birth that Jews evince trepidation at the reaction or the lack of reaction of Christians. Our anguish, compounded at times by anger, has a twofold thrust, one directed toward the past, the second pointing to the present. On the one hand, we cannot understand the world's silence during the trauma of the death camps. Even more horrifying, the deliberate decisions taken by leaders of the Allies not to bomb the rail lines leading to Auschwitz and some of the other camps lead us to believe that Jewish lives were and still are considered "expendable."

We have spoken of this period of time as being one of God's silence. *More pertinent and of greater anguish is the silence of the world.* How do we confront the silence of the world in the face of hundreds of thousands of preventable, needless deaths? Arthur Morse's *While Six Million Died,* an acid indictment of the world's passivity in the face of evil, suggests that Hitler counted upon the discounting of Jewish deaths as a mandate toward the furtherance of his genocidal plans. *What made such passive acquiescence possible?* What were the factors involved in statecraft, in political process, and in the stance of Christianity toward the various forms of government which were the preconditions for the occurrence and continuance of the Holocaust Kingdom for five full years? It is these questions that I raise on the purely human plane vis-à-vis the past. I am neither a historian by vocation nor a political scientist by trade. But if we are to prevent any possible future Holocaust, then we must be aware of the answers which historians and political scientists are qualified to give to the questions adumbrated above. I do not think that these questions have been adequately addressed.

The Problem of Power

Insofar as understanding the past can be mustered, this is all to the good. But understanding is not yet action. The usual appeals to repentance, to being responsible, even to being generous, do not actually tell us what to do. If Christians confine themselves to calls for contrition alone, the world will remain the captive of burly sinners masquerading as saints. The question which I raise for discussion is: *What has Christianity to say about the handling of power?* Bonhoeffer is, to my mind, an excellent case in point. One gets from his writings no clear picture of what type of action he would be recommending now, but one gets the clearest picture of what Bonhoeffer means if we locate him within the context out of which he wrote. For in Nazi Germany, and indeed in all of Europe during the 1930s, the Christian role was, at best, one of suffering witness. Bonhoeffer lived this role. To him it meant reliving the passion of Christ. When nothing else remains for a Christian, this role remains. But we seek to prevent the recurrence of Jewish powerlessness. How then does Christianity face the problem of power?

I have spoken until now of the past. Present realities are more pressing still. Both historically and theologically Auschwitz is not isolated. *It is conjoined with the birth of the State of Israel.* But in no way is it to be considered a compensation for the Holocaust. Such a restoration of "meaning" would be blasphemous. But there is no other nodal event in Jewish history where the slaughter of millions in the most abject and degrading circumstances was linked temporally with the most intense and energetic efforts toward a new beginning. That is why Jews reacted as strongly as they did to the passage of the infamous United Nations resolution equating Zionism with racism. To us the mocking silence of the world of the 1940s was merely transposed into the demeaning speech of 1975.

The hesitancy of many Christian denominations to take a forthright stand on this issue is a reflection of the ambiguous position of many, if not most, Christians to questions of power. To a religious Jew, Israel represents an attempt to concretize

Judaism within the political and social structures of an incarnate community. Israel does not answer the agony of Auschwitz. But it is the most viable response that Jews have and can make to the Holocaust: "I shall not die but live!"

Jews would want their Christian friends to understand the State in that light and not merely as "part of the problem of the Middle East."

The Crisis of Belief

The mystery of evil is deepened agonizingly by the outrage of Auschwitz. But in my judgment it is not thereby transformed into a qualitatively unique event. Were it to be so, there could be neither answer nor response to this crisis. Only despair would reign. We see in the works of Elie Wiesel a contending with God built upon a dialectic of rejection. Man rejects God as God abjures man. Faith is lost, regained, and lost again. But not every survivor lost his faith as a result of the Holocaust. And not every one who perished rejected God. Jews did walk to the gas chambers chanting *Ani Maamin* (I believe with perfect faith).

This heroism of the religious is exemplified by the question posed by an anonymous Jew to the late Rabbi Meisels.[2] Both were then in Auschwitz. The year was 1942. The Nazi S. S. decided that all Jewish boys under fourteen who were not fit to be slave-laborers were to be sent to their death. The selection was made by building a horizontal pole attached to a vertical column and set at a predetermined height. All those too short to touch the horizontal bar were sent to special barracks, kept there without food and water, and sent to the crematoria that night. When the youngsters recognized what was happening, the shorter ones tried to walk on tiptoe past the scaffold; when they did so, they were immediately beaten to death by the guards. Several hundred youngsters were eventually gathered in the building, and after being counted by the S. S., they were guarded by the Kapos, the Jewish police.

Parents panicked, and many of them who had some money or small jewelry on their persons immediately ran to the Kapos and tried to bribe them so as to release their children. The

Kapos could not do so, because if the count of the condemned Jewish boys was not the same as that which the S.S. had, the Kapos could be killed. One exception they did make. They would take the bribes if they could capture some other Jewish child who had been spared. They would then put him into the condemned group in place of the Jewish child who was to be ransomed.

And so this Jew from Oberland came to Rabbi Meisels and said, "My only son, who is dear to me as life itself, has been taken to the barracks. I have enough to be able to give to the Kapos so as to ransom him and let him live. But I know that in order to save him, some other Jewish child must die in his place. What is the law according to the Torah? May I save my only son or must I let him die?" Rabbi Meisels tried his best to dodge the question. There was no answer he could give. What he did say was the following: "My dear friend, the Sanhedrin itself would ponder such a question deeply for weeks. Here am I in Auschwitz, without any other rabbis to consult, without books, without texts—how can I possibly give you an answer to your question?" The unknown questioner then answered: "If you do not answer me, it means that you are really afraid to tell me the answer, namely, that it is forbidden to ransom my son. Therefore, I want you to know that I accept the decision of the Torah fully and with joy. My son shall go to his death, but I shall not violate the law. As this is Rosh Hashanah (when the story of the *akeidah*, the binding of Isaac, is read) so am I to follow in the footsteps of our father Abraham, and this day I shall offer my child as my *akeidah*." Must not this story elicit our undying admiration, at least in the same measure as the anguished debates with God that characterize Wiesel's stories?

Both Fackenheim and Wiesel aver that the Holocaust was qualitatively unique. This would mean that it transcended every past persecution. Yet the Jews of the fifteenth century experienced the Spanish Expulsion as unique and in the words of one of their leaders and thinkers—Don Isaac Abravanel—as equivalent to the departure of the first human pair from the Garden of Eden. The Holocaust in the scope of its decimation far exceeds all past persecution. Fackenheim's sole argument for the existence of "radical demonic evil" is that the Nazis deliberately compromised their own war effort on the Russian front by diverting rolling stock to the death camps. One has to remember, however, that one of the prime goals of the Nazis was to strip Europe of its Jews. There was no contradiction in the shunting of railroad cars to the camps. I cannot, therefore, accept as sufficient this argument for the qualitative difference between the Holocaust and past Jewish persecutions. It is as difficult and painful to believe in God today as it was when the second temple was destroyed.

The Holocaust has, I think, dismissed any easy use of omnipotence as an attribute appropriate to God.[3] After Auschwitz, we can assert with greater force than ever before that an omnipotent God would have to be either sadistic or totally unintelligible. But if God is to be intelligible in some manner and to some extent—and to this I hold firm—then his goodness must be compatible with the existence of evil, and this is only if he is not all-powerful. Only then can we maintain that he is intelligible and good, and there is yet evil in the world.

Through his self-limitation God therefore *acknowledges* man as a being in his own right and as one who has the power to act on his own authority, even contrary to God's will and plan. *Once man exists in history, God is endangered.* He must be so threatened because he has risked himself upon the freedom of man. He has delegated a portion of what was his preworldly omnipotence to human beings. In so doing, he has foregone the guaranteeing of his self-satisfaction by his own previously unlimited power. In so doing he can also choose not to interfere with the physical course of events "with a strong hand and an outstretched arm," but to allow man the full weight of responsibility for his actions. He can withdraw and hide his face.

The Holocaust disclosed the depths to which man had sunk and the degree to which God withdrew. Dare we not say today that *the founding and preservation of Israel is God's gesture of faith in the midst of his silence?*

Notes

1. Reprinted from *Conservative Judaism,* vol. XXXI, 1–2, Fall-Winter 1976–77, pp. 21–5. Copyright 1977 by The Rabbinical Assembly; used with permission.

2. I owe this example to N. Lamm, "Teaching the Holocaust," *Forum,* Summer 1976. Although the veracity of this incident is open to question, the intent of the tale is true.

3. I believe this theological position to be one held in common by both Heschel and Hartshorne.

15

Prospectus for the Future

David A. Rausch

We came from many different areas of the United States and a plethora of academic and religious institutions. One of the participants came from as far away as Israel; another flew in from Vancouver, British Columbia. Many of us were apprehensive. Few knew exactly what to expect. A broad spectrum of the Jewish community was represented and some wondered whether it was worth the effort to dialogue with evangelicals. Were not differences, such as the area of proselytism, too awesome? Were not the barriers insurmountable? How could they demonstrate that their Judaism was fulfilling and meaningful— that they needed no other religion? The evangelical participants also varied greatly. Some questioned whether or not they should accept the label *evangelical* because of the misinterpretation the term had suffered in the last decade. A few wondered if dialogue was even possible. Would they be asked to totally throw out their theology—to do away with traditional beliefs in which they had found substance and meaning? Would they be labeled as narrow and intransigent if the dialogue did not produce immediate and significant results? Those few in both communities who had experienced close fellowship between Jews and evangelicals questioned whether some scholars from both communities would be sensitive enough and would actually "listen" to what the other community was saying. Would they talk past each other? Would they be honest? Would they exchange pleasant niceties and then return to their environment unaffected and lacking understanding? A Jewish scholar left a newborn baby daughter to deliver a paper; an evangelical scholar had not finished making up his final exams and was missing class. Another had flown in from speaking engagements in South America, tired and overtaxed. The conference coordinators, Rabbi A. James Rudin and Dr. Marvin R. Wilson, had spent untold hours on complicated details, disrupting their lives for more than a year. Was it worth it? Frankly, it was with a great deal of apprehension that both communities came together in Chicago on a chilly, windy day in December.

And yet, the accomplishment was well worth the effort. Reports in the press and lack of communication had given each community a distorted view of the other. Reported comments by Rev. Bailey Smith and Rabbi Alexander Schindler had caused such misunderstanding that Nathan Perlmutter, national director of the Anti-Defamation League of B'nai B'rith, declared in a press release, "There are good Christians and bad Christians, good Jews and bad Jews . . . to hear some of the talk lately we'd also have to say there are foolish Christians and foolish Jews!" The conference participants needed perspective and just getting to know one another was a great accomplishment. Jewish participants indicated amazement at the depth of scholarship represented within the evangelical community and the diversity of opinion among the evangelicals. Evangelicals were surprised at the number of issues in which they agreed with the Jewish community. Evangelicals also became sensitized to statements and terminology that were offensive to the Jewish community. The process of getting to know one another was enhanced from the outset because of the complete honesty exhibited in the early discussions. Such frank discussion characterized the entire conference because the participants were embued with the philosophy that effective and meaningful dialogue could only be rooted in honesty.

Friendship developed as caricature began to dissipate. Some of the greatest accomplishments were realized during individual discussion over meals or late-night fraternizing in the coffee shop. This led some to believe that small group discussion sessions would be valuable additions to future conferences. Participants had to chuckle at times during vigorous ad hoc discussions when they realized that a Jew and an evangelical were on the same side arguing a point fervently while a Jew and an evangelical on the other side zealously opposed such a view. Diversity of view *within* each community was very apparent!

Participants worked exceptionally hard (four to five hours sleep was not uncommon), and important groundwork was laid. The area of "Mission, Witness, and Proselytization" was perhaps the most volatile issue, and yet the discussion on it proved to be one of the most rewarding. As the issue began to be methodically sorted out, it was apparent that within this complex issue there were subsidiary parts that were blown out of proportion. Both communities were horrified about unethical evangelism; both communities felt that something should be done about it. There was also a consensus that the lack of definition of terms and the historic use of language within each community had contributed to a barrier of misunderstanding. What was the exact biblical imperative for the evangelical? What was the relation of witness to both communities? How is proselytization affiliated with cultural genocide of the Jewish people? Again, *within* each community there were diverse viewpoints that complicated discussion, but a definite foundation for understanding was accomplished. A candid airing of fears and frustrations was helpful. Nevertheless, the questions certainly were not resolved. I feel that the greatest danger is impatience. The Jew asks, "Why can't they simply give this up?" The evangelical asks, "Why can't they see my predicament?" Both communities must realize that this issue cannot be hammered out in a few hours or even properly understood in a few hours. It took years for this barrier to be entangled and encrusted with alienation and misinterpretation. Patience is needed to unravel it—much work needs to be done.

Another area in which significant groundwork was laid was the common realization of the challenges of the future. For some evangelicals it was a revelation that "morality" and "moral imperatives" were not foreign terminology to modern Judaism and that the Jewish community feared moral disintegration as much as any evangelical did. On the other hand, for some in the Jewish community, it was a surprising revelation that evangelicals were concerned about social justice and had not limited themselves to singular, peripheral concerns. Once common concerns were recognized, the automatic question that arose in both communities was: "Why on earth haven't we worked together on these issues?" It was followed quite quickly by the exclamation: "Let's get busy and work together on these important concerns!"

While important foundations were laid in several areas, there were areas that needed to be addressed in structured educational dialogue and, hopefully, will be addressed in the future. One of these areas is the Holocaust. While the one evening public session on "The Holocaust and the Reality of Evil" was stimulating and fascinating from the philosophical perspective, there is a great deal of interaction needed by the Jewish and evangelical community in this area. For the Jewish community, it may be difficult to understand how in the face of the mass of Holocaust literature and the popular movie portrayals in the past few years *anyone* could not be acquainted with the facts and ramifications of the Holocaust. Indeed, scholars within Holocaust studies have recently been delving into more "interesting" and "complicated" issues surrounding the reality of evil, guilt and forgiveness, and the psychological impact on survivors and their children. However, in spite of all the publicity, those of us who teach the Holocaust on the undergraduate or graduate level never cease to be amazed at the total ignorance about the Holocaust among secular as well as Christian college students. Educational institutions are also notorious for asking why a course on the Holocaust should be taught, and some colleagues are quick to assert that one should be emphasizing the positive virtues of mankind rather than one negative incident. At the same time, it must be noted that individuals who learn about the Holocaust in class are the first to understand the importance of such a course, and educational institutions are soon very supportive of the effort.

In general, evangelicals do not understand the history of the

Holocaust, and even worse, are unaware of the importance it holds for in-depth understanding of the Jewish community. A Jew may make an impassioned plea for the evangelical to refrain from "cultural genocide," but how effective is that plea to a person who does not historically understand the awesome ramifications of genocide on the Jewish community? When one realizes the pain with which the Jewish people have been inflicted in the past by those who called themselves "Christians," it is a sobering experience. When church fathers wrote letters filled with hatred, when Hebrew Christians were forced to persecute the Jewish community to "prove" their allegiance to Christianity, when crusaders could march around a burning mass of Jews in a synagogue and sing "Christ, We Adore Thee," the word *Christian* takes on a different connotation. When Martin Luther becomes impatient with the Jewish community in their persistent "unconverted" state and in a lapse near the end of his life writes shocking anti-Semitic statements, *Reformation* Christianity takes on a different connotation. When Hitler uses the name of Jesus and claims biblical support in exterminating over six million Jews, *biblical* Christianity takes on a new connotation.

It is no wonder that the Jewish community opposes evangelism. Often, it has been an attempt to eradicate Judaism. The Jews' only escape from Christian persecution throughout the medieval period was to convert to Christianity. In fact, the Nazi regime was the first time in history that the act of conversion could not save the Jew. Anti-Semitism had been "modernized" to such a point by that time, that anyone with a Jewish grandparent (even a faithful church member) was considered part of the Jewish "vermin" and unworthy of life in a "Christian" republic. Therefore, when Jewish people meet an evangelical they *expect* to be put under considerable pressure to convert. Jewish people experience the same irritation during evangelical witness as do most evangelicals when a pair of very knowledgeable and proof-text-laden Jehovah's Witnesses rap on their door and begin evangelizing. The evangelical must understand the Holocaust as a culmination *as well as* a perpetuation of this sad history. It is relevant to the tendencies we view today with such alarm.

With all due respect to the "German church struggle," it seems that only a few evangelicals, a few Protestants, a few Catholics, a few Orthodox, a few agnostics, and a few atheists (not necessarily in that order) helped the Jewish people during their persecution. I feel that the evangelical community must be asked what made the difference? Why did a few put themselves, their families, their possessions, and their careers on the line for a persecuted people, while most did not? What is in evangelical theology that should make one react differently from other groups in the face of prejudice, scapegoating, caricature, oppression, and outright physical violence to a race or religious group different from one's own?

Without an understanding of the Holocaust, we cannot understand groups such as the Jewish Defense League or why the Anti-Defamation League constantly patrols injustice. Without an understanding of the Holocaust we cannot fully appreciate the fears surrounding something as simple as the "Christian Yellow Pages" or the full implications of a "Christian" republic. Without an understanding of the Holocaust we cannot understand the importance of Israel to the Jewish community or why Israel does not "bargain" more. Nor can we fully understand the fear associated with Soviet Jewry—and, in the same vein, Soviet evangelical Christianity. I believe an understanding of the Holocaust is important in understanding one's Jewish neighbor.

However, an understanding of the Holocaust goes far beyond the Jewish community. The Nazis had enough gas left over to kill twenty million more people. There were not nearly that many more Jews to be exterminated. Who was next? Would an evangelical have fared any better in the end? Without an understanding of the Holocaust, we can neither fully appreciate the ability of human beings to be inhumane to other human beings nor contemplate the indifference of those not being directly affected—even in a civilized society. I fail to see vast differences between "civilized" Germany in the 1920s and 1930s and the "civilized" United States today. I do not believe that we

are more "Christian" than Germany was or that deluding ourselves that we are can keep us from similar error. The history of
the Black American within a "Christian" America should sound
some alarm at how one can theologically legitimize any stance
or action. For the student of the Holocaust, the increase in
scapegoating, racial tension, and overt acts of violence as our
country becomes more economically troubled is very disturbing.
How one's latent prejudice against any group can be nourished
and cultivated is a reality we must think through together—Jews
and evangelicals in conversation over a matter that directly
relates to the specter of evil that could engulf us all.

Another area that needs to be addressed in the future is the
topic of "Christian Zionism." There is a great deal of support
for Israel in the evangelical community. While such support is
appreciated in some segments of the Jewish community, there
is also a great deal of apprehension about *why* many evangelicals support Israel. Some American Jewish leaders caution that
the widespread support for Israel among fundamentalist evangelicals is not based on a healthy respect for the Jewish people.
The argument usually goes like this: "Fundamentalist evangelicals believe that Jesus cannot return for the second coming
until the Jews are regrouped in their biblical homeland and
then converted to Christianity." Such a statement appears to
twist the actual historic fundamentalist evangelical eschatology,
and it seems that Israeli scholars understand this eschatology
much better than the American Jewish community. This may
be because Israelis have been in dialogue longer on the specific
relation of the evangelical view of the future to Israel's interests.
At any rate, questions relating to Christian Zionism have to be
explained. The evangelical community needs to ascertain if it
has relegated the current Jewish community to an "ancient"
status that can miss the complexity of modern Judaism. Jewish-
evangelical dialogue is also important in clarifying whether or
not the evangelical eschatology can be turned against the Jewish
people by future events that would appear to be supported by
prophetic passages of the Bible.

Such an issue comes at a time when the nation Israel is
under constant criticism by most of the world and when many

Jewish leaders are discussing the importance of support for Israel. Arnold Forster and Benjamin R. Epstein's *The New Anti-Semitism* (McGraw Hill, 1974) found that attitudes toward Israel must be reevaluated. While Forster and Epstein note that one can oppose Israel's position on specific issues without being anti-Semitic, they also caution that "many of the anti-Israel statements from non-Jewish sources, often the most respectable, carry an undeniable anti-Jewish message" (p. 17). Robert Loewenberg, a professor of history at Arizona State University, wrote in *Midstream: A Jewish Monthly* (May, 1977): "Why, since the brief respite in Jew-hatred, between 1945 and 1967, one liberal group after another has turned upon Israel—the people and the land. Is the pattern purely accidental?" (p. 33). Evangelicals and Jews need to dialogue about their mutual support of Israel and whether or not negative attitudes toward Israel hurt Judaism and the Jewish "peoplehood." They also need to clarify why their respective communities support Israel.

The Holocaust and Christian Zionism are two topics that should be on the agenda for future evangelical-Jewish dialogue. But most important, I believe that Jews and evangelicals cannot afford to wait five more years before gathering again in national dialogue. Too much is at stake. Furthermore, a solid groundwork has been laid in several areas and a basis is there for intensive small-group hammering out of differences within a historical, theological, biblical, and cultural framework. As Rabbi Tanenbaum explained in a closing statement: "All beginnings are difficult, but no one said it would be easy." I would hate to see such a good beginning dissipate because of lethargy on the part of either community.

A concern of most participants in this conference must also be quickly pursued in the future; i.e. in what areas can we work together and how do we initiate immediate action? Certainly we who participated in the conference have also the responsibility to maintain correspondence with each other and to relate our new-found attitudes to those about us. In addition, an important question to be asked is how the Jewish and evangelical delegate can impart this information to the mainstream of each community. Caricature, stereotypes, and distorted views of either group radically impede the search for knowledge and truth. The local communities must experience the same opportunity of interaction as we did.

May I suggest that the average evangelical needs to be encouraged to know more about the Jewish community and to get to know Jews personally; and the average Jew needs to be encouraged to know more about the evangelical community and to get to know evangelicals personally. May I further suggest that a viable interaction must be based on sensitivity to the feelings of the other community and that an attitude of learning, humility, and love rather than of "conquering" should characterize such personal relationships. I believe that evangelical ministers and rabbis need this experience, but I am convinced that it is also necessary for their congregations. I am well-aware that this is fraught with danger. For example, one evangelical group associated with Pat Boone's movie on Israel began passing out "gospel tracts" during the Oneg Shabbat in a local temple. Such callous disregard of Jewish hospitality was unforgivable. Nevertheless, the same Jewish community welcomed evangelical church groups and found many of them to be conscientious, studious, and honest in their endeavor to understand Jewish worship and Jewish people. I believe to remain ignorant is a far greater danger than the lack of sensitivity that might occur. Besides, I believe each community should be honest when offended and should not stereotype any group by isolated experiences. I have spoken to Jewish groups and asked, "Have any of you had dealings with an evangelical?" Without fail, a horror story is related. I have spoken to evangelical groups and asked, "Have any of you had dealings with a Jew?" Without fail, a horror story is related. When one gets down to the basics with both communities, however, one finds they actually know very little about each other—personally. It seems to me that accurate, personal information and actual interpersonal relationship is the only key to viable interaction between communities. Any friendship entails time, risk, inconvenience, work, and patience. Leaders can minimize the risk through education, but they cannot substitute on the local level for personal time, interaction, or patience.

Something happened at this conference that should tell Jewish and evangelical leaders about the potential of interaction. They saw walls that had taken decades to build begin to crack—walls of caricature, insensitivity, and misinterpretation. In less than seventy-two hours this accomplishment was quite significant. When Dr. Kantzer asked Rabbi Tanenbaum to conclude our last session with prayer, the power and fervency of his prayer to God encompassed all of us. We knew we were leaving new-found friends and profitable personal relationships. We had become family.

On the way back to Cleveland on a DC-10, I was given a seat next to an older woman with a radiant personality and energetic speech. She was Jewish and had lost her entire family in Czechoslovakia during the Holocaust. "Do you know," she said, "no one would believe that it happened?" She related that when she was first brought to Cleveland in 1948 she was standing in a store when the manager said: "*All* these refugees say they lost their families to the Nazis. I don't believe it ever happened. I think they just want sympathy." When she piped up and told how she lost her family, those present told her the man did not really mean what he had said. She seemed surprised that I believed that the Holocaust occurred. I explained that I taught a course on the Holocaust and how necessary I believed a knowledge of it to be. She was pleased. She told me about losing her husband two years ago, her loneliness, the vandals in the neighborhood, her love for cats, and her deep sorrow over her only daughter's marriage to a Gentile. "I can hardly forgive her," she said. "What about the children? The worst of it is they don't worship anywhere. What about the children?" We talked the whole trip, this pleasant lady and I. We shared the pictures that we carried, our hopes, our dreams. "It has been so nice to talk with you," she took my arm and grasped it firmly, ". . . to share." "I do hope our paths cross again," I replied, and made a mental note to remember her name and hopefully visit her in Cleveland. I had to run to catch my commuter plane to Mansfield, and again I felt that I had left a friend. A hollowness encompassed me and a sadness that such relationships had to be so rushed. I thought about that dear old lady, her difficult life and her immense courage. I thought about the conference, the new acquaintances, the interaction. Tears filled my eyes. It was painful, but very encouraging. You see . . . I understood.

DATE DUE